Praise for Memoirs of a Coney Island Clown

"Jellyboy the Clown is a renegade wizard freak, weaving us into a hypnotic, breezily psychedelic story of his journey to become a sideshow performer. We peek between our fingers as he describes sword swallowing injuries, hold our breath with him as he barely survives an intense house fire, and laugh nervously as he fights off bouncers with beer bottles. This is not a book for the faint of heart or the easily offended. This is for those who want an insider's view of sideshow, for historians of the avant-garde oddity arts, and purveyors of vaudevillian road chaos. Whether you're a seasoned sideshow aficionado or a curious bystander, prepare to be swept away on a wild ride through the twisted psyche of Jellyboy the Clown. The book reads like you're peeking over the shoulder of Anthony Bourdain as a circus freak while he's getting stoned with Hunter S. Thompson as he writes *Zen and the Art of Motorcycle Maintenance*, and it is beautiful." - **Jenn O. Cide, international performer, producer, and professional weirdo**

"Jellyboy is a clown unlike any other. Driven by an insatiable curiosity for pushing the limits and a family tragedy, his adventures into the world of sideshow take him on a journey filled with daring creativity, danger, love, and extraordinary perseverance. *Memoirs of a Coney Island Clown* is your ticket to join him for the truly weird and wonderful ride." - **Marc Hartzman, author of** *American Sideshow: An Encyclopedia of History's Most Wondrous and Curiously Strange Performers*

"I warned Jellyboy not to do most of the death-defying deeds in this sideshow saga of his insane early carnie career. Don't Screw Up, I yelled at him again and again. Stranger than Fiction! Read all about Jellyboy's struggles: accidents, blood, fights, and fire! Drinking at a wise guy's hangout or getting kicked out of the Mermaid Parade, falling apart, or making sideshow history, it's one hell of a read." - **Dick D. Zigun, permanently unelected mayor of Coney Island, and founder of Coney Island Circus Sideshow**

ERIC BROOMFIELD

"It's a masterpiece that is truly captivating. Wild and hypnotic (su)real stories that actually happened and pull you in right from the beginning. A must read. Highly recommended."
- **Ramana the magician and mentalist**

"It is a ferociously funny road trip packed with characters that are tough, funny, and smart. It is also a search for artistic identity that is gritty and brilliant, tragic and triumphant. You will not forget Jellyboy the Clown." - **Strange Eye, festival and event photographer**

"From the first sentence, Eric Broomfield grabs you and takes you with him into the global underground of sideshow freaks. The book delivers the shock and madness you'd expect from a sideshow memoir, but what's so wonderful is how much heart it's all told with. Broomfield's passion shines through and is contagious. It's an exciting and dangerous life, but Broomfield has lived to tell the tale, but only just. Death came close, real close...In the best Chaplinesque clown style, the book showcases all the facets of the clown: funny slapstick, insane journeys, and deep tragedy. Through it all, Jelllyboy the Clown plods a steady course with a smile painted on his face, even when a sea of emotions roils beneath."
- **Captain Frodo, internationally renowned circus performer, director, writer, and host of the** *Way of the Showman* **podcast**

Memoirs of a Coney Island Clown
Jellyboy's Sideshow Saga

Eric Broomfield

Outside Talker Press (an imprint of Vaudevisuals Press)

First Edition

Copyright © 2024 by Eric Broomfield

All rights reserved. No portion of this book may be reproduced in any form without written permission from the publisher or author, except as permitted by U.S. copyright law.

Layout by Nathan Wakefield
Edited by James Taylor, Jenn O. Cide, Julie Tibbott
Cover design by Lisa Marie Pompilio
Suit in cover photos painted by Marie Roberts
Front cover photograph by Kenny Lombardi
Back cover photograph by Norman Blake

ISBN: 978-1-737-2036-6-7

Published by Outside Talker Press, an imprint of Vaudevisuals Press.

www.outsidetalkerpress.com

To my surrealistic older brother
Jason Broomfield
1970-1999

Contents

Foreword	1
One Spark Is All It Takes	5
1. Carnivolution	6
2. The Misfit Mother of Death	16
3. Skull Boy's Psycho Rodeo	31
4. Freaks and Fire	44
5. The Unholy Sideshow	54
6. Foot in the Door of New York City	63
7. After Dark at the Amusement Park	78
8. Traveling with the Show	88
9. The Unicorn Goat	99
10. Coney Island Clown	111
11. Other Side of the Pond	124
12. Wild Women and Wise Guys	134
13. Children of the Sword	147
14. Holding It Together While Falling Apart	165
15. Faster, Faster We Ride	173
16. The Elemental	186
17. Squidlings Around the World	204
Afterword: The Creative Process	211
About the Author	216

Foreword

The very first time I ever saw Jellyboy, I had finished a long day at the grind show in Coney Island Sideshows by the Seashore, involving 8 to 9 rotations of an hour-long smorgasbord of dangerous, scary, or freakish stunts presented by a 4 to 5 strong cast of which I was the "Natural Born" freak (sideshow parlance for some physical difference from birth), so I was tired.

I was hanging around at that six to seven p.m. time between the day and the night. The bar was empty, with just Jamie the long-serving rockabilly bartender, and me. Then I saw him, and he looked like the *most* tired human I'd ever seen, a floppy, downtrodden looking gentleman in dirty ragged clothes, blotchy black and white clown makeup on his face, with tufts of hair in strange places on his face as well as his head...he had a world-weary expression that neither I nor anyone else could have imagined the depths it had come from. He hoofed himself up onto one of the bar stools, looked in the middle distance, and said one word: "Beer," and I thought to myself, "*That is the saddest, tiredest-looking clown I've ever seen in my life.*"... turns out he was working at Cha Cha's, a kind of rival! I was a cast member of Coney Island USA Sideshows by the Seashore, with Dick Zigun our boss, and he didn't like any other sideshows being in Coney Island. But with Jelly's talents and charm, it was never going to be long before he and his maverick Philly crew of Matterz his brother, Penguin Boy, Betty Bloomerz, and other crazies from their world of "Carnivolution" would become infamous players in the USA sideshow scene, and beyond.

My name is Mat Fraser, I'm a disabled actor and writer, with congenitally shortened arms, no thumbs, and flipper-like hands. As a personal research and experience journey, I worked in sideshows between 2001-2015 ish, in historical cultural heritage to "Natural Borns," the disabled performers in sideshows of yore, taking the mantle of "Sealboy" for such work, after the famous performer Sealo the Sealboy, who like me also had phocomelia (seal-like limbs). It's deep, personal, and I loved it, though it is certainly not for everyone, especially the faint-hearted or particularly sensitive types. I grew to love the sideshow, with its dangerous stunts, scare acts, stomach turning skills, and shocking abilities, as a peculiar form of entertainment unlike any other.

The sideshow I knew back then was still mostly "traditional," harking back to older days, a retro experience of outsider Americana, perhaps typified by Donny Vomit's style (one of the very best!), but things were changing. Post Jim Rose, post grunge, post Bush, post depression of USA, a new breed of sideshow performer was coming, and Jellyboy was for me the best of these newbies, with his chaotically hilariously bizarre Squidling Brothers Circus Sideshow, a theatrical, crazy, drug-fueled, fantastical theatrical experience with music, overgrown puppets, and messy sideshow, all roughed up and punky, as if the entire scene had just discovered acid and moved into a squat, all with a ferocious intention to entertain people by scaring and thrilling them with their sheer danger and revoltingness. Not at all quaint or old-fashioned! And yet, Jelly is old-fashioned in some ways, the good ways: he has great respect, love, understanding, empathy, kindness, and will be there with a sledgehammer, a machete, or a rubber chicken to fight any foe alongside you if you need it.

This book covers about ten crucial years of Jellyboy's life, as he navigates his understanding of his own experiences and the world through the prism of his earth-shattering family trauma, and the following tribute of developing skills and performances. We go on tour with his life, and it's as wondrous as the rock formations in Zion, Utah, or an endlessly moving fractal image. A revolutionary roller coaster for sure, covering the inception, development, and touring life of him and his brother's dream…knives, puppets, metal music, booze, dollar bills, staplers for scrotums, nails in noses, weed, electric coils to threaten this mortal one, and of course, swords, for the entertaining swallowing of! But of course, Jellyboy doesn't only swallow swords, he swallows a whole rifle! The one thing he won't swallow? Shit, from other people. My guy!

Jellyboy has almost died three times since I've known him. Inevitably maybe, in a crash on the road while on tour. The smoke inhalation in a lethal fire was the worst I think–his brother Matterz made a great documentary about that–and me and Julie Atlas Muz, my better half, were amongst the many performers who turned up to perform in his benefit at the old House of Yes in NYC. Another time, he fell off a roof he was painting with no safety precautions, and broke both his heels–ouch! A year of wheelchair, then crutches, then sticks, limping, and finally back to walking followed: somehow, he bounces back, again. He's the only man I've known to become disabled and non-disabled again, twice! So far, that is...

His accounts of the early noughties American sideshow scene really do paint a picture of the outsider life that touring sideshow traditionally is and has become. From the older-fashioned presentational style of the classic tricks to lifetime squatters hanging from flesh hooks as an almost anti-showbiz ritual, Jellyboy manages to straddle these two worlds and make them one, for me the most successful person to do that.

He did Theatre Bizarre in Detroit, huge shows in their hometown Philly, conquering Coney Island, and on to nightlife, where Jelly ended up on the stage of the Slipper Room, (legendary and original house of burlesque and variety), working the Ripley's "Believe it or Not" street pitch on Broadway amongst the tourists, and The Box, where prestigious rich people club and watch shock acts, where I also worked. Now Jelly was performing to people who were not at all like him or had his values, but they loved him just as much...of course by the time you read this, he will have been on *America's Got Talent* for an audience cheering and chanting his name, so who knows what is going on now?

Jellyboy is one of the special people, a living and joyous embodiment of universal loving awareness through shocking and dangerous entertainment. Not special in any lesser way; to me special is extra, more, beyond, wonderful, free of ordinary-ness, and utterly individual.

I'm talking about a non-religious spiritual level of special, a kind of almost subconscious understanding of humanity, and how to heal it through often scary, boundary-pushing entertainment, in the pursuit of harmony of the universe, understanding the demise of loved ones in his soul, containing his brothers...

So, sometimes you maybe have to watch Jellyboy swallow a sword that he just wiped on his pants leg, or observe him risk his life with a bolted string of electricity that throbs from his homemade Tesla coil to the nail in his nose, and if not, then surely stapling one hundred dollar notes to his scrotum to make "batwings" will lead you to an escape of the...ugh...normal.

People seem to like Jellyboy, I've noticed. I think it's because he's so in touch with himself, so honest, unpretentious, and funny, gentle; he listens, and he remembers (with the amount he drinks and smokes just in this book, how does he do that? Must be magic!). To some of you, much of this book might seem like a madman's diary of an erratically modulating, living hell. The constant smoking and drinking, squatting, sleeping in and on various ill-designed slumber areas, the fights that occasionally break out, the sometimes near death experiences of sideshow mistakes, the relentless scrabbling around to get shows and acts together under the often squalid conditions that Jellyboy so gleefully describes, would put most people off perhaps, but reading about it is fascinating, and anyway, dear reader, you love all this stuff don't you, otherwise you wouldn't have got even this far!

I've not written a foreword before, and this book is utterly unlike others I've read, so if you've made it this far, you're really going to enjoy this frikkin' book! Read on: you have nothing to lose but your FEAR!

Mat Fraser, New York City, April 13, 2024

Mat Fraser, Sideshows by the Seashore, Coney Island, 2010 (Laure Leber)

One Spark Is All It Takes

R eached through waves of thought. Past, present, future, all equally in clear focus. Saw lights shine through the smoke. Figured time was up on earth. Being suffocated and devoured by a constrictor snake that was pure elemental fire. In its grip, jaws dripping down hot digestive juices on my skin. After so much time chasing each other, I was finally caught in the grip of the elemental itself. The Misfit Mother of Death slapped me in the face to keep me awake as I burned. Beams of light came closer through the smoke. Not the light at the end of the tunnel, but two firefighters with a life preserving respirator mask.

I was carried like a battering ram, headfirst, face down. The floor passed under as they ran out the door, descending the stairs. I felt weightless in their cross-arm carry. The firefighters gently placed me on the sidewalk. Covered in soot and burns, Brian sat on the front steps of his building. I'd always loved fire, but this was too much! An ambulance pulled up. While placed on a stretcher I wondered: *How did I get **here**?*

Chapter 1

Carnivolution

The World's Greatest Nipple Lifter called on the telephone. We met up at the Bean Cafe on South Street with Red Stuart, the sword swallower. They were looking for an inside out sideshow talker. The lip flapper with a nail in the head, a presenter of bizarre mind bogglers from out of time. Red was sketching contraptions in his little black book of shadows. The old road carnie inhaled a cigarette and savored the smoke before releasing it through his nose. He sat still, a little like an iguana staring into the midway of his mind. His shoulder-length red hair was tied back between a white Japanese headband and a choker necklace made of beads.

"It's all in the mind, you know," he said as he looked up at me over the lenses of his spectacles. Red's eyes were shining as if he wanted to tell me about the secrets behind his leathery grin. He and I had a job working in the jazz section of Tower Records down the street from the coffee shop where our meeting was taking place. The year was 2004 in the city of Philadelphia. I had just hired him and his sideshow partner to perform with my space rock band, the Hydrogen Jukebox, in a street festival we called Carnivolution. Our band was becoming an art collective variety show. The tentacled concept brought in poets, dancers, puppets, painters, fire, and, of course, circus sideshow. They were impressed with the way I presented the acts on the microphone in between singing songs. "Nipple Man is just checking on his car. He'll be back in a minute."

As if on cue, the World's Greatest Nipple Lifter emerged triumphantly through the door. He was glowing with pride as he said, "I was so close to a parking ticket. The cop was writing it and I walked up to him and said, 'Do you realize you're giving a ticket to a man with the strongest nipples in the world?' I pulled out my pitch card, and the cop started laughing and ripped up the ticket."

He looked like a mix between a pirate and a circus strongman with muscles rippling through his clothes. Long, skinny, rope-like locks were woven into his brown hair, and his ears were pierced with thick gauged rings that left hollow spaces in the lobes. On his face a well-groomed beard sat tightly with a mustache, his sideburns and chin whiskers all separated by the fine work of a razor.

"Nipples strong enough to bend the law," I said, looking at the pitch card.

"Why are you dressed as a clown? This is a business meeting. You should save some things for the stage," the pierced weightlifter said disapprovingly. I was dressed in neon green spandex pants covered in black polka dots, a striped, sleeveless, multi-colored tailcoat, a red clown nose, accompanied by vintage 3D glasses with red and blue lenses. My hair was short, messy and brown attached to a ginger beard, sharpened to a point on my chin.

"Life's a show; I'm just being a natural eyesore," I responded. "Dirty looks are just as good as smiles."

In 'the business,' making a fool out of yourself is a bad idea, unless you are a fool hired in place. Either way, bad ideas are dangerous, and danger is entertainment. A clown with no makeup is an unfinished work, confusing to the eyes. Some people say you should go to clown school, learn the tradition before declaring the profession. However, it was as if clownhood had declared me, and school isn't the only place a person can learn. Anguish could be turned into laughter. Torture acts could morph into antidotes for human tragedy. Reality with the occasional gaff or swindle; prick your finger on the spindle to show you are more powerful than poison.

"Let's get down to business," said the World's Greatest Nipple Lifter, joining us at the table. "Red and I have a group we'd like you to join."

"Sounds great, but I don't know any sideshow tricks. I'm more of a clown and a barker."

"You need to know the terms for what you're talking about, Jellyboy. It's not a trick when Red swallows a sword. He is literally risking his life: it's called a stunt. Magic has tricks; it's fake. Sideshow is absolutely real." The pierced weightlifter looked over to Red.

"The lingo we use in the carnival and the circus are how we tell the normies from the freaks," Red added. "You're still green yet, Jelly. People are really touchy about the words you use. Not everyone will take the time to explain it, so listen up: the term 'barker' is an insult. You're an artist, not a dog. It's called talking. You are an outside talker delivering a pitch to gather a crowd, or you are an inside talker who guides the madness on the inside of the tent."

When Red was done explaining, the nipple lifter thought for a second and said, "By the way, sideshow and clowning are two different things. You should think about changing your name and getting a costume that makes you look a little tougher."

"But I'm a clown. Can't you be both a clown and sideshow performer?"

"There's no written rule, it's just not really done," said Red. "It doesn't seem like you're interested in the rules all that much, Jellyboy, but you should learn what they are before you bend them or break them. Sideshow as it was in the old days is dying. There aren't traveling shows any more, the way there used to be. Things have to change to stay alive."

The World's Greatest Nipple Lifter wanted me to learn a list of stunts from Red and get us a monthly show. Spitting up molten lead, dancing on broken glass, walking up a ladder of razor-sharp swords, putting a cigarette out on the tongue, and of course, the human blockhead. Passing on information to the next generation. Scrawny, poverty-stricken proportions became the makings of a freaked freak with a nail in the head.

Red opened a metal tube, inside of which was a collection of stainless nails of various sizes. All shining, each one menacing. He picked one of the smaller ones and handed it over to inspect. It spun like a screw that was flattened and polished. He put his thumb on his nose and said, "Make a pig nose, aim the nail, and drive it in." After I removed my clown nose, I held the nail up to a pig nosed nostril and considered the consequences. Red saw the angle was wrong and helped guide the nail. It was frightening, like getting pushed, like when you can't see where you're falling. Red's thumb was on the flat end of the nail, which was lodged in my shocked but smiling skull. "Your eyes may tear, and you may want to sneeze, but those reflexes will go away after a while." The old stunt was passed on and fear was replaced with confidence; pompous arrogance, déjà vu in a blender, innocence lost in the outfield.

"Now you try yourself, but don't screw up," said Red. That was the start of our partnership.

Someone who saw us perform on South Street was fascinated by the sideshow. He was having a surprise party for his friend, Al. The Carniv'Al had the title, "A Latin Carnival." After the old people and children went home to go to bed, we arrived. The party's host greeted us with an envelope containing payment. There was a gracious welcome, and introductions were made with Al, the guest of honor. The show took place in a large suburban backyard, with a deck overlooking a garage. Inside was a DJ and dance floor. We were given sangria and told that behind the garage was the "backstage dressing room" where preparations for the show could be made.

Getting everyone's attention was easy. Red opened the show eating fire with three torches. He extinguished the flames with his mouth like he was tasting cotton candy and relit them with the remaining torch in a subtle dance of concentration. Fire eating was followed by the human pincushion: hat pins through the cheeks. "If you ever have a problem holding your socks up, jab one through the calf. It may only bleed a little, and it lets a person know they are still alive. Ladies, if your brassiere strap keeps falling down, ram a pin through your chest: guarantee that strap will give you no more trouble," said Red, dressed in a black robe embroidered with Japanese characters. His chest was covered in a Buddhist mandala tattoo.

"Necromancy, alchemy, witchcraft, ESP, mind control, Hinduism, voodoo, and black magic are ways of allowing the subconscious mind to overtake the conscious; they are all very real. The mind has power over the body, and just as the ancient Sumerians did six thousand years ago, I will swallow a sword." Red had a vast collection of swords from around the world, from a dagger to a claymore. He stretched his throat, making the cold metal vanish down to the pit of his stomach. Over time his Adam's apple had calcified, making it possible to swallow a serpentine blade. He had a sword that curved in waves from side to side, causing his Adam's apple to move back and forth along with the curves. The bigger or stranger the implement, the louder the applause.

"What's that on the end of your sword, Red?" I asked into the microphone.

"Pizza," he replied, and the people moaned, touching their throats.

At the end of Red's act, I held up a screwdriver and said, "I've got a screw loose. Who wants to see me rip off this clown nose to spite my face?" The people yelled, "Do it/Don't do it!" in the intoxicated comfort of their friend's backyard. It happened with one hand and the other slowly sank a screwdriver up the right nostril to the back of the head, tightening the gears in the hollow space of my clown skull. For a moment Jellyboy became Screwy Louie, up close in people's faces to give them a better look at their own fear's excitement.

The World's Greatest Nipple Lifter took the stage with a headset microphone. The thing about his act is the sensitivity of other people's nipple empathy, coupled with the brute strength and elasticity of his freakish areolas. Humans tend to quiver when tender flesh might tear. We dipped the tip of a cigarette in gasoline before the show. The strongest known pierced weightlifter on the planet attached a metal grinder to his nipple harness. He announced that the clown would stick his face into the sparks and light a cigarette, so I stuck my face into a spark shower. The cigarette just wouldn't light, which sent a tremor of laughter through the audience. Red dipped the cigarette in gasoline, this time so everyone could see, but again nothing happened. We asked for a volunteer from the audience to use a lighter so I could at least smoke to end the nicotine fit. Even the lighter had a hard time starting our gas-dipped cigarette, so it seemed like it was all part of the show. We were forgiven with a round of applause.

After the party we went to a diner, where Red told us his life story as a carnival showman. He had notes for a book and wanted to share them, so we'd know where he'd been. "The person who broke me in the business of swallowing swords was Toni Del Rio, a half-and-half sword swallower, both male and female. That was in 1967, just before I went off to Vietnam. That same year, most of the carnivals with sideshow acts were shut down by 'do-gooders' who thought the 'freaks' who were our royalty were being exploited and abused. The crowds were also fading because people had TV and movies. The carnival started becoming more about rides than live shows. I signed up for 'Nam in '68 and was a Navy Seal for sixteen months before being discharged with a purple heart. My commander was killed trying to defuse a bomb." Red revealed the scars. "Shrapnel from the bomb and pieces of my commander's bones were lodged in my legs."

"What did you do?" I asked.

"Screamed and screamed. But they sent me home. Of course, once I got home, there was nothing to do, so in the summer of 1969, after I got my head straightened out in Woodstock, I started hitchhiking around the country doing shows in different towns. While I was doing that, I ran across my old friend Toni Del Rio, joined up with a traveling show where I met Bill Fitch the Son of a Bitch. He was a son of a bitch, too. He was run off the show for freaking out some of the dancers with his human pincushion act. When he left, I picked it up. It's one of those things you've just got to do. The first time I did it was on stage. It got me feeling a little lightheaded but then, standing there with pins in my face, I figured there was nothing to it. I picked up stapling from my tour in 'Nam and applied it to the show to collect tips, 'cause field surgery was Crazy Glue and a Swingline T50 staple gun with stainless staples being used. I was the first one to do this in '69 on the road with the sideshow. It felt like fate running into Toni again. We had a strange relationship. Toni was half man, half woman. Eventually she had the operation and became a full woman, but that wasn't until years later. In '71, I met Ward Hall in Waterloo, Iowa, working the Thomas Shows. Ward had one of the last legitimate freakshows. He traveled with the strangest. Some people called him the King of the Sideshow; some called him the queen."

Red laughed and the waitress came over to take our order of late-night breakfast. "In '72, I studied Buddhism in Colorado for a while. In the beginning of that winter, Toni and I performed a show that was way out there. Crowds of people came to see the sickest show ever. Toni worked the peep show; I geeked pigs and chickens. We made more money doing that than anything else we ever did."

"What do you mean 'geeked'? Like, you bit off their heads as a performance?"

"Something like that, Jellyboy. I'd twist the chicken's head and bite down on its neck, let the blood drip down my face like a wild man. With the pigs it's a little different. You stick your hand up their ass, after you catch 'em of course, and rip out their intestines. They run all over squealing and bleeding. That's when people start getting sick. I'd throw vomit and intestines at the audience. Guaranteed to clear the house, fast. We got their money though. We sure got their money." Red laughed proudly and continued.

"I'd spend the end of the winters in New Orleans. Eventually, around '76, I started working with large reptiles. Cops don't mess with reptiles, so I made a little extra scratch smuggling. We would extract venom from the cobras and inject small amounts to build immunity to the poison for the Kiss of Death, where the venomous snake bites down on your tongue and you take it into your mouth. Through the '80s, I did electrical work and managed some rides before getting back with the World of Wonders and reviving the live freakshows on the carnival lot."

My imagination and my stomach were filled at the end of the night. I was ready to help with the reinvention and revival of the freakshow. A superstitious feeling told me I would find all the others on the same path, or they would find me, one mysterious way or another. Where does someone go when freakshow antics are unwelcome? When the time of the merry pranksters came and went before you were born? Red and the World's Greatest Nipple Lifter had a place in mind. They were performing at the sideshow, tattoo, and motorcycle convention called Inking the Valley in Wilkes-Barre, Pennsylvania. All I needed was a way to get there.

I took a road trip with my berserker poet friend, Frank Walsh, in his pickup truck to the convention. Frank grew up there, and his father still lived in the same house, so we also had a place to stay. I had recently met Frank at a puppet slam while scouting talent for the Carnivolution, and we became fast friends. The night we met, he was wearing Nordic war paint from a thousand years ago. Frank's hair was wildly different lengths, some curly, some straight, some matted into knots, and balding on top. In drastic contrast to the hair on his head, his mustache was neatly trimmed, like a swashbuckler's. He paced around the stage with sweat dripping off his head, reading poetry about puppets into the microphone, the way a warlock would conjure a fire elemental.

Wilkes-Barre, Pennsylvania is an old mining town full of ghosts and radiation that was frequented by traveling shows until they were replaced by televisions. Still, there were some beautiful forests and waterfalls for the creatures of myth to dwell in, almost forgotten, near the house where we slept. The Clownicals of Jelly the Chronicler unfolded the sheets and hid under the covers, mummified in a basement guest bed, the night before the sideshow gathering. There was a twilight-zone sensation of sleeping in a new place under the ground with brick walls, cement floors, wooden floorboards above, populated by two large spiders and their collection of insect corpses. I slept with the lights on, and dreamed in black-and-white, like forgotten childhood dreams.

The gathering was at the Holiday Inn in the center of town. We arrived late in the afternoon after sleeping in, and there was time to kill before the evening performances. The sideshow was off to the side of the tattoos and motorcycles. Frank, from the Underground Literary Alliance, aka the ULA, had a printed press pass on the brim of his detective hat. Wherever we went, it was the reporter and the clown, carving out the story. People came out of their shells to spill the sauce of the tale. All of it is important; every encounter, every turn to the next sign in the road.

The sound of a marching band from far off drew us into the excitement of a large group of people. They were gathered around a football field behind a school near the convention center, practicing for a national competition. Horns and drums cracked into the air, carrying the sensations of the old-time traveling shows. People were spinning flags; twirling, throwing, and catching in flawless sequences. We belonged there. Frank took some pictures and interviewed one of the coaches for the ULA's imaginary "Paw Print Newspaper." We didn't stay long, but the music never left our blood.

When a clown is walking down a country road, conversation jumps out from behind the trees. One train-hopping young man with black eye makeup named Scarecrow stepped out from behind a rock in a cornfield. He looked up from under the brim of his farmer's hat into the unusual. A traveler with no place to go. We told him about the sideshow convention. Frank gave him money and cigarettes. Scarecrow's eyes were lost, hopeful, new wave, home bum, lenses materialized from a storybook realm.

We parted ways with Scarecrow and went over to Frank's aunt's house. She wasn't home, so we decided to go back to town for beer and food. On the way from the bar to the hotel, there was a fistfight on the sidewalk between teenagers. Two boys were laughing in hysterics while punching each other in the face repeatedly. There was a teenage girl smiling and watching as her two scrapping friends punched as hard as they could. One of the boys was knocked down. I reached my hand from just outside the realm of possibilities to help him up. Then they went back to punching each other in the face, as if we were never there.

As soon as Frank and I walked into the convention, we met Ward Hall and his friend, Pete the fire eating dwarf! Red had mentioned to me that Ward had been called the King of the Sideshows. For the past sixty years, Ward Hall had been the keeper of the flame, who lived and traveled with the strangest people in the world, including Schlitzie, the pinhead star from the movie *Freaks*.

Ward Hall gave us an order form for his book, *My Very Unusual Friends*. "Meet the baseball playing Siamese twins. Meet some very strange ladies. Learn of the love story between the alligator-skinned man and the monkey girl. Meet the world's fattest entertainers."

Pete the fire eating dwarf looked about as old as Ward, except there was a childlike gleam in his shiny blue eyes. I sunk a large nail into a red bulbous clown nose and hammered the nose and the nail onto my face. Pete's smile grew, remembering the old days. We told Ward and Pete about our show called Carnivolution, and asked if they would take a picture with us holding our poster. He was happy to take the photo, but according to him, it was too small to qualify as a poster.

"That there is an 11 x 17 handbill," Ward said. "A show poster is something you can read from far away while driving in a car." Dimensions aside, at least the picture on it was to his liking. In the center, there was an image of my band the Hydrogen Jukebox's mascot, a ringmaster named T.H. Box. The character had four arms and squid tentacles for legs, holding a flaming sword and a marionette. We explained to Ward that T.H. Box was an interdimensional being who pulled acts out of portals through the rings in his circus tent.

The performance room and the hallway leading to it were covered in old carnival banners from the '50s and '60s. Banners that attracted crowds by being larger than life. The banner on the stage was the largest in the collection: it said *HOW STRANGE IT IS* in bold letters about the size of a highway billboard. Old sideshow banners hung around the room. "*There's a sucker born every minute.*" "*Who's got a dollar? 100 pennies, 20 nickels, 10 dimes, 4 quarters, one crisp cool bill.*" "*The money you spend here today you'll forget about tomorrow, but the things you see you will remember for the rest of your life.*"

Out of all the performances that night, the Lucky Devil Sideshow from Coney Island left the strongest impression. Tyler Fyre, Magic Brian, and Insectavora were all artists who were keeping the sideshow tradition alive while pushing things forward. Tyler Fyre was a jack of all stunts, the kind of talker that makes you check your pulse. He had eyes tattooed on the back of his head that took me with him, into a crazy smile stretched ear to ear. You have to believe it when you see it.

Magic Brian was a master of audience manipulation and slapstick illusion. Insectavora was a self-made freak in the truest sense. Half of her face and neck were covered in tattoos reminiscent of the Māori people from the South Pacific, spirals mirroring each other in thick, black ink. The other side of her face had a line that traveled down her body, to the bottom of her leg, past a lucky horseshoe. Clowns, snakes, mermaids, and a Ferris wheel illustrated the rest of her skin. She had eyebrows full of piercings, with rings like fangs through her bottom lip, and dyed dreadlocks with 1950s-style bangs. Her movements and clothing were out of the 1920s, bouncing through time like a punk rock Betty Boop, with venom and flames. These performers were adding new spins on old stunts that sparked my imagination.

Tyler Fyre and Magic Brian did a double human blockhead act with choreographed, synchronized hammering. They hung signs from nails driven into their nostrils. Tyler Fyre swallowed his sword with a mad look in his eyes, bowed, and winked. He stood up, tossed the sword out of his throat, and caught it. Down the hatch without a scratch. Magic Brian blindfolded a lovely volunteer from the audience. He gently toyed with her, which caused her breasts to accidentally walk into his hands. She had a great sense of humor about the whole thing and walked off stage giggling to a large round of applause.

Insectavora walked out onto the stage like Eve eating the forbidden fruit. She sucked the worm out of an apple, let it squirm, and slurped it up like a string of spaghetti. She chewed, swallowed, and devoured a bag of crickets like it was the most delicious thing she had ever tasted. She then unfolded a fan to shield between her legs, lifted her skirt, and began pulling a chain of Jolly Roger pirate flags from inside of herself, past the folding fan. The longer the chain got, the wider her smile, and the louder the applause. Insectavora walked up a ladder of razor-sharp swords, protected by only a thin layer of dirt. An amazing feat with her amazing feet. Burlesque, sexy, gross-out sideshow was in my face while I was seated on the floor in the front row!

Tyler Fyre said, "We have one act left, but it must be done outside, behind the hotel. Put your hands into your pockets. For five dollars a head, you can see Insectavora's "freak pussy" breathe fire." That dangerous, don't-try-this-at-home stunt made the Lucky Devils quite a chunk of change that evening. Afterward, on our way out the door, I asked Insectavora how she did it. She replied, "Very carefully," and wrote in my sketchbook *'Jelly the Klown, thanks for the love and support.'*

Frank and I walked out of that sideshow gathering with stars swirling in our eyes and cartoon birds flying around our heads.

Insectavora, Coney Island, 2011 (Norman Blake)

Chapter 2
The Misfit Mother of Death

S ometimes something is so old, it's new.

Ellen Powell Tiberino, painted by Joe Tiberino, The Ellen Powell Tiberino Museum, Philadelphia, 2008 (Geoff Hall)

The end of civilization has already happened and has begun again, so long ago, so many times, it has been forgotten. The feeling of never again in this lifetime, in this form. This strange will never change. A feeling that won't let go. Flames that don't consume their embers continue to burn until the nerves burn away, but they never burn away.

There are people whom you've never met but always know upon introduction. Call her a flaming radical burning for attention, but Kathy Chang's real intention was to spark a discussion of how we can peacefully transform our world. During her life, she haunted the students at Penn University on their way to the library and held happenings in front of the Philadelphia Art Museum. She used theater, dance, poetry, music, and nudity to wake up the dead and end business as usual. She was a half-naked woman in a marijuana leaf costume thrusting her pelvis with a missile strap-on in broad daylight. This was her pattern from the early '80s to the mid '90s, using psychedelic art and sexual energy to transform the universe. No change came; the new world order had no room for Kathy Chang(e).

In her final performance, she left her body behind in a willing self-sacrifice. On October 22, 1996, Kathy set herself on fire outside the giant peace sign on Penn's campus. None of the people she dropped notes to were home, so no one was there to try to stop her. She died a few hours later in the hospital. Transformed herself in the hopes of changing the dark ages of the future to a renaissance of human harmony.

When I first heard of Kathy, she was already gone but she still had work to do. Why not lend a hand and be "Kathy's clown" for a while? It was eight years since her self-immolation, and she had become a local legend. Many people remembered her fondly, and everyone said they wished she was still around.

Frank Walsh had taken me under his intense, master poet wing into the West Philadelphia house painting community. It was getting close to the anniversary of Kathy's suicide, and Frank's friends were all talking about what to do for the memorial that year. Every year on October 22, the friends of Kathy Chang(e) got together on Penn's campus and haunted it with art of all kinds, spreading Kathy's message of transformation.

The Spiral Q Puppet Theater was founded by a friend of Kathy's who lived with her at a place called Kill Time that hosted legendary parties in the 1990s. Spiral Q had an enormous warehouse filled with giant puppets they made for parades and rallies. The puppets were built with backpacks for a person inside the body to support paper mâché heads on flagpoles. The hands were on sticks with a rope down each sleeve to create lifelike movement. Spiral Q had made a puppet of Kathy Chang(e). I was determined to get this puppet for the memorial, so I helped Spiral Q with their Parade.

The Peoplehood Parade was a couple of blocks long and headed for the dog bowl in Clark Park. It really was something to see. The entire Spiral Q puppet army, junk band, marching free punk jazz, old-time, and ragtime on stilts had taken over the streets. When the parade arrived at Clark Park, the puppet show emerged, accompanied by a Q card orchestra of horns, accordions, drums, and my effects pedal-driven amplifier for psychedelic noise and creature sounds. It was true fun for the whole family.

There was no elaborate plan for the memorial. We brought signs that had Kathy's quotes and a boombox to play her music. Her old boyfriend brought a couple of joints made from marijuana that Kathy had grown. It was an amazingly well-preserved, beautiful substance that we smoked openly outside Penn University library. I brought along a megaphone, a monkey mask, an evil clown mask, and the giant Kathy Chang(e) puppet. Dancing in a mask is different. There is a feeling of invisibility for the actual persona and hyper-visibility for the bodily form.

Frank was reading what he had written about Kathy, causing my mind to wander into a video I had seen of Kathy dancing outside the art museum. Her legs were long, thin, and muscular, kicking out far and straight. My monkey mask clown dance started in the legs, ended up in energized fingertips. While I danced to the rhythm of Frank's poem, the Misfit Mother of Death whispered a song in my ears that felt like the weaving of a spell, allowing me to see the spirit world in full color with my eyes closed.

As I danced for Kathy Chang(e), I felt my older brother Jason with me. He lived in a small, one-bedroom apartment above an old woman in Monsey, New York. While he stood six feet five inches tall, his ideas were too big for his body. The surreal science fiction of his imagination could not be truly contained. Empty pockets overflowed with paintings, sculptures, costumes, movies, adventures, stand-up comedy, and songs. Before being dishonorably discharged from both the Army and the Navy, he studied sculpture in the basement of the Cathedral of Saint John the Divine in Harlem, New York.

Mental breakdowns and angry clashes with our parents were always a problem. Yet to me, everything my big brother did was magic. Jason was extremely critical of himself but hugely complemented others. The hourglass had run out. Everything was broken beyond repair. On a couple of occasions, he had told me that he wanted to drive off and blow his brains out. We spoke long and tearfully about it. At the time he was seeing a psychiatrist. I never thought he would go through with it.

My younger brother Matt and I were summoned to the psychiatrist's office at Temple University, where we were students at the time. We did not know why but would soon find out, called into a room where our mother and father were waiting. They pulled us in, standing in a circle facing one another, linking arms.

My mother said, "Jason has done something horrible to himself. He's dead; he shot himself." We all began to cry. It was an uncontrollable disbelief that swelled up and burned as tears tried to put out the fire.

We drove home to Suffern, New York, by the railroad tracks on 52 Prairie Avenue to make funeral arrangements and take care of Jason's belongings in his apartment. My mother had been the one to find him in his bedroom. After missing phone calls, she drove over to his place and walked into an unlocked apartment. The door to Jason's room was partly open; what she saw inside would haunt her for the rest of her life. She didn't believe her eyes, so she got another person to confirm the reality of what she saw. That person did so by vomiting.

Jason took his own life at the age of 29 in the year 1999, but that is not who he was. How people die sometimes overshadows who they were and what they did. The last memories I have of Jason are horrible, almost unreal gore and sadness. I cried for months walking down the street. If anyone asked why I was crying, I told them, and they would start crying too. Riding the razor into music and poetry was the only medicine for the inescapable images of my brother's remains.

Matt and I were the only ones in the family who truly knew Jason's creative side. We knew what was important to him and what should be kept or thrown away. So along with our Aunt Margie and her partner Maggie, we went to his apartment. His landlady followed us up the stairs, frantically telling us that the walls would need to be painted. When we walked into the room, I knelt down by the bed and bowed my head. Everything was splattered in blood. The wall at the base of the bed was thickly coated in the chaotic design of Jason's mind. His brains had soaked into the rug under the bed and pieces of his skull were scattered around on the floor. A nearly finished bottle of vodka was on the windowsill. My old unicycle was covered in blood under his bed and whatever paintings were hanging were splattered as well.

His body had been taken away for an autopsy, but I would view it one last time before the casket was closed. We threw away what was unnecessary and took paintings, sketchbooks, recordings, and other art objects. The blood was not frightening; it was Jason's essence. It somehow comforted me to know that he wasn't completely gone. I put a few pieces of his skull in my pocket, and we were off, leaving the unicycle behind.

Matt and I were only a year and a half apart and had always been best friends. Jason was just as close in age as my cousin John. We all grew up together in the '80s. John and Jason were in high school while Matt and I were in elementary school. All our lives changed one day in 1989 when John died in a motorbike accident. I remember being at a little league baseball game chewing on purple Big League Chew bubblegum with Matt, in our uniforms, when we were picked up by a friend of the family. They took us to their house while the older people processed what had just happened. John was riding his quad bike with a friend in the woods and caught his neck on a low hanging wire that was dangling over a trail. He was my mother's sister Margie's only child. Ten years after that, in 1999, Jason and John were both gone.

Some of Jason's closest friends got drunk at the old foundation of a house in the middle of the woods off a suburban highway. We had all spent many nights drinking there with Jason, the only light being the moon and cigarettes in our dark imagination party.

At home, my mother played Don McLean's song about Vincent van Gogh's suicide on repeat. The wake was a closed casket. My father, Aunt Maggie, Uncle Kenny, Matt, and I went to see Jason one last time. He had put the barrel of a shotgun in his mouth and pulled the trigger. The top of his head was gone, covered in a black cloth by the mortician. His lips and jaw were all that was exposed. The unreal deal was all too true but the eyes in my head saw Jason's jaw as rubber.

"Why is he wearing a mask?" I asked, starting to feel dizzy.

My father put his hand on my shoulder as calmly as he could. "That's not a mask, it's what is left of his face." The mortician's makeup made it look fake.

Shaking his head from a head taller than the rest of us, my uncle Kenny Kolb said, "That's not him anymore; he is somewhere else."

I kissed Jason's crooked lips with my swollen eyes, and the casket was shut.

It was a Catholic funeral and the priest said that Jason "wasn't necessarily in hell;" he was "probably in purgatory." Jesus loved him, and Jesus loves us all, but Jason wasn't even Christian. In the choir loft, I played a song called "Alright Jason" that I had written the night that he died. I then walked down to the podium to make a speech.

"I want everyone to focus on the casket and think of a good memory you have of Jason. Send that thought to him. What I want people to remember is that he was funny. He was a good person to hang out with. I learned about life and art from him and will never take that for granted."

To honor Jason's memory, Matt and I decided there would be no fallback plan: we would become professional artists. Matt was a film student; I was studying comparative religion, creative writing, and modern dance. We had played in rock bands together throughout high school, where Matt played bass as well as keyboard while I played guitar and sang. Just before Jason died, we had started a new band called the Hydrogen Jukebox. Jason's creative spirit fused with the music, and we gained a new focus that was unstoppable.

As I twirled for Kathy Chang(e), I twirled for Jason and for all those who broke the mold but couldn't stick around. The ones embraced by the Misfit Mother of Death, who I had come to know as the spirit, who guided me to the circus spark and gave me the name Jellyboy. The warmth of her presence attracted me to the strings of fate that I followed into the mist, where I met the others on this path, alive and dead. The daydream drift carried thoughts through shadow material and back into my brain. Past experiences exposed, naked to oneself. No clothes, no skin, no bones, no blood, only thought, and thought only thought it was.

Kathy Chang(e) wished to break the hypnotic spell of the worker drone feeding the status quo in the face of Armageddon. Violence seemed to her the best way to get the attention of the media and the people; however, she was morally opposed to inflicting violence on others. After the dance, the poetry, and the visions of death, we looked around and wondered why the Penn campus was so empty. It seemed that classes were not in session. It was a "wellness day" for the students so we decided to take our performance off the campus and into the streets. The puppeteers marched the giant Spiral Q puppet of Kathy Chang(e).

The fifteen-foot-tall puppet got its head caught in the trees but caught the eyes and smiles of the curious people on the sidewalk who wanted to know what it was all about. We gave them photocopies of essays Kathy had written that spoke to who she was. Individuals approached us, saying that they remembered Kathy and were happy to see us. We bounced like rubber balls in a particle accelerator and took to the streets in the name of Kathy Chang(e). A peaceful warrior who fell by her own hand in the ongoing war of symbols and ideas.

The South Street Headhouse District Association had put me in charge of organizing the Philadelphia Halloween parade and Day of the Dead festival. They gave a clown a budget of five thousand dollars and said, "Hire whoever you want." Salvador Dali's work was going to be displayed in the Philadelphia Museum of Art, so the Headhouse Association wanted us to raise the spirit of our surrealistic brother in the dance of the dead. It was advertised as the biggest Halloween party in Philadelphia. We had to distribute hundreds of posters and thousands of postcards, along with coordinating the parade and the show. We were to handle the sound, set up and break down the stage, and run the costume contest.

When hiring performers, I tried on a new persona and became Malerkus Squidling, Professor of Circusology. It's easy to get people to work together when a budget allows you to hand out one-hundred-dollar bills. The South Street Headhouse Association came up with the Day of the Dead poster design, a skeleton head with Salvador Dali's hooked-up mustache. We had boxes of postcards and posters with our band's name on them. All that was left was the almost daunting task of distribution. Distribution would be retribution because if we really were in a war of ideas, we finally had the ammo to help us fight. We split into divisions in cars and on foot, dissecting the city of Philadelphia, covering the walls with our posters inspired by Chang(e), not to be ignored.

Using the budget for the South Street Halloween parade, I would be able to hire my favorite artists and search for performers I'd seen and heard about but never met. Fire, dancing, and sideshow would be heavily represented in the lineup. Red Stuart joined us as well, swallowing swords and sticking pins through himself like a bloodless pincushion. I told one of the fire dancers about a dream I had where a clown on a unicycle broke out of a straitjacket while breathing fire. She said, "I know someone who does all kinds of stuff like that. This crazy kid named Barry Silver." She gave me Barry's number and I called him that night.

Dance and sideshow transcend the human form by using the human form. Dance, however outside of the mainstream, has been kept alive in universities and community centers. Sideshow, on the other hand, springs up wherever it can fit before it is chased away by an angry mob. Barry Silver lived sideshow and had done so his entire life, even though he was only twenty years old. I called him on the phone and said, "Hello, this is Malerkus Squidling, Professor of Circusology, I represent Carnivolution. Do you have a previous engagement for Halloween weekend?"

"No, I don't; what do you have in mind?" Mr. Silver was very enthused and the plan for his talents to come forward in the public eye had jumped out of a clown car like fifty drunk clowns, through the receiver and into his ear.

"South Street on Halloween with Red, the sword swallower. I hear you can break out of a straitjacket." The realm of possibilities linked us to bring old stories to the surface.

"Red doesn't like me very much; it's a long story. Yes, I can break out of a straitjacket. I do everything except sword swallowing. You know, Malerkus, I was in your show before, spinning fire, but the troupe leader wouldn't let me breathe fire because I'm only twenty."

"That's ridiculous. I don't remember you. I never like to see people's talents go to waste. If you say you can breathe fire, you have my okay. What are the most dangerous stunts you perform?"

"Someone could break a cinder block on my head with a sledgehammer," Barry offered. "I can also sandwich myself between broken glass and a bed of nails and let four people sit on me."

"That sounds great; I'd love to see it. What's the deal with you and Red?"

"Well, when I was fifteen, I wanted to learn to swallow swords, but he wouldn't teach me unless I gave him fifteen hundred dollars. We had words. Basically, I thought he should have taught me because I wanted to learn so badly. He told me I was a snot nose with a silver spoon in my mouth because I went to magic school and clown college. My parents wouldn't pay for sideshow and getting that kind of dough was impossible."

"Well, you were young, I'm sure we can patch things up. You two would be a great team. Red understands show business. He's got some perspective."

Other aspects of the Halloween weekend spectacle were live painting and liquid light projection. I rented two Spiral Q puppets. One was Kathy Chang(e), and the other was the pierced blue freak-sister.

Jellyboy the Clown became Malerkus Squidling, so I bleached my hair for the first time ever and dyed it bright orange. Using Elmer's glue and a hair dryer, my friends crafted spikes like a small gothic castle on my head. Electricity led the way. Malerkus Squidling wore someone's funky old suit and a new pair of old dress shoes. The suit had red and white zigzag patterns running up the legs into the jacket, a checkered vest and space frog bowtie, and an orange berserker Civil War beard with mustache spikes, ready to howl at the moon's cartoon lagoon.

The Hydrogen Jukebox band jumped in our black and silver short bus to South Street. We were our own roadies, setting up the stage, the PA system, and equipment. While the band was sound checking, I walked down the street to set up the parade. To gather the crowd, the megaphone was painted as a monster with a big mouth full of shark teeth.

People were being painted into skeletons outside of Isaiah Zagar's Magic Garden, a mosaic installation full of broken mirrors, bicycle wheels, and bottles embedded in the walls. We were surrounded by skeleton puppets. Soon motorcycles pulled up and trucks with floats followed. "Come one, come all! Have your face painted, be part of the parade. Don't be shy, when will you have another chance like this? We need puppeteers and strange ladies, ghouls, and children of all ages. Please join our undead march." Reporters snapped pictures of Salvador Dali's horse-drawn hearse.

Drummers and horn players began showing up and playing to gather more of a crowd for the parade.

"Witness the surrealist Salvador Dali rise from the great beyond and dance the rest of the dead out of their graves. We will march to Headhouse Square and breathe fire for your entertainment. Melt clocks and the boundaries of what is possible."

The colorful costumes quilted the sidewalk and overflowed into the street. It seemed like the beginning of a race, and I was thinking someone would fire a pistol and the entire crowd would start running for the finish line. The crowd was ready to march when the men in suits and mustaches showed up to give the order to the police to begin. Horns played free jazz and we danced down South Street, followed by crazy bicycles and camera men.

A frequent member of the Hydrogen Jukebox's wind section, with his single dreadlock Elliott Levin played saxophone as if his mortality was on the line. He was sandwiched between a fifteen-foot puppet of Kathy Chang(e) and the Movement Lounge modern dancers, who were dressed as pixies. Elliott looked like a werewolf and sounded like an elephant gone mad, sending funny farm smiles into the air following rhythms from the marching drums all around us. The monster megaphone blasted the buildings with vocal airplanes. They bounced back into the eardrums of my mother and father, who for the first time ever were seeing our self-realized lives as we marched with the party of death.

The Carnivolution had the ship's wheel, the compass, and the star chart, but would soon realize that's not all it took to lead the way on the most beautiful of days. The parade was ten blocks long. It ended at the stage in Headhouse Square.

To create the atmosphere for the sideshow performance, the Hydrogen Jukebox improvised, led by my brother Matt's five string electric bass guitar. He became Matterz Squidling as his long straight hair bounced to the rhythm of the Carnivolution. Trombone and flute followed the bass line, weaving counter melodies. The free jazz trumpet, saxophone and clarinet sounded like a flock of angry birds following a strong double bass kick drum. Echoing guitars screamed, sticking the chaos together into a contagious eruption. Sweat poured off us, and the horn players looked like blowfish.

Red swallowed swords and jabbed himself with needles. He made quite a lot of loot that day having people staple money to his chest, arms, and face. No flinch of pain while people frenzied around, fascinated by such a casual response to the snap of a staple gun. Barry Silver stood with his bare feet as real and unprotected as a newborn's bottom on broken bottles while holding a cinder block over his head. Red took a sledgehammer to the concrete block and shattered it. Barry fell to the ground and pretended to die. He then sprang up full of life.

Giant pieces of wood were being painted by undead bloody artists pulling colors out of the eyes all around. A nonstop variety show straitjacket escape into the sunset. Fire blasts lit up the street while people danced. The Misfit Mother of Death smiled a warm glow around me in the autumn chill as I walked around handing out one-hundred-dollar bills to the performers, and everything was about to change.

The Squid was born of fire. Tentacles screaming, soothed by liquid lullabies. The Misfit Mother of Death opened up a jar and beckoned compassionately, when the pain became too great, for the small creature to crawl inside. She would have put the Squid child on a shelf in the wall of history at the timeless dime museum, but it was not time for silence. The tentacles' call would sound from the great beyond, into the fantastic eardrums with eyeballs waiting for the signal. The unknown is what kept the frail Squidling alive and gave it an appetite. The baby chose to live through the birth burns. It needed a guardian—but who could love such a monster?

Malerkus Squidling stepped forward into acceptance and touched the infant tentacle. Suction cups took hold and clung to the hand that had pushed through a dimensional door. There was not an immediate sting or recoil. The Squidling wailed long into the night for its mother. She dared not interfere directly. The child needed life to reflect light in its shadows. The Misfit Mother was too busy caring for the gone and the lost ones, though the living marvels and oddlings remained strong in her mind. She wanted this monster-birth to be strong enough to bridge the living and the dead. Her hands would only burn the child.

"Boy, you know what your problem is? You don't know what your problem is. That's your problem. You want to take on the world and you're not even here. Take in your surroundings, or they will take you in," said the carnie showmen from beyond the grave. Then all he did was laugh like it was a clown routine that he had never seen and disappear with the Misfit Mother back into the shadows of the timeless dime museum.

After the snows of the winter melted in the spring of 2005, I started going to planning meetings at an art gallery on Lancaster Avenue, coming together with a photo gallery, the Community Education Center, and the Tiberino Museum. Representatives from the University City District partnership were there too; they were the West Philly equivalent of the South Street Headhouse. The idea was to put artists up and down the avenue leading the way from the Community Education Center (CEC) to the Tiberino Museum. I convinced them to give us money to have a roving sideshow parade with drums, horns, fire, and belly dancers.

The Carnivolution met at an old Quaker school turned into an arts center on May 14 to start the roving ruckus through the street. Lining the sidewalk were artists selling their work in tents and galleries. The Carnivolutionists gathered on the green garden lawn of the CEC just inside the gate. Frank Walsh was there first, painted green. The green man poet shouting in the spring. A cosmic clown named the Great Quentini showed up, with beard braids down to his nipples in a scraggly white robe and a light up spaceship helmet. He played a drum made from a plastic water jug with mallets in a fine marching beat. Elliott Levin was there with his industrial saxophone, howling like a mechanical animal. Barry Silver was breathing nonstop fire geysers. A belly dancer brought her finger cymbals and sparked them in time with Quentini's plastic drum.

Joined by a few other costumed friends and members of the Hydrogen Jukebox, we walked to each gallery, did a quick show, drank the free wine, and wandered off down the block, spreading organized chaos. The first stop was the Photo West Gallery. We went in with live music blasting and gathered a crowd by dancing. I hammered a nail in my snout and Frank Walsh, dressed as the green man, recited a poem to Quentini's rhythm. We were on our way to Saunders Park where the band was set up with a generator.

When the electric music concert was over, we marched to the Ellen Powell Tiberino Memorial Museum, and found our new home! The drunken congregation who dwelled there danced to the music, screamed for the sideshow, and kept calling for more fire. Joe Tiberino's family compound courtyard was made up of five backyards full of three-dimensional murals with strange faces that came alive out of the walls.

The Ellen Powell Tiberino Museum, Philadelphia, 2008 (Geoff Hall)

Carnivolution with Jellyboy, The Ellen Powell Tiberino Museum, Philadelphia, 2008 (Geoff Hall)

Carnivolution funhouse mirror with Jellyboy and Andrew Cabeze, The Ellen Powell Tiberino Museum, Philadelphia, 2009 (Geoff Hall)

The museum had a magical pull, a wine-soaked gravity, and a turpentine soul that sent us all into a haunted web of Philadelphia family history. Joe Tiberino saw through the facade of South Street and University City like a wine-drinking, white-bearded wizard. He drank with Bacchus, Che Guevara, and Pablo Picasso, in a world of his own design.

The March of America mural was a backyard masterpiece where immigrants and African slaves joined the chaos caused by our nation's birth. The wooden figure, oil painted cutouts lined the outer walls in the back of Joe's house. The three-dimensional paintings mixed with a collage of found objects. Fusion, transfusion, and the social lore of West Philadelphia depicted the MOVE revolution, evaporated into spirit vapor from a firebomb dropped by the city of Philadelphia. A sign that we were home inside the courtyard walls of the museum was a mural of Kathy Chang(e) dressed in a marijuana leaf costume.

Inside the house, bones and taxidermy cluttered the bookshelves in Joe Tiberino's open door study. It had the feel of an Old West saloon because of the giant buffalo head mounted to the wall. We overflowed like the books on his shelves into the yard, pulled by an unknown magnet. Ever-flexible rubber band orbits of art, stretched to launch the good time, tumbling through the air.

Joe Tiberino raised his glass and smiled a wine-stained grin. Under the brim of his hat sat a painter, a gangster, and a welcomer of weirdos, the king of the court of sages and fools. An image of his wife, Ellen Powell Tiberino, looked over everything from the center of the main mural, sculpted and painted into a doorway. She gazed upon the shanty town bar and the spiraling church stairs leading to nowhere, because she was everywhere in the yard.

The baby Squid knew that Ellen Powell Tiberino's spirit was mother to those who didn't fit the mold, friend to the misfit, and bridge between worlds. Kathy Chang(e) used to frequent the Tiberino Museum before she and Ellen became friends and allies of the Misfit Mother of Death who, it seemed to me, was the one who invited us all there in the first place. The party was for the living and the dead. The garden and the sculptures rising from the plants made them all want to overstay their welcome and howl till the sun came up.

University City District made it clear that the Carnivolution wasn't the image they were looking for to represent the Second Friday art happenings. I then made it clear that they were not the image we were looking for with Lancaster Avenue, or West Philly. Frank

Walsh and I decided we needed to crash their parties and steal their "work in progress" signs of gentrification. And that's exactly what we did.

The Hydrogen Jukebox got a gig at a camping festival in Lancaster, Pennsylvania, where I ate some mind-bending mushrooms by the campfire and got lost in Elliott Levin's flute playing. Elliott was one of those musicians that seemed to be in every band in the city and had been since the '70s. He played saxophone for the most part, but also carried a flute that he played equally well. He was an old head, poet, musician, who only played music to get by. He could riff on any melody, mutate it into abstract jazz, and come back into the song with a harmony. The Hydrogen Jukebox was lucky to have him wander in and out of our practices and shows. That night, his wise and mischievous flute playing was speaking to me, trailing off down deep scales, as I stared into the fire. Eventually, Elliott wandered off and I started wondering why I had a plastic festival wristband on, tagged like cattle on the farm. I asked if anyone had a knife to cut it off.

When I held the knife against the bracelet, all I saw was blood flowing through my wrist inside the veins of a psychedelic bloodstream. Distracted by the sight of my transparent arm running with life force, I was afraid to cut away from the body towards the wrist. I tried instead to slice it upward. The pocketknife wouldn't cut the thick plastic bracelet locked on my wrist. I applied more pressure. The blade jumped up and bit me in the lower lip. I stood up immediately and took off my shirt, placed it on the cut to soak up the blood that was pouring out as I backed up behind the tent, up against one of the parked cars.

All images doubled, then doubled again and again, until there was only one color. The sound did the same, feeding back until only one ringing tone sounded. Warm water ran down my leg. I was no one for a while, then my friend Lance, who had given me the knife, was standing overhead explaining what had happened. The knife had gone through my bottom lip all the way to the gum. I passed out and pissed myself. After a minute of realizing who and where I was, fragments of the situation came back in quick flashes.

"Why did you give me the knife?" I yelled, embarrassed to be alive.

"Because you asked me to." Lance couldn't help smiling as he answered my question. He was a good friend of our drummer and was having a crack at managing the band.

"I'm stupid, stupid, stupid!" I shouted, licking the knife wound and touching my face to assess the damage. "This is crazy, I'm going to have a huge scar."

"It's not as bad as you think," said Lance as he helped me up. "Stop touching it though. Why don't you wake up Styx Latte so we can get in his car, turn the lights on, and look in the mirror."

I opened Styx Latte's tent and woke him up. Our shaggy, red-bearded, long-haired, drummer with A.D.D. opened his eyes. It took a second for the story to sink in, but Styx understood all too well. A few days before the show, Styx had torn his Achilles tendon on a screen door and had to get stitches. He hobbled out of the tent with a pair of crutches to get us into the car.

When staring into the mirror, a clear, calm, sober mind took hold and let me go into laughter. The wound was deep but only as wide as the knife tip. "Now I have another mouth to feed," I said aloud and everyone in the car started laughing too. As I mouthed the words, the cut on the right corner of my lower lip moved open and closed just like a mouth. When I spoke, it spoke; when I laughed, it did too.

I woke up by the campfire embers in the morning with a crusty lower lip and we all went out for pancakes. It was almost time to go back to being Jellyboy the Clown, rather than Malerkus Squidling. To provoke the shadows and amuse the monster-birth. To be the punchline punching bag of controversy wherever it was in need.

The clown makeup was calling to my skin. Barry Silver helped me design a face and applied makeup in a way that wouldn't smear or melt into my eyes. Under the eye was painted the shadow of my thin spectacles, with long, black, half diamond-like daggers pointing down my cheeks. Two black lines on the center of the brow were surrounded by mirror image eyebrows, arching up the entire forehead like thick S hooks. Nose red followed my nostrils. The knife wound was painted on the right corner of my lower lip as a much-needed reminder of mortality.

Chapter 3
Skull Boy's Psycho Rodeo

I tried to climb for a good view of history in full clown face for the first time. Standing on the shoulders of geniuses and giants, we found the wind to fill the sails of our artistic airship. Later that year in the winter, Hurricane Katrina brought down the levee and flooded New Orleans into a war zone.

Asbury Park, on the boardwalk of the New Jersey shore, called us in to haunt them. It was a big art festival which our sideshow would headline. The boardwalk is the ruins of the turn of the last century, bookended by beautiful old architecture covered in graffiti. Vegetation grew, overflowing through broken windows, but the beach was still open, and people still came out. Ghosts dressed like proper ladies and gentlemen still promenaded with the seagull sounds in the salty air. Asbury Park was an overgrown graveyard inhabited by punks, greasers, and a mixed bag of Jersey nuts. A fantastic place to light flaming torches and make a show.

Skull Boy was the name of the guy in charge. His face was painted boldly like chiseled bone. The bazaar sprang up from the boardwalk like weeds out of the cracks in sidewalks. Clowns in on the haunting were brought out from the walls by the character of the red-faced Masked Perfesser, with a long nose that knows too much.

The original Howard Johnson's '60s diner was the host of the show. Vendors of all kinds of arts and crafts sold their wares along the route while live music blasted out front. We set up on the boardwalk and waited for the sun to fall, which brought the rusty orange moon out on the water.

Frank Walsh, the Masked Perfesser, 2009 (Geoff Hall)

The Masked Perfesser's slapstick was slap-happy that night. Crossing the line from our heads over to the heads of a few people watching. The beginnings of the combined revolutionary assembly of fire, music, dance, poetry, and sideshow. A mannequin's head, launched in a long arc into the unready skull of a man named Monkey.

The show was such a success that Skull Boy asked us to perform at another event he was hosting in Belmar, New Jersey, called Skull Boy's Psycho Rodeo. "Hee-haw!" We galloped in our minds to the Belmar biker bar. When we got there, we were met with a rude welcome from the Jersey Devil.

Held in the back room of an enormous biker bar with an unusually large number of security guards and bouncers in staff jerseys, Skull Boy's Psycho Rodeo was not a rodeo at all. It was a misplaced show of mismatched bands. Skull Boy had his makeup on, wickedly contrasting his surroundings. He enthusiastically greeted me, as I was not Jellyboy but Malerkus Squidling, and folded a few hundred-dollar bills into my hand. "This is in case we get too busy later. Thanks for coming out. By the way, very nice frog bowtie, Malerkus."

"Thanks, Skull Boy. What should we do about loading our gear?"

"Just wait until the band before you is set up, then bring your stuff from the car to the side of the stage."

Not a rodeo at all unless looked at abstractly through a crystal lens. A state of mind culture clash, Old West saloon, where the cowboys were really New Jersey bikers. A different breed of weirdo than Carnivolution. We were as frightening to them as they were to us.

Our crew was getting the creeps from the place. There were a bunch of us. We came in three vehicles. Our band was six people deep: Styx Latte, the drummer; Matterz Squidling on the bass; Bunny Savage, the guitarist; Jim Kydonious on flute; and Royce Pape with the clarinet. Along to enjoy the show was our friend and acting manager Lance, who had lent me the knife I used to accidentally stab myself in the face at the festival. Barry Silver and his girlfriend, who was his assistant, were also with us. We were a crew of nine, intimidating but outnumbered.

The band before us was self-indulgent and off-key. They were slowly driving away the audience as we were bringing our equipment to the side of the stage. Styx Latte preset his drums and went to sleep in his car. The trouble started when we were bringing in the sideshow gear.

"What's all this?" said the stage door guard.

I responded, "A fire extinguisher and a bed of nails."

"What's in the bucket?" he asked.

"Broken glass," said Barry Silver.

"You guys can't perform here. It's a liability issue."

"Maybe we should talk to Skull Boy and the manager," I said. The door guard got on the radio with the manager. We walked across the room to have a meeting. The conversation we had wasn't really much of a conversation.

"There is no way you guys are doing a show in my bar with that kind of equipment," said the tough looking little manager, with a wild look in his eyes and powder on his nose.

"We are a circus sideshow."

"I don't care what you are; no way are you doing a show here."

"We came all the way from Philly. We don't have to use fire, glass, or nails. There are other things we can do that are safe. Like the straitjacket escape for instance," I suggested, still trying to be nice in the face of all this nonsense.

"No, no, no: no way!" He was getting more and more angry, and that was making the two huge, bald bouncers on either side of him stand up straighter with their arms folded.

"Do you even know what a sideshow is?" I asked, taking the nail out of my pocket.

"I don't have to know what it is, and I don't care what it is. The only thing that matters is that you are not doing a show here tonight."

"So, you mean to tell me we can't do something like this?" I put the nail up to my nostril and slammed it into my skull with the palm of my hand.

That set the manager off. He started yelling at the top of his lungs, "Remove them!! Get them out of my bar."

The bouncers smirked and assumed bulldozer formation. Matterz Squidling was standing next to me. Being the Squidling Brothers from the same mother and father, we are very protective of each other and don't take kindly to being pushed around. When the bouncers started pushing, so did we.

After rapidly removing the nail, I leapt on the back of a man twice my size, all one hundred and thirty pounds of Malerkus Squidling in a red and white zigzag suit and matching polka dot shirt with a green space frog bowtie. The bouncer grabbed me from behind his head, flipped me over his shoulders, and I was locked in a wrestling hold on the floor. *That* was the real psycho rodeo.

Meanwhile, Matterz was being forcibly backed up towards the stage door by the bar manager. Royce Pape, the clarinet player in our band, was about as big as the man on top of me. He rushed over and caught the goon off guard, grabbing him by the shirt. He pulled him up and I scrambled around the floor looking for the spectacles that had fallen off my face.

"It's not going to happen like this," said Royce, looking like a Samoan warrior, with his long, curly, dark hair and stocky frame. "Back off, no more fighting." The guard actually listened to him although they were nose to nose, on high alert. Things weren't going so well on the other side of the room: Jim Kydonious, our pacifist flute player, already terrified by New Jersey, had run to wake up Styx Latte, who was passed out by his drums after just napping in his car a few moments before.

"There isn't going to be a show, Styx. There is a brawl in the bar! We have to get out of here fast!"

Barry Silver had been hastily bringing props out to his vehicle, holding his coffin-shaped bed of nails in front of him like a spiked body shield. Matterz was backed up to the door with a half bottle of beer in his hands, overwhelmed by a bouncer and the manager of the bar. I saw him snap from across the room as the manager was winding up to swing a punch. His long, straight, heavy metal hair came to life like the rapids of an angry river. He seemed to grow as his chest expanded: he threw beer in the manager's face, and then broke the bottle over the man's head.

At that moment, our lead guitar player Bunny Savage came running in to support Matterz who was outnumbered two to one, and pushed the already bashed man into the spikes that Barry Silver was carrying towards the door, cutting him up pretty badly. The bouncer backed away and the manager tried to run, but he tripped and started crying like a child with road burns on the parking lot pavement just beyond the stage door.

Adriano Moraes, 2024.

Royce became diplomatic and stood at the door talking to the bouncers as if he was one of them. "Things have gone too far, gentlemen. We don't want any more violence. We just want to get our stuff out of here." In a matter of minutes, the cars were loaded, and most of the Hydrogen Jukebox made a grand getaway. Barry was in a panic, having just shredded the manager with his bed of nails. He and his tiny, pink haired girlfriend ran to their pickup truck and took off as well. Word was the police were on the way.

Jim Kydonious and I stayed behind to talk to the cops who arrived just as the others had driven off. Jim had recently joined the band to play flute. His main love was heavy metal guitar, though he was too much of a perfectionist to plug in anymore. He was about fifteen years older than me with a whitening beard and shoulder-length brown hair. Strangely enough, I met him while he was playing stand-up bass with a West Philly bluegrass band called the Flat Possum Boys. His flute melodies tied together the high end of our often-cacophonous sound.

It's a good thing the police showed up when they did, because the story had just spread throughout the bar. Bouncers and patrons alike began to gather around the bloody, shocked manager. A growing crowd of dirty looks would have turned very ugly, but a patrol car pulled up with its lights flashing. The officer was a tall, honest looking fellow with an even temper. He was trying to find out what really happened. First, he approached the bloody manager who was in shock, trembling slightly, surrounded by friends. They talked for a few minutes. Then the officer walked over to me. I was standing next to the large bouncer who I had the tangle with.

"Okay, does somebody want to tell me what happened here?" said the cop.

"This guy attacked us," said the bouncer, pointing his finger at me like a child reporting to the principal. The policeman smiled and took a long look at both of us. I was calm and polite with shrugged shoulders.

"So," he said, "you mean to tell me that this little guy in the frog bowtie attacked you and the rest of the security staff?"

The officer decided to question us separately. "So, what's your story?" he asked me after he talked to the bouncer.

"Well, our circus act was hired to perform here, but the guy who hired us didn't clear our act with the bar. We drove here from Philadelphia to do a job. When the staff saw our equipment, they told us we couldn't perform. Things got heated and the manager ordered his bouncers to forcibly remove us rather than just asking us to leave. There was a fight and now here we are."

"Sounds about right. Can I see your identification please?"

"Oh no, I left it at my house."

"I'm afraid I'm going to have to take you in for disorderly conduct."

"I'm sorry, it's just that the clothes I'm wearing are a costume. I left my ID in my other pants at home. I can gladly give you my social security number and you can check my records. I really can't afford to go to jail. I have to go to work tomorrow."

The officer thought about it for a moment, took my information down on a pad and walked to his car to check it out. When he came back, he said, "Your record is clean. I would say for your own safety you should get in your car, go home to Philly, and not come back." The crowd was bloodthirsty and staring at us.

"Thank you so much for being understanding, officer." Jim and I got in his truck and took off, but we didn't get far before we rode right into a DWI checkpoint. Jim was nervous, because he had a pipe and some weed in his glove box.

A flashlight shined in our faces and an intimidating policeman said, "Been drinking this evening? Have any drugs or weapons in the vehicle?"

"No sir," I said, not giving Jim a chance to talk. "Just did a circus show at a bar down the road, now we're headed back to Philadelphia."

"Circus, eh? What kind of circus?"

"It's an old-time sideshow with stunts."

"What kind of stunts?" he asked, shining the light in my eyes.

"Would you like to see?" I quickly pulled a nail and a mousetrap out of my pocket.

"Okay, humor me." His attitude had changed from menacing to amused.

"Alright, sir, then for your entertainment I will use this mousetrap to hammer this nail up my nose into the skull, just missing the brain." The wooden mousetrap made a nice sound as it knocked the nail back.

The cop started howling with laughter and he called all the other cops over to see. "Let me see that nail," said the officer. I wiped it off and handed it to him. He checked it was real. Then came the human blockhead part two. All of the police were laughing and saying, "Can you believe this guy?" To end the routine, I snapped the mousetrap on my tongue and thanked them with a lisp.

"Good luck in showbiz, and safe trip back to Philly," the officer said, and we were back on the road. Jim was so wound up and nervous about everything that his driving was all screwy. He was ranting about how much he hates New Jersey and how we could have been in jail. He stopped at a green light and was driving sporadically from fast to slow.

Next thing we knew, we were lost, and that made matters worse. A patrol car spotted Jim's erratic driving and pulled us over. There it was again, a flashlight in the face with blinking lights behind us.

"License and registration, please. Do you know why I pulled you over?"

I spoke up, "Officer, we are lost and can't figure out how to get back to Philadelphia. We were already inspected at a DWI point just a few miles back." He took the license and registration back to his car and returned a few minutes later.

"Your story checks out," he said, and gave us the directions back to Philly.

When we got home to 4811 Chester Ave, everyone was sitting in the living room going over the events of the night. We told them what had happened to us. Barry Silver said, "We had to stop at that checkpoint, too. It was frightening. I told the cop there was a fight at the bar that was really bad, and I just wanted to get my girlfriend home. When I told him that, a call came in on the police radio about it and he let us go without searching our car.

Then Styx said, "Jellyboy, you have to stop fighting at our shows. Now we have to pay out of pocket for all the gas."

"I know, Styx, but the best part is that Skull Boy paid me before the fight. Who knew that sideshow would be so dangerous?" I said, jumping up and down, so pleased to be out of that mess with all our money.

"It's New Jersey that's dangerous," said Jim. "I'm never doing another show there for the rest of my life."

We celebrated our freedom for the continuation of the night. Some spirit out there was protecting us as we were protecting the baby Squid monster-birth while it stretched and grew towards its potential. The Squidling had ideas of its own which would be inoculated in our minds.

What if we made a sideshow horror movie? Slasher, zombie, vampire, with black magic and circus freaks? A contagious idea, and our whole collective was inspired by shadow versions of our alter egos. Matterz, Frank, and I began talking about the story. In no time, Matterz, who had gone to film school, began writing a script for *The Unholy Sideshow*, our movie!

Since I was a kid, I was always into special effects makeup. I used to keep a disguise kit under my bed in the finished basement room I shared with my brother Matterz. It was one of those weird things that I had waited for an opportunity to use in just the right situation. I used to carry a snake bite kit around too, but I never had the chance to use it. I imagined rattlesnakes were more common than they are. The day I got to use my disguise kit for a practical reason had to do with a family emergency. I was in junior high school. The family was getting ready to go see Matterz perform trombone at a school concert. About an hour before it was time to go, my brother Jason walked through the door in quite a shocking way. His hair, which had been long, brown and wavy, was cut short and bleached blonde. He also shaved off his eyebrows. My mother said, "Oh my god, he is on drugs!"

Jason had been an apprentice to a master sculptor who had a huge art studio in the basement of Saint John the Divine's church in Harlem. He had witnessed a sexual assault on a New York subway platform, tried to stop it, and a gun was drawn on him, so he ran! In his imagination, that man would follow him home to murder all his family. So as not to be recognized, Jason cut off his hair, bleached it blonde, and shaved off his eyebrows. He walked through the door ashamed of the way he looked and how he had reacted to what happened to him in New York. He wanted to come to the concert with us but told me he was afraid people would stare at him because he had no eyebrows. That's when I had the idea to use the makeup kit.

"I can make you some very realistic eyebrows," I told him.

"How can you do that?" he asked, with tears running down his cheeks.

"I've got clear sticky wax and realistic hair in my makeup kit: I can fix your disguise so no one will think you look strange at all!" I excitedly ran down the stairs to get my makeup kit, whipped him up some foolproof eyebrows and gave him a baseball cap to cover his crazy haircut. When I held up the mirror to his face, he looked surprised at how good it was. With uncontrollable tears of joy, he embraced me and said, "My little brother! You fuckin' did it! My little brother, man, you really fixed me, I can't believe it!" The whole family went to see Matterz play music that night.

That Halloween, we were set to perform at the Tiberino Museum, the Day of the Dead on South Street, with an afterparty at the Rotunda. The Headhouse asked us to resurrect the spirit of New Orleans.

The Hydrogen Jukebox playing at Carnivolution, with Jellyboy on guitar, Jim Kydonious on flute, Royce Pape on clarinet, Rob "Bunny Savage" Newman on guitar, The Ellen Powell Tiberino Museum, Philadelphia, 2005 (Geoff Hall)

Angel the Clown, 2005 (Geoff Hall)

As our circus grew, thoughts of a clown named Angel spitting fire and telling stories of her adventures were inescapable. We met during the summer of 2003 in Ithaca, New York. The Hydrogen Jukebox had moved as an experiment to see if we could make it in the festival scene of upstate New York. Just before we arrived, Angel moved there to study medicinal plants with an herbalist named 7Song.

We started spending lots of time together, exploring the woods, gorges, and waterfalls, and finding places to swim. We learned each other's stories, and the deepest wound I ever had in my spirit started to heal with a growing idea called Carnivolution. I told her of my brother Jason's suicide. She told me of her Pentecostal Christian childhood, and her escape into the punk rock circus, traveling all over the country in a bio-diesel bus and hopping freight trains with legendary freaks from the End of the World and Know Nothing Zirkus Zideshow.

Angel had a curly mop of red hair in between stages. Her earlobes were stretched, filled with animal bone, and she wore a crooked septum ring. She truly came to life while spinning fire on poi chains. She sparkled with fairy magic, slight freckles, and bright blue eyes that reflected death-defying trails of fire. Figure eights of flame dazzled by her hairy armpits, way too close to her face, leaving a sweet stink that felt like a love potion in its wake.

After Angel finished her studies with 7Song, she got on a plane to move back to northern California. The winter hit hard. The ice dripped in long daggers from rooftops and the snow piled high. My car broke down. I lost my night job cleaning movie theaters and was stuck indoors. Styx Latte and I decided to move back to Philadelphia. Public transportation and couch surfing in Philly would be better than being broke and trapped in frozen upstate New York. Carnivolution was planted in my mind, and I was determined to make it a reality.

Two years later, I had a job as a house painter in West Philly, with a circus collective on the rise. It was time to show Angel how she had affected my life with a plane ticket to perform at Carnivolution on Halloween!

I was dressed as a roach for the party at the Tiberino Museum. We had a great sideshow and the fire crew teamed up with Frank Walsh and the Hydrogen Jukebox. My roach costume consisted of an old green Russian paratrooper suit full of strings, tubes, and valves. The wings were wires with door screens lashed to them, fixed to a backpack frame with a hubcap at the center. Thick rubber tubes were attached to an upside-down bicycle helmet, spray painted brown.

After the Tiberino's living backyard was set with speakers on the stages, Angel and I put on clown makeup together with a shared mirror. We forgot about everything but what we were doing amidst the paintings coming out of the walls.

The party was an all-night dream, full of costumes, but before we could open our eyes, a flash flood of humorous memories overwhelmed us, like diehard roaches refusing to be exterminated. During the party, Angel found a fledgling artist named Tommy Toons who wanted to turn all of us into a comic book. He was a student studying animation at Drexel University and was immediately adopted by the Carnivolution. Tommy Toons walked home with a circus spark glowing in his hands to bring future dreams to light.

There wasn't much sleep to be had. The party that took us so long to set up needed to be broken down and packed away as soon as it bloomed. All the equipment was loaded into our black and silver short bus, only to be unloaded again early the next morning on South Street for the Day of the Dead. Sleep knocked me out like a sucker punch: I couldn't figure out when or where it landed, but when I awoke, life was stirring in the big old house getting ready for the parade. We had done it before as the pack animals of show business: set up the stage, test the sound, organize the parade, play the show, and break it all down again.

The Headhouse wanted us to start the concert before the parade arrived. We refused and I ran down to the launch site of the march to get things moving. Angel agreed to take charge of our part of the procession and launch it before the rest. I ran back to start the show, knowing that Angel was leading the fire performers and our Fear puppet, which we needed in our plan for the beginning of the band's performance.

The main parade was paralyzed. The police, the fire department, a mass of tall bikes, a marching band, vintage cars, and tons of people in costume holding giant skeletons awaited the order to march. The Carnivolution wouldn't let that stop us from having a renegade promenade with fire and fear to start it all off. The Hydrogen Jukebox started improvising music to a small crowd who were awaiting the arrival of the parade, when behind them appeared a giant puppet with painted, paper mâché heads on sticks. The Seven Faces of Fear could be seen from over the tops of the audience's heads, each operated by a separate puppeteer, surrounding a striped circus tent on wheels as its body. The band improvised as the puppet, encircled by more people holding torches, made its way through the costumed crowd.

The puppeteers got in formation with the fire breathers on the front and sides of the stage. Frank Walsh, otherwise known as the Masked Perfesser, took to the stage with a new persona: Lazari the Dark Magician. He would resurrect the spirit of New Orleans as we were asked, except not in the way expected. Zombies led by a vampire ripped apart politicians while the band accompanied the poem *Hurricane Land*. The main parade arrived in the middle of our spectacle and the Halloween dance party erupted in the streets.

Red was happy about the show because New Orleans was dear to him. His sideshow with Toni Del Rio used to winter there for the Mardi Gras. As I gave Red his money, I asked him the question that had been burning on my mind. "Would you teach me to swallow swords? I can pay you of course, a bit at a time over the course of the winter."

He looked at me as if seeing me for the first time and said, "Sure. If I can do it, so can you."

"Really? Thank you so much! I know it won't be easy, but I'm up for the challenge and ready to dedicate myself fully." We shook hands and both felt relieved. Red hadn't had a job since Tower Records and now he knew he would make it through the winter.

I ran over to Angel and told her. We hugged each other tight, jumped up and down and squawked in glory. When Angel was around and dancing, everyone else felt it was okay to do the same. She naturally had and gave freely that contagious spark of life.

Chapter 4
Freaks and Fire

Red got me started by bending a wire hanger into the shape of a sword. We looked through a catalog and I ordered three stainless steel medieval replica swords, one of which was a cane with a dragon's head for a handle that Red wanted for himself. Part of learning sword swallowing was preparing the blade and giving away power to receive power. Gifts are common among sideshow people. While waiting for the swords to arrive, I tried to put the hanger down my throat. It seemed completely impossible.

I convinced Red to take Barry Silver on as a student as well. It was Barry and my New Year's goal to get a sword down. We practiced together with the hanger to no avail; only horrible sounds of mucus and bile rejecting the metal, as we tried to tackle the first of many gag reflexes which lead down to the opening of the stomach. We could hardly get the hangers to stay in our throats, let alone push it past into our rib cages. It was do or die, and dying wasn't an option—although that was the chance we were taking if we screwed up.

Fall turned cold after Angel moved to the west coast, just as two years before. This time, however, things were coming together rather than falling to absolute zero. Painting outside lasted until it was too cold. Then, thankfully, some inside work came along.

A circus group from California called the Yard Dogs Road Show was coming to town. Information was passed along, and a batch of their posters arrived at my door by mail. Canvassing with posters was one of my specialties around Philadelphia. They were performing at a little club on Bainbridge just off South Street. Their show was more like vaudeville with a live band, storytelling, burlesque, and sideshow. They had an amazing old full-length tour bus going all across the country, living a dream on wheels. Their sword swallower was a lanky, calm magician of a man with striped pants and a thin mustache who swallowed a neon tube which made his entire neck glow through the skin. He also ingested a long, skinny sword that he sliced through a lemon to prove its sharpness. He stood out among the rest, then faded into the background, seated for most of the show, playing percussion with the band.

At their show, I bought a book called *Freaks and Fire: The Underground Reinvention of Circus* by J. Dee Hall. On the cover was a puzzle piece-faced clown with a lizard's tongue. The introduction of the book talked about the connection of clowns and sideshow to shamanism. It introduced the do-it-yourself circuses of the 1990s that shocked and mystified their audiences. Groups like the Bindlestiffs, the End of the World and the Know Nothing Family Zirkus Zideshow, the Brothers Grimm, Circus Contraption, and the Jim Rose Circus out of Seattle. Two individuals had their own chapters: Zamora the Torture King, famous for his deep muscle human pincushion, and the Enigma, the sword swallower tattooed from head to toe with blue puzzle pieces.

We had the swords delivered to Red's place at the old pet shop where the original *Rocky* movie was filmed. He called and said it was time to prepare the blades. I took the subway to his spot, and he opened the bars of the storefront smoking a cigarette. Coughing, Red said, "Put another nail in my coffin. Come on in, Jellyboy. I'm going to show you the difference between life and death." He had the three swords by a metal grinding wheel. The one I chose had skulls on the handle and sheath. The other two had dragon heads on the handles. One was the cane sword that would be Red's. The other I gave to Barry for all his guidance. It was nice to be able to help him with his dream of swallowing a sword.

"Listen close, and watch closer," said Red. "If there is the slightest nick or burr on the sword when you swallow it, that might be the last thing you do. One little snag and you could rip yourself open from the inside. Make no mistake, it is deadly." Then he leaned over the machine like an old pro and sparks began to fly with the smell of burning metal. When he was finished, he wiped it with a cloth. The sword was smooth and beautiful. Then he licked the blade. "One of the reasons I lick the blade is to make sure it's smooth." He put the sword up, let it fall down his throat and tossed it out like it was nothing. "Now it's been test driven," he said and laughed long from the gut of smoker's cough. "Now you know it's safe…well, as safe as it can be."

Red recommended that Barry and I come to the Philadelphia tattoo convention. He was working the door and would get us in for free. The following week, I took the train back to Philly after visiting my parents in Lancaster, PA, reading about the Enigma in *Freaks and Fire*. The tattoo convention was at the Wyndham Hotel in Center City, Philadelphia. Red let Barry and me in as his guests. In a sea of people, through the buzz of tattoo machines, I stopped dead in my tracks at the sight of the Enigma, the blue puzzle piece man! He was standing right in front of me with horns implanted under the skin of his blue, bald head.

Enigma was holding an armful of trophies for the tattoo contest. At first sight, the most striking part of him was how orange the long goatee on his chin was, and how white his teeth looked next to his blue skin. His blue eyes had the sparkle of a snake oil salesman. Opening the book to his page, I walked up to him, and said, "Hey, I was just reading about you and didn't realize you would be here. Did you know you were in this book, *Freaks and Fire*?"

"Why no, I didn't; that's puzzling. Oh, wait a minute, I remember being interviewed for that. I didn't think she was actually going to publish it. What do you know? Say, I've got to bring these trophies over there. You can come with me if you like."

I followed the Enigma to the stage. "My name is Jellyboy the Clown."

"Funny, you don't look like a clown."

"Well, I'm not in makeup."

"That's the problem with makeup, it washes off...so two cannibals are eating a clown, one looks up at the other and says, 'Does this taste funny to you?'"

He put the trophies on the stage and said, "So, what's your name when you're not a clown?"

"Oh, it's Eric," I answered shyly.

He took the book out of my hands and signed it next to his picture. '*To Eric the magnificent from your Big Blue Pal the Enigma.*'

"Thanks, Enigma. I just recently started learning how to swallow a sword. Can't quite get it though."

"Sword swallowing is not how, but why. Why would a clown want to swallow a sword?"

"Because it's the most amazing thing I've ever seen."

"Well, the answer is different for everybody. As long as you don't stop wondering why, it should come to you. Ask the right questions if you want the right answers."

Just then the Enigma was swarmed by people with cameras and questions.

"Didn't I see you on *The X Files*?" one asked.

"I get around," he responded.

"Did all those tattoos hurt?" another asked.

"Only where there are nerves," he said.

"Is your whole body tattooed like that?" said another.

"You wouldn't just paint the front of your house," he stated.

"How long did that take?"

"It's like painting a barn with a toothpick."

Every person who had a question wanted a picture with him. The Enigma didn't mind. He acted like a mix between a knight and a jester. I stood there the whole time watching and waiting for a chance to continue our conversation. Eventually, I got a chance to get a word in.

"I'm making a horror movie about zombies and black magic circus performers called *The Unholy Sideshow*."

The Enigma got really serious for a second and said, "I make soundtracks—I'm a musician as well as a sideshow performer, you know."

"So am I. I mean, I'd love it if you helped with the soundtrack. Hell, it would be easy to write you into the movie if you like."

"Sounds like a great premise for a film."

He wrote his email address on a piece of paper and gave it to me. "Let's be in touch, Jellyboy. Check out the show later on tonight."

"I wouldn't miss it. Thanks, Enigma."

The convention was amazing. Overwhelming amounts of brightly colored human canvases proudly displayed themselves throughout the hotel. It wasn't just tattoos: artistic scars and branding, split tongues, implants on foreheads and forearms, piercings all over the body, faces stretched to impossible proportions. We were in the heart of the hive of the modern primitive movement, and there I was without one piercing or tattoo.

I was there to see the sideshows with Barry Silver. We were like little kids running around a carnival. Then it was showtime! We got up front, close enough to see everything but not so close that we were in the performers' faces. Enigma did a one-man show with a blue puzzle piece-shaped guitar.

"People keep asking me, 'What's next?' as they sit and grow old in front of the movie screen, worshiping the scripture of *Star Wars, Raiders of the Lost Ark*, and for some of you people, *Sesame Street*, with popcorn as your communion wafer and soda your blood of Christ. 'What's next?' I can see it now…the Church of Cinematology! All hail the LA Mecca, a free movie every week coming out of an LA writer's melon!"

Enigma had programmed his own backing track of drums, bass and synthesizers. He played guitar while he spoke. Then he picked up a hammer and nail.

"We're going to start real simple, with only a hammer and nail, just like the Romans." He crossed his arms and said, "I'm a suicidal carpenter; don't cross me." He put the nail up to his head. "Why did Jesus die on the cross? He forgot the safe word. Do you want to see me hammer this nail into the center of my brain?" Everyone screamed.

"Okay, on the count of three—1, 2, 3." He paused, just before driving the spike into his head.

"So, you're just going to let me do this? You're looking at me like I killed the Lindbergh baby." Then he hammered a nail up each of his nostrils. He looked around. "What? It's a tattoo, okay." He pried the nails out of his head and let them fall to the floor.

"Now it's time for the most dangerous part of the show. I know you're thinking it, and I'm thinking it too: balloon animal routine!" He pulled a condom out of his wallet and opened it.

"I got this balloon out of the balloon museum in my wallet." He snorted the condom up his nose and pulled it out of his mouth. It came out with a bit of blood on it.

"You'll have to excuse me, I'm spotty, it's my time of the month. Now, to reverse the process." He rolled the condom up on his finger and put it toward the back of his throat.

"I'm doing this for you guys because I know you love it. I'm sticking this balloon, wet with nasal debris, back into my cranium. Rhymes with geranium." He pinched one nostril and inflated the condom, making it pulse out of his nose.

"I think it likes you. It's not a little kitten; it's not a puppy; I think a sea cucumber best describes this balloon animal." He soloed on the guitar a bit, then leaned down to pick up a sword shaped like a cross.

"I've had religion forced down my throat every day of my life. Why should today be any different?" He put the sword up, dropped it down into his guts, and bowed while playing guitar.

While Enigma was working people up to a frenzy with his jokes, he picked up a chainsaw and pulled the string to rev the motor. The smell of gasoline filled the room. "Yee haw, just like back in Texas!" Enigma yelled, while windmilling the chainsaw and making the revolutions of the motor pulse. The sound of danger ripped through the air.

Then the blue puzzle piece man placed the running chainsaw by his feet and pulled a bandana from his back pocket, which he tied around his head as a blindfold. He put an apple in his mouth, fumbling around with his hand searching for the chainsaw, picked it up, and quickened the speed of the rotating chain, sending out shockwaves into the audience. He held his hand up to his ear and everyone in the crowd freaked out in a mess of sound. He ran the chainsaw into the apple, shooting sprays of applesauce all over. 'X marked the spot' in the apple of the human jigsaw. He removed the bandana to reveal the delightfully demented face of a self-made show devil.

The friendly monster man then asked that the lights be lowered. He turned around and came back with a glowing red neon tube. "Luke, I am your father; surrender to the dark side." The most dangerous thing a sword swallower can swallow is a neon tube, because it is a glass tube filled with mercury. Enigma made the entire tube vanish down his throat leaving only an electric cord and a jack-o'-lantern glow coming out of his mouth. He pulled it out slowly and said, "I just swallowed a lightsaber! Take that, Darth Maul!"

For the final stunt, he pulled six feet of medical tubing attached to a giant syringe out of a suitcase. Enigma fed the tubing up his nose and swallowed it down the back of his sinus passage into his stomach. He pulled out a bottle of blue liquid and chugged it down with one gulp. He pushed out his stomach, making him look like a mortal genie. Pulling on the plunger inside the syringe made the blue contents of his stomach flow green through the tubes. As the liquid filled the giant syringe, Enigma started in with the banter.

"I wish I could get that much back on my taxes." Little pieces of mostly digested food were filling the syringe through the tube.

"Looks like I've been eating seafood, and there is an oyster."

When the syringe was full, he poured the green liquid into the container and made a toast: "Here's to recycling, good for the environment." He downed the funky green liquid from his stomach back into his throat from which it came and took his final bow.

After the area was cleaned, a horde of performers from Brooklyn, New York took the stage. It was the combined forces of the Disgraceland Family Freakshow and the Coney Island Circus Sideshow, and what a show it was! A classically creepshow young man named Diamond Donny Vomit made the introduction. He was tall and thin, in a button-down shirt, a suit jacket, and rockstar striped circus pants, with sideburns that went all the way down his jaw.

"Ladies and gentlemen, what you are about to witness is not for the faint of heart or weak of stomach. Freaks, wonders, human curiosities, nature's mistakes, the bizarre, the downright strange; right here on this stage tonight for your demented and perverse pleasure. If you're ready to be entertained, say, 'YAH!'"

He then began conducting the crowd in a game of screams. When his right hand went up, the right side of the room yelled until he cut it off abruptly and switched to the left. To make it more interesting, he added a silver spoon. Whenever the audience saw the spoon they yelled, "SPOON!" Donny Vomit stirred up their energy: *SCREAM....SCREAM...* "SPOON!" yelled the audience, until the enthusiasm and humor were where they needed to be to start the show.

A man named Roc Roc-It hit the stage with the gusto of a post-apocalyptic clown. Instead of makeup, his face and head were covered with tattoos—spaceships and alien creatures and hot chili peppers for sideburns with burning dynamite wicks. He blew up a long balloon with no effort at all and began to twirl it. Counting to three, he pretended to put the balloon in the air and attempted to ingest it. It wasn't working so he took a drink and tried it again. This time it began to disappear down his throat. He grabbed his neck and moved the throat around a bit and puffed out his belly, which was quite large compared to the rest of his body. The balloon eventually disappeared into his mouth completely. He made a guilty face, turned around, reached into the back of his pants, and pulled out a balloon animal in the shape of a poodle, to a roar of laughter.

Insectavora drunkenly danced onto the stage in a black dress and safety goggles. I had seen her before at the sideshow gathering with Tyler Fyre; however, this felt like a different Insectavora. She took off the dress, revealing a colorful canvas of inked skin. Roc Roc-It picked up a bed of nails and placed it on the stage. Wearing only a black leather bikini, Insectavora laid her back very carefully across the sharpened spikes. Roc Roc-It placed a cinder block across her chest and cracked it to rubble with a sledgehammer. It looked like some of the block jumped too close to her face, but she got up from the nails seemingly unscathed.

Donny Vomit took cables connected to a battery and threaded them up his nose and out his mouth. He then lifted the battery with his sinus passage. Smiling through the discomfort, he removed the wire, which was a little spotty with blood.

I was mesmerized by Heather Holliday. She was so wacky and lovely all at once, like a 1940s pinup all punked out, wielding a blade. Greedily licking her sword, with eyes open wide, she put it up and let it fall down her throat with great and careless ease. She pulled the sword out, patted her stomach, and ran offstage.

Spliff the Amazonian Affliction walked onstage. His dreadlock mohawk, put up with a hairband on the top of his head, made him look like a pineapple, high on a Viking battle potion, ready to rage. He turned around, dropped his pants, and sat on the nail bed. He invited two volunteers to stand on his thighs. Up comes a photographer named Lunchbox (whose size matched his name), and he and his girlfriend Joy stood on Spliff's legs. Spliff's back was a little bloody, but he laid his stomach on the bed of nails. Another bed of nails was laid on top of him that GanJeesh rested his stomach on in the opposite direction. A third bed was placed on top of GanJeesh that Donny Vomit laid his back on. A fourth and fifth were placed on the stack where JiJi the Carnie Girl and Heather laid. In order from top to bottom were Heather Holliday, JiJi, Donny Vomit, GanJeesh, and Spliff anchoring the bottom. Roc Roc-It placed a porcelain piggy bank on Heather's stomach and cracked it to pieces with a staple gun. They hastily got everyone out from all the nail beds, stood next to each other, and took a bow.

Barry Silver was feeling the same way I was about the show. He knew Roc from talking to him on the internet. Roc and Spliff introduced us to everyone in their crew as sideshow performers from Philly. We followed them up to the upper level of the hotel to have a smoke. A couple of people knocked on Insectavora's room. She poked her head out, looking a bit disgruntled to see us. Heather Holliday was in the background. We told them if they wanted to smoke with us that we would be in Spliff's room. Insectavora shook her head and told us, "Heather and I don't smoke." A bunch of guys gathered in Spliff's room and lit up. Roc Roc-It had carabiners in his ears and was making people pull his earlobes as hard as they could.

Heather wandered into the room out of nowhere and my heart almost stopped. Then it started beating very fast. She unwillingly transformed me into a blabbermouth.

"Wow, your performance was something special, really. So cool, and so funny."

"Thanks," she said a bit sarcastically and made a buck-toothed rabbit face by tucking in her upper lip and batting her eyes. We started talking about different swords and Red Stuart's collection.

"My favorite one of his is the sword cane," she said. "Sword canes are so cool."

My eyes lit up. "That's the one I got him!"

"No way! You're just saying that because I said I liked it."

"No, it's true. I've been learning to swallow swords and I got him that as a gift."

"Really? Well, if you say so. The kind I like best are the showman cane swords. I want to do a cane spinning, tap dancing, sword swallowing act."

"That's a good idea. I will get you one."

"No way; you don't even know me."

"I don't have to know you to want to get you a sword. Your whole show was out of this world, really. I will never forget it as long as I live."

"Now you're talking creepy." Everybody started laughing.

After that, I couldn't stop thinking about the Disgraceland Family Freakshow and the Coney Island Circus Sideshow. Red sat with me looking through his catalogs for the right sword cane. We found it! A tan varnished wooden cane with a nice hook on the end. I ordered two and had Red prepare them on his wheel to be swallowed. I did a bit of internet research to find out when the next Disgraceland/Coney Island show would be: March 4, 2006. A photographer friend and I went to Brooklyn to a place called the Funhouse. I kept one cane for myself and the other I took as a gift for Heather Holliday. I realized it might be perceived as a bit creepy, but I was serious and wanted her to know that I wasn't just talking. As soon as we walked in, I spotted her and twirled the cane.

"Hey Heather, remember me? I know it's been a while, but I got you that cane sword."

She looked at me in disbelief and hesitated, then started laughing and hugged me. Then she brought it all around showing Donny Vomit and her other friends. After that she kind of disappeared and I got lost in the party.

It was a big warehouse space with a stage and a bunch of side rooms. The entertainment that night was wonderful. The Knuckle Up Cabaret started with a punk bluegrass group with a washtub bass, a banjo and fiddle, followed by the hardcore music of the Jungle Junkies. The sounds and the feeling in the room were an added bonus, but I had come for the sideshow. The performers were just as entertaining off the stage as on.

Insectavora was drunk, wandering around looking for her boyfriend. He had the word *GODLESS* tattooed on his head in bold letters. Donny Vomit emerged from the shadows with blood pouring down his hand. Insectavora said, "Donny, are you aware how much you're bleeding?" He didn't seem to mind, but I told him to put some direct pressure on it to make it stop. Heather Holliday seemed to vanish. I asked Donny where she was.

"She took off. It was really nice of you to give her that sword but let me give you some advice about Heather: she is best dealt with purely in business."

A juggler comedian named Brendan the "Pretty Good" balanced on a rolla-bolla and juggled a knife, a torch, and an 'apple of death!' He said, "Everything you do should end with the words 'of death' or 'of doom.'" He was a skilled street performer, much better than "pretty good."

I stayed awake all night at the Knuckle Up Cabaret and had the pleasure of meeting a German punk traveling with Roc named Larz Vegas. Larz was in his middle 40s, wearing a vest covered in spikes that revealed muscular arms decorated with tattoos that told the story of a life of adventure. He was immediately kind and curious about me.

"You're on the trail, vibing out the sideshow, I see," he said with a German accent, noticing that I was sketching and making notes in a book. He couldn't have been more accurate. I had the strong feeling I would be seeing a lot more of Larz and Roc as time went on. They were the friendliest in a fairly standoffish crowd. Perhaps it was because they were travelers, or perhaps they saw in me what I saw in them: that ancient spark of wonder blooming out of the circus seeds. Perhaps they could feel that I was a guard of the monster-birth, and they too were in league with the Misfit Mother.

Chapter 5
The Unholy Sideshow

A horror movie was bubbling in the Squidling's cauldron.

Zombies from the Unholy Sideshow movie, 2006 (Geoff Hall)

Matterz graduated from film school at Temple University in 2001 and was more than ready to do something with his degree. He wrote the script, was the camera man, the editor, the director, organized the set builds, and put together the team of makeup artists. We did the casting together and had lots of help from enthusiastic friends who got carried away with us. Our crew was solid with major effort from Beth Hand and Naomi Little. They were jacks of all trades, determined to make the movie happen, doing everything from set design, makeup, coaching the actors, boom stand operation and lights, whatever needed to be done.

We shot a winter scene with at least forty zombies and a handful of makeup artists. The house on 4811 Chester Ave was our lab for creating a zombie army as well as the house where the murderous sideshow family lived in the movie. Frank Walsh was Lazari, the undead dark magician, leading an apocalyptic zombie platoon through the icy back streets of West Philly.

Enigma and I started talking on the phone all the time, exchanging creative ideas. We decided to write him into the movie as a gumshoe supernatural detective from the Order of Mystery. He came to visit me, and I showed him a banner we were working on for the scene where the sideshow murders a member of the audience and brings her back to life onstage. It was an orange banner with a split face—half clown, half Malerkus. At that point, I could get the sword halfway down my throat and leave it there with no trouble, but it kept getting stuck somewhere before entering the rib cage.

"I knew there was something important about you," said Enigma. "Sword swallowing is like doing pushups. The more you use the muscles, the more control you have. It takes time and patience." We were plotting the story and he agreed to be in the May Carnivolution show, as well as film a scene at the Tiberino Museum that same weekend.

Barry Silver got the sword down just in time to film the scene at the Triangle Theater. When the day of the shoot arrived, I tried one last time to swallow the sword, and with a small shift in my posture the sword fell past the point where it was getting stuck and went all the way down to my stomach! It was magic. I thought it was a fluke, so I tried again. Sure enough, the sword went down like it was nothing: it was meant to be! My character was written in the script as a sword swallower and now it was true. I called Red to thank him. That night Barry and I stood side by side and swallowed swords ten times in row while the camera rolled. It was a long night of take after take. During one overtired magic take, I ripped the intestines out of a blonde woman from the imaginary audience, then brought her back from the dead on an operating table in the middle of the stage. A gruesome end to an epic film shoot.

The 2006 Coney Island Spring Gala was plastered across my computer screen. It called for all enthusiasts to come out and be a part of history. Dick Zigun was going to organize buying the Sideshow by the Seashore building they had been leasing for many years. Rumors said that Coney Island was about to be redeveloped in a way that would not flatter its old title as "the Playground of the World." The price of a ticket to the gala was one hundred dollars, but I felt compelled to attend the spectacle. The entire sideshow would be there along with some very special guests. I wanted to see if I could convince some of the Coney Island Circus Sideshow to be part of our *Unholy Sideshow* movie.

Going in clown makeup was tempting, but not a good idea. You never know how that will go over. But I couldn't resist bringing a few gags in my pockets: the blockhead clown nose, with two spikes to hammer into my face; a lot of laughs and screams; a cane sword; and a mousetrap on the Chinatown bus. Twenty dollars round trip for a two-hour ride from Philadelphia to Manhattan.

The Spring Gala was an upscale carnie fundraiser of hobnobbers and hobgoblins. Wonderful costumes surrounded by games, lights, music, and action. A circus train of people danced in a joyous line that picked up strays and stragglers on the corners of the huge ballroom, unifying the party. Everyone was dancing, drinking, and enjoying hors d'oeuvres. Getting carried away, I scared a couple of burlesque-looking ladies by removing the clown nose of death from my nostrils. "WHAT? I'm allergic to glue!" Screaming and bubbling giggles died down when Dick Zigun, the artistic director and unofficial mayor of Coney Island, spoke into the microphone.

Standing next to him onstage was a shirtless man, with short arms and four fingers on each hand. His name was Mat Fraser the Sealboy, and Dick Zigun started the show by challenging him to a pushup competition. Never challenge someone with short arms to a pushup competition: you will lose. That was probably the point, but it was unexpected. Mat devastated Dick Zigun with rapid fire pushups while the audience went berserk, egging on the animosity between the two showbiz gladiators. Mat was a child of Thalidomide, and because of this, his arms didn't go past his hips, and he had no thumbs. However, the man could *wail* on a drum set. It seemed that he could play any rhythm flawlessly and kill anyone he wanted to by kicking them in the face with his lanky, grasshopper legs. He was a force of nature, an intellectual and a true wonder of the world.

After the competition, a Russian aerialist climbed up to the ceiling with two pieces of red silk. She was accompanied by a beautiful man in makeup who played classical music on a Theremin synthesizer. He pinched, pulled, and wiggled an invisible field surrounding an antenna on a wooden box to produce perfect pitches that harmonized the hypnotized room. Donny Vomit, Roc Roc-It, Heather Holliday, and Insectavora did quick versions of their sideshow acts with ironic safety goggles on. Safety first, of course. The night ended with a live art auction.

I tried to explain our *Unholy Sideshow* movie to Donny Vomit, but we were both a bit too drunk. Heather Holliday walked up to me with a red and white striped box of popcorn.

"You want this? It's too salty for me."

"Of course, thank you, never salty enough for me." It's nice to boogie with a box of popcorn as a prop. I told Heather I finally figured out how to swallow a sword.

"I was practicing cane spinning with the cane sword you gave me," she said. "I dropped it a few times, and now it's all loose. I think I ruined it."

"Oh no, should I get you another one?" I said, dancing and eating popcorn.

"No, I'll probably break that one, too."

We danced and talked for a while, then she disappeared into the party. Other people started filtering in and the lights changed to lasers. After a bit, the only people left from the gala were me and the girls with mustaches painted on their faces who had been serving hors d'oeuvres earlier in the night. I danced with the mustache girls until the sun came up, then took a bus back to Philly. I never threw away that popcorn box.

In Carnivolution, I started the Clown-Centric Sideshow between band sets on a small stage on the other side of the yard at the Tiberino Museum. It was an ongoing cliffhanging narrative tale of high adventure. After all, I was a new sword swallower in the world and needed a chance to test my metal.

I unveiled the tale of a young Jellyboy, lost in the medieval woods, at the beginning of a long journey. While running away from the responsibility of a life revolving around hard work, I wandered into a mystical forest and stumbled upon a mysterious clown maiden named Snarlena Piranha. She had the problem of the vagina dentata. While wearing Peek-a-Boo, the squeaky clown head baby toy, with hands to cover his eyes, I swallowed the skull-handled sword to woo the maiden. Snarlena and I jumped towards each other and bounced back and forth in seemingly innocent clown sex.

After a lot of squeaking, Snarlena gasped as her stomach began to grow rapidly with a baby on the way. "*Breathe, breathe, push!*" I coached from the sidelines of labor pains. Her water balloon broke, and an adult child began to crawl her way out of Snarlena's giant fanged vagina. The full grown, naked, newborn woman oozed out from between Snarlena's legs, covered in tapioca pudding. She stood up quivering and holding her own umbilical cord, waiting for the placenta to fall so she could be named. To Jelly's shock and horror, the afterbirth fell out with the name *bitterness* written across it. She had given birth to a curse.

Enigma came running out of the woods wielding a chainsaw. I had been tricked by the forest into giving birth to a curse, and ran off, never to return: a fugitive from the laws of nature, giving the first cliffhanger ending to the Clown-Centric Sideshow. "Come back next month for the rest of the story!" I said to those present at the Tiberino Museum.

The Hydrogen Jukebox was in full effect that night, playing loud until the bar ran out of alcohol.

Out of the blue, Angel called and told me she was leaving California to attend nursing school on the east coast and wanted me to take a trip with her to Portland, Maine, a twelve-hour bus ride with a transfer in Boston. Portland was a picturesque town by the ocean, boats and seafood everywhere. Angel had a good size house with a front lawn, a backyard, and a driveway. I could only stay for a day, so after walking around town, we went back to Angel's place where she cooked, and I practiced making a mist with small mouthfuls of water in preparation for fire breathing. By the time the sun went down, I had a mighty fine mist with no splash or dribble down my chin.

"It's very important to use the right fuel and to keep it a secret among serious circus people. Whatever you do, don't swallow any, or you will be pooping rainbows. Keep it in the front of your mouth." Angel lectured me about flash points and how different fuel combusts at different temperatures. First, she made a few small fire blasts off one of the torches she made in the misty night of her backyard. She had a couple different types of fuel; one to dip the torch in, and one for the actual fire breathing. She showed me how far to hold the torch from my face and handed over the bottle of fuel.

"Don't use too much, only a shot glass full, and keep it as close to your lips as you can, then give it all you've got. Oh, and breathe through your nose."

After putting the bottle to my lips, I raised the torch in front of my face and sprayed the fuel onto the head of the flame. To my surprise, there was a huge explosion that nearly burnt my lips but sent a fireball forward and up, lighting up the backyard. She gave me a few more safety tips about breathing to prevent the fire from jumping back towards my lips. After a few tries, I was able to control the size and shape of the fire blasts. Angel heard there was a Spiral Q puppeteer in town who was going to drive back to Philly, and I could catch a ride with her.

The puppeteer and I drove back to Philly but had to stop at her parents' house in Rhode Island to pick up a trunk of her stuff. On the way, while chatting about our art forms, it started pouring rain and her windshield wipers stopped working. Visibility became zero, so we pulled over to figure it out. We tied a rope to the windshield wiper and pulled it through the passenger side window. My job was to pull the rope when the windshield filled with rain. It felt like we were Vikings on a longship, rowing our way home.

One of our housemates, who was a professional cook, had just moved out with his two dogs. This opened the best room in the house for my brother Matterz Squidling to move into, with his studio of video and recording equipment. It was the third-floor room looking over the street. The walls were painted orange with golden trim, the floor was old, varnished wood. Moving into that room left a vacancy down the hall. The Enigma called from Las Vegas and asked if he could move in to escape his girlfriend. It was perfect: my brother and the Enigma on each end of the hallway, and my room in the center.

Enigma came back from Vegas loaded with cash, his guitar, a few suitcases, and all his sideshow props, just whatever could fit in his Jeep. He was trying to downsize, always leaving pieces of himself behind to amuse and puzzle his friends.

The Enigma was a lot of fun to have around the house and to drive around with. To walk through the world of American superstores with a puzzling blue man with devil horns was a hilarious thrill. Jaws would drop, questions would fly, followed by wisecrack replies. In Pathmark, we started to dance when we walked into Barry White's voice blasting over the speakers. The people who worked at Home Depot recognized the Enigma from *The X Files*, where he played a character named Conundrum. He bought me a machinery bit for my power drill so I could blockhead it—a big improvement from the shiny little nail I had been using. He also gave me a big, twisted flooring spike to hammer up my nose. At home, we stayed up all night doing dishes and cleaning the house. Enigma loved cooking for big groups of people. We watched *Holy Mountain* by Alejandro Jodorowsky, and he gave me a copy of the classic book *Memoirs of a Sword Swallower* by Daniel P. Mannix, which I read more than once.

Enigma was a blue genie in the temporary service of a clown who found him in a book instead of a lamp. One day over a cup of coffee at the Satellite, we struck up a life changing conversation about tattoos and the full body concept.

"You see, Jellyboy, you might as well think big. Having little tattoos here and there is cool and all, but you can do anything, so why not think of your body as one unified piece of art with a theme? You have no tattoos, so you are a fresh canvas. I could tattoo you from head to toe in mazes. You could be the Amazing Maze Man!" Enigma said with a straight face, deadpan and with a wink, trying to sell me on the idea.

"Yeah, but as wild as that is, it isn't me," I said. "I think of myself more as a death-defying cartoon. Maybe my body could be one unified cartoon story?"

"Now you're on to something, Jellyboy. You could be the Living Cartoon!"

"I see an image in my head, of a face on my foot, of a philosopher looking into a periscope that goes all the way up the leg and rib cage, up to the elbow where his eye is looking out. The periscope would turn into a railroad track that a steam-powered circus train would ride up, pulling some fantastic show."

I decided to get my first tattoo, but it wouldn't be the train. As my mortal genie, Enigma agreed to tattoo an old ship's wheel in the center of my chest, representing the cycle of reincarnation. He warned me, however, that circles are the most difficult to tattoo. We cleared the table of my circus altar and scrubbed it down, turning it into a temporary tattoo studio.

To make circles, Enigma traced a bullseye on my sternum, using a coin for the center, a medicine bottle for the next ring, and a clown figure with a mouthful of yellow fangs with a jack-o'-lantern grin for the last ring. They weren't perfectly lined up, but it didn't matter. The small, heavy tattoo machine buzzed like a hive of bees. The needle vibrated the bone while injecting ink under the skin. I was the captain of my own imperfect ship that would take us to faraway lands. The Enigma passed magic into the center of my being with the wand of his tattoo machine, leaving a fairly crooked outline of a ship's wheel in the center of my chest.

I was a bit sad when I saw the results. "I like it, but it's crooked. Can't fix that, can we?"

"We could always inject lemon juice in it to try to wash out the ink. I think it's a cool tattoo. It reminds me of *Dungeons and Dragons*." We both liked role-playing games. To us, life was a role-playing game. The more I looked at it, the more I liked the tattoo.

Through a musician friend who knew people in New York, I was given a show at the cabaret stage at a party space in Brooklyn called Rubulad. The theme was dungeons and drag queens. Enigma drove a car full of us there. He helped me brainstorm a solo show the night before, a snappy arsenal of setups and jokes with punchlines to knock 'em dead.

Rubulad was a huge maze full of rooms with stages, bars, and art filling every inch. The stage I was to perform on was small but in the center room, bridging the corners of the compound. There was a grand piano on the stage, which was perfect, because Matterz would be able to accompany the act.

When we first arrived, the Rubulad was vast with emptiness, but that soon changed. Because the theme was dungeons and drag queens, many of the attendees were crossdressing with swords by their sides. Some were on leashes, playing a dominatrix/submissive game. A lot of the girls had mustaches painted on their faces. The boys looked so dashing in stockings and lipstick.

The guy running the stage was a musician named Aaron Goldsmith. He was a circus enthusiast living at the Rubulad space, one of a long tradition of artists who had come and gone while keeping the place in business. Aaron was working the sound board and managing the stage, as well as booking the entertainment. He welcomed me and told me Rubulad had been a home away from home for the End of the World Circus and the Know Nothings. Rubulad loved the underground circus sideshow.

I had a twenty-minute set, opening with an eyeball helium balloon puppet who walked across the air on two tongues, then jumped to kiss someone in the front row. This got people gathering around while Matterz played creepy circus melodies on the baby grand. I took a feeding tube out of my pocket and swung it around like a lasso, then attempted to stick it up my nose. At that point, I had the undivided attention of the entire room.

I pretended not to be able to feed the tube up my face and raised a finger in the air with one hand while reaching for the power drill with the other. "It helps to pre-drill the hole," I said into the microphone. Looking frightened, I put the drill to my nostril and asked, "Should I do this?" The room screamed, "Do it!" The drill sunk straight back into the center of my head, in and out at a fevered pace, until it stopped in the back of my head. "It's stuck, it's stuck! What should I do?" I yelled out. "Reverse!" yelled back a few clever people. I flicked the reverse switch. Out came the drill, covered in snot. I licked the snot off the drill bit to the moans of the observers. "It tastes funny," I said with a thoughtful look on my face, "like a salty clown." Then the tube went right up the nose with a rubber hose and out the mouth, north to south, like dental floss for the brain.

Matterz passed me a glass of wine from the piano. People started clapping and stomping a rhythm, chanting *chug, chug, chug* as the wine ran up through the tube, changing the color to red as it wrapped around my head like a loop-de-loop roller coaster. When every last drop of wine was gone from the glass, I asked, "Which way should I pull it out?" People started shouting in all different directions as I ran back and forth on the stage, pulling it this way and that. Finally, I threw the slimy tube into the audience and one person grabbed it like a trophy, jumping up and down.

The sword with the skulls on the handle was next. I asked for a volunteer to come up and inspect it to verify that it was real. A man in a Guy Fawkes *V for Vendetta* protest mask came running to the stage, wearing a shirt that said, "Investigate 9/11.' He confirmed the sword was real, so I put it up and let it fall past the heart, lungs, and liver, deep into the ribcage, to the pit of my stomach, and took a bow. I motioned to the masked man to pull the sword out of me. He did and held it up in the air to a rain of cheers from the audience.

The show was so strong they asked us to come perform with our whole group on New Year's Eve, 2007!

Chapter 6
Foot in the Door of New York City

All this new motion brought us to a place in Brooklyn called the House of Yes. No, not the House of Maybe, but the House of Possibility, with a welcome mat that said *YES*. Aaron Goldsmith, who hired me for the Rubulad cabaret stage, made the connection. The entire second floor overlooked a junkyard. The ceilings were high enough for aerial, with a stage and an open space big enough for a huge dance party. The bar jutted out of the kitchen with a giant puppet head of a wild thing over the counter. Behind some red curtains was a place to sit down and relax away from the dancing mob. It was an opium den setting, where dreams held down the fortress of a team that screamed, "Why not?!"

The Hydrogen Jukebox was due for a trip to New York. We had tried in the past at places like the Lion's Den and CBGBs, just before it closed down. Those types of shows are difficult for out-of-town bands. The House of Yes was a homemade venue with a built-in party that couldn't even be stopped by a blizzard. It started snowing on our way there. We were in Styx Latte's black and silver short bus. For us, missing a show was always out of the question, no matter what the weather.

When we arrived, Aaron greeted us and made introductions to the people of his house. We met Keelan Kelly, a blue-eyed gentleman with a psychedelic gleam, and Lauren Larken, a graduate student/expert grant writer, and her cat Pilgrim. We also met the beautiful intellectual aerial duo of Kae Burke and Anya Sapozhnikova, both of whom were costume makers for the conceptually rich speedy sewing machine. Before the party started, we sat together for a smoke and chatted about our dreams of creating our own eco-circus tent show. The question was how do we do it? How would we become our own traveling circus festival?

Larken thought if there was a clear enough plan, then perhaps a grant could be written. I shared with the group my vision of the carnival tent show as they listened with wide eyes.

"I want a tent with the face of a monster where the entrance is the mouth. People would enter the tent by climbing aboard a Gravitron, spun around, sucked to the walls and released on the other side. There they would be met with a world of unicycles and juggling clowns, morphing the atmosphere. Outside the tent would be two hot air balloons as the eyes of the monster with aerialists hanging off the bottoms, giving a show before the show."

Kae and Anaya's eyes lit up. "We want to be the aerialists on the hot air balloons!" they proclaimed, seeing it clearly in their minds.

"If there is a way to make the show produce its own electricity, I might be able to write a grant to get it off the ground," said Larken.

More than a foot of snow fell that night. The audience and the entertainers were snowed in at the party. Kae and Anya performed amazing silk acts from a rigging point on the ceiling before the Hydrogen Jukebox blasted the party to life. We were mixing circus acts into our set, so Anya and her friend Mike Dirt performed an electric act with a lightning wand and two metal plates while we improvised. Mike Dirt was a fire spinner who used a staff to twirl flames dangerously close to himself and the audience with great skill. Anya acted as the lovely assistant, switching on the machine. She ran the fluorescent light along Mike's skin while he twitched, and sparks flew off his body.

In between the circus acts, the band would strike the audience with a few songs in a row to get them dancing. "Johnny's a Space Frog" got them hopping to a bebop rhythm. Lyrics like, *"Don't you cross my path no, I'm a lost squid. Lost squids try to understand I'm doing the best I can with the thoughts I got, cause I'm a five-legged frog! Little tuna fish John's tripping on islands...say you're on acid? Is my face cracking? Clowns never had it so good, said the lion tamer in Hollywood."*

The songs echoed through a blur into the next morning. We shoveled out our bus and rocked it out of the plowed-in parking space, heading home to Philadelphia with the whole band feeling wonderful.

That week, I got some help making a *MySpace* page since I had always been bad with computers. The main photo was of my face framed with two machetes, and a mousetrap on my tongue. *MySpace* became a tool for me to find other circus performers and events. Each person's page had a row of "top friends" so you could keep zooming in on friends of friends of friends. You could contact whoever looked interesting. While searching, I stumbled upon a burlesque clown in New York City named Hot Dottie Lux, with blue triangles under her eyes. She was having a birthday party called the Clowns of Coney Island, at a venue in Brooklyn known as Galapagos.

All the performers from the Coney Island Sideshow would be there doing their acts, dressed as clowns! It was Dottie Lux's birthday wish, and my dream come true. I wrote her a message explaining who I was and the acts I did. I told her that her birthday was my dream show and asked if she could include me in the lineup doing my mental floss and human crazy straw acts. She wrote back that she was pleased to meet me, but that the show was already booked and advertised, with no room for other performances. I wrote back that I understood and would still be attending the party with some friends.

Finding the right gift was a challenge. In the end, I decided to customize a baby doll that I had found on one of my house painting jobs in Powelton Village, down the street from the Tiberino Museum. The man who hired me said I could keep whatever I found. There was a rack of clothes from the '70s with a white polyester button down shirt with red stripes and red polka dots. I'd been wearing it in the *Unholy Sideshow* movie and at my shows. The other thing I found was an entire bathtub full of dirty baby dolls with genitals drawn on them in magic marker; we used them in the movie as well. The doll that I liked best was missing her legs and had blue eyes with long lashes, whose lids opened and closed. I put her in a new dress, then wrapped her in a box with a *Curious George* funhouse mirror. I knew it was creepy, but I figured a clown like Dottie would find the humor in it.

I took the Chinatown bus to New York and got to Galapagos a bit early. Roc Roc-It was there drinking at the bar. It was the first time we had met while I was in clown makeup. He was talking to a tattoo artist from Staten Island named Magie Serpica, who was dressed as a retro rockabilly pinup, with hair done to match. We started talking about tattoos and how Roc met Dottie, because he has a clown face tattooed in the center of his chest. I showed them the wheel that I had recently tattooed on my sternum. It was just a black outline.

I said, "It's a bit crooked and didn't quite turn out the way I intended."

Roc smiled. "Those are the best tattoos."

Magie chimed in, "It has character. You should get it finished."

"Oh, I definitely will. It's grown on me the longer I have it, but I have an idea for a full body concept to become the Living Cartoon." I told Magie and Roc about the philosopher on my foot looking through a train track periscope, standing on the shoulders of geniuses and giants. They loved the idea.

"I would totally do that for you," Magie said. She told me how to get in touch with her and the forces were set in motion.

The show whizzed by in a blur of confetti and clown makeup on performers I had previously only seen in the flesh of their human skin. Donny Vomit was a classic hobo with white face and five o'clock shadow. Insectavora was a demon clown with a smile of ear-to-ear fangs below evil eyes. The snake charmer Serpentina was all sunshine with rosy cheeks, red nose, and a blue armored body, with metal grinders to shower sparks off her armor. Heather Holliday had a big red heart painted over one eye of a painted white face. Roc Roc-It was the only one who didn't need to change his appearance: he was a clown in everyday life with his jolly green eyes, tattooed eyebrows that said *What? What?* and chili pepper sideburns topped with cannon fuses.

Red hot Dottie Lux jiggled and wiggled her naturally beautiful, voluptuous form in hypnotic waves. Dottie's colorful face stayed still and peaceful while her body danced a whirlwind of fleshy motion. At the end of the performance, people began to come forward, bestowing gifts upon her, which she graciously accepted. I handed her the box which held the legless doll with the funhouse mirror. "Oh my God, I love it!" she exclaimed. "She is going right in my room of creepy, freaky dolls!" A clown after my own heart.

It took a while for the party to disband after the show was finished. I stayed around the bar drinking with the gang of clowns I had arrived with until Heather Holliday caught my eye. Once again, I was beamed into her energy field, blabbering, attempting to amuse her. She had enough to drink to find me amusing.

"I was thinking, since I'm a sword swallower now, and I've pulled a sword out of you, it's only fair that you should pull one out of me."

She looked a bit annoyed, and cleverly responded with a heart over one eye, "You pulled the sword out of me at my show. If I ever happen to be at your show, you can pull me onstage as a volunteer and I'll pull it out of you. It wouldn't be right to do it here. I don't like showoffs."

My face turned red under my white makeup. "You're right. That would be unshowmanly of me. If you're ever at one of my shows, I will take you up on that for sure." After that, we joked a bit. She introduced me to her younger brother and hit the road.

I was so distracted by my conversation with Heather Holliday that I had lost track of my friends. They were gone, my phone battery was dead, and the bar was closing. I couldn't remember how to get back to the apartment, so I just paced around outside, hoping my gang would come back for me. They eventually did and teased me about being so ridiculous with Heather. They had gone to a different bar for a drink to get away from my silly, starry-eyed spectacle. I apologized, and we all walked back to the apartment to sleep in our makeup.

Enigma was still living down the hall from me in Philly. One day, shortly after the Clowns of Coney Island show, he said, "You really like New York, don't you? I have an email for the guy who runs the entertainment at the New York City tattoo convention. You should see if you can get in on that. Just don't mention my name. I don't want to deal with them, but it would be a good show for you, since you're just getting started." I emailed them but got no response.

The Enigma had an idea for a comic book mirroring his own life, called *Mortal Genie*. He was the genie trapped inside a shard of glass who escaped imprisonment, on the run from a fire elemental who burned down towns and cities to return him to his master. In his travels, he served who he thought was worthy, and took off when the elemental was nearby. This left in peril those he cared for and those he served after he was gone.

Enigma looked a bit tired. He was in a pickle, frantically smoking a cigar and pacing around like a madman, packing and talking. I was listening and helping him get his Jeep ready. I thanked him for all he taught me. I was in his debt and would help him in my own way as long as I was able. He said he understood and appreciated my friendship. In the middle of the night, leaving a half smoked, mostly chewed cigar in the ashtray, the Enigma gave me the rent for the next month and was gone. After all, you can't hold onto an escaped genie forever.

That week, in Red's out of business pet shop under the train tracks of Fishtown, Barry Silver, Red Stuart, and I built a huge, foldable bed of nails from 1,500 spikes. When I brought it home, my brother Matterz's eyes lit up the way they did the first time my mother brought home a used piano when we were kids. "I want to learn how to do the bed of nails! I can't be left behind on all this sideshow mania!"

When Matterz was five years old, my mother brought home a used piano for my older brother Jason, who had started learning some songs on the synthesizer. The day she brought it into the house Jason told her he had lost interest. As my mother sat crying in disappointment, Matterz came over to comfort her and said, "I'll learn to play piano." "But you're only five years old," my mother answered, wiping tears away. Matterz was determined, so he started taking lessons with a piano teacher who lived down the street, launching him into a life of music!

When we started our first band in high school, Matterz played the keyboard, but he quickly learned electric bass guitar when he realized that's what we needed to make the music work, and he's played it ever since. Now with this new bed of nails, not only could he create the sonic atmosphere for the sideshow, but he could also take part in the action as well. The Impenetrable Music Man was born. We began testing the limits of his body on the bed of nails.

Matterz Squidling, 2011 (Lunchbox)

The New York City tattoo convention at the Roseland Ballroom sent me a message. They decided to take a chance on me. Rivers of thoughts ran through my head: there were new acts of my own design I wanted to try. What better place to debut the new, than in a scene that had seen it all? The show was happening in only a few days, so I set my mind on scripting the acts. A friend of mine named Cobweb Jon shared his insights, as he was a fire spinner, body piercer, and scarification artist who had been very involved in the convention world. He told me the New York conventions were run by the Hells Angels. He warned, "Don't talk to the Angels unless they talk to you. Don't joke with them unless they joke with you. They know you're a clown, but they don't care. Just do your job well and don't get too carried away. In fact, I haven't been to a convention in years, but I'll go with you." Cobweb Jon even went so far as to lend me a tailored black zoot suit with white stripes running from top to bottom, and it fit me perfectly.

I had just bought six rubber chickens that could scream in polka dot bikinis. They would be the bed of rubber chickens known as the Henrietta Sisters, retired Las Vegas show chickens, given another chance at fame in the circus sideshow. They fit perfectly in a suitcase. Frank Walsh bestowed upon me the Masked Perfesser's slapstick, so I could smack myself over and over in the head with it to start the show.

The trick was carrying all the props to New York on the bus. I had six chickens, two swords, a slapstick, a power drill, an easel, a blank canvas, a syringe, paint, a paintbrush, a pair of scissors, a fish tube, and the clown nose of death. Along with Cobweb Jon's suit, I wore my older brother Jason's boots. The boots were a bit big on me, painted green with monster faces, eyes on the ankles and teeth along the edges of the sole, with nasty red gums. The only ingredients missing were the helium balloons that I wanted to tie to the handle of my sword, but I hoped to somehow find those on the way.

The ticket taker who worked the entrance at the Coney Island Sideshow was giving out wristbands to people entering the Roseland Ballroom. Remy Vicious was her name, a smiling showgirl of the weird with bright colors inked into her skin. The way Cobweb Jon and I were dressed and the props we were carrying made it obvious that we were there as entertainment. She greeted us warmly and told me that Tyler Fyre, Insectavora, and Heather Holliday were inside the convention. Amidst the buzzing of tattoo machines and the wandering of tattooed minds, we eyeballed the art as we weaved our way to the stage.

Two Hells Angels guarded the stage door. They were heavy metal bikers with invisible wings. We got along just fine. They were amused by us, and opened the curtain backstage where I could keep my props.

Once we took a look at the space, Cobweb Jon took off to find some balloons. While unpacking and setting things out, a sly man named Johnny Fox appeared across the room. He introduced himself as a sword swallower and owner of the Freakatorium banner collection hung throughout the convention. He asked me in a polite, but curious way, "Who are you, and what do you do?"

"I'm Jellyboy the Clown. I'm the Living Cartoon. I'm going to beat myself over the head with this slapstick, put a power drill up my nostril to pave the way for this fish tube, attached to this clown nose with a paintbrush sticking out of it in the left nostril. I will pull the tube through my face until the clown nose goes on my nose. The paintbrush will go up my other nostril and I will paint a portrait of a beautiful girl with my nose, while drinking wine out of a glass she is holding, using the tube that is flossed through my sinus passage. Then I will lay on a bed of rubber chickens and have a girl stand on me, holding a sword with many helium balloons in one hand and scissors in the other. I will stick a syringe in my neck full of super serum that allows me to swallow swords. While standing on the chickens, I will swallow the sword and leave it down as the girl cuts the balloons off the sword, allowing them to float to the ceiling. Then I will bow to the girl, and she will pull the sword out of my throat. The End."

Johnny Fox looked a bit stunned following this imagery, quickly darting his eyes with a smile creeping on and off his face. In a prophetic tone he said, "Well, I'm what's happening...right now. You are what's happening in the future." Then he went on stage and grabbed the microphone. He announced himself and the opening of the NYC tattoo convention with feats of prestidigitation, manipulating cigarette smoke, and flipping coins in between his fingers. He mocked the jaded tattoo convention crowd by making dumbfounded noises to build browsers into a swarm of intrigue.

When he had an audience, Johnny Fox revealed his shield full of swords. He twirled and spun a dagger, put it down the hatch and tossed it out of his throat, swallowed several swords, a thin saw, and a long corkscrew. The spectators were wowed, then wandered off back into the slow drift of the convention. When he came back to the side backstage curtain, I told him how much I enjoyed his demonstration and interaction with the audience. He looked down at my feet and noticed the green monster boots I was wearing. "Nice magic boots," he said.

"Thank you, Mr. Fox." I smiled and thought of my brother Jason creating boots for his character Zer Garow Bon Lelgin Purv the Stangester. He was a son of a star, a man of golden skin who was an interdimensional inspiration to a few Hydrogen Jukebox songs.

While waiting for Cobweb Jon to come back, I wandered around the convention floor. Insectavora was looking at some clothes when I noticed her. She seemed a bit shy, like she was not expecting to see me.

"Hey, Insectavora, can you believe it; I'm performing here tonight. I hope you get a chance to check out my show. I've seen yours so many times now. It would mean a lot to me." She just smiled and nodded.

Shortly after, Heather Holliday and I noticed each other at the same time. Moving towards her I said, "Heather, remember when you said you would pull a sword out of me if you were at my show?"

"Yes, I do," she said, hesitantly, holding back a laugh.

"Well, I'm performing today. Will you be my volunteer?"

"Umm...okay." Her eyes searched the room for reasons to say no, but she decided to stay true to her word.

"Great! Oh, wow. Well, I'm performing really soon, so I have to go get ready. This is going to be fun." I took off for the stage. As I got there, I saw Cobweb Jon triumphantly walk through the door carrying a bouquet of helium balloons of SpongeBob SquarePants, Bert and Ernie, and Bart Simpson. He quickly went backstage and tied the balloons to the handle of my sword. We set up the easel with the canvas and brought all the props to the stage.

To start it off, I ran out on the stage, wild with the slapstick in one hand, and the microphone in the other. I began shouting, thwacking myself on the head in between the words.

"My name is Jellyboy" *thwack* "the Clown" *thwack* "with the upside-down frown" *thwack, thwack* "turned upside-down" *thwack, thwack, thwack* "the Living Cartoon" *thwack* "and I'm not quite right in the head." At that point all the foot traffic had stopped in front of the stage while people stared. "Come closer if you dare, and I will show you the secrets of primitive brain surgery." I gestured for everyone to move closer, and it worked!

"First, you need to open your head so you can see the brain," I said, falling down and getting back up, over and over again. "Since my head isn't doing such a good job of opening like a coconut, I must turn to technology. That's right, folks, if you can't crack it open by hand, we have power tools!" I picked up the power drill, pulled the trigger full speed ahead into the center of my head, pre-drilling the hole to get at my brain. The drill came out covered in a brain matter-like substance called snot. I licked the drill bit and said, "I think you are starting to doubt my artistic ability."

The people shouted, "Yes!"

"Well, all I need is some inspiration. I am looking for a volunteer, I mean a beautiful woman! You, back there, yes, you! Come up on the stage."

Heather Holliday ran onto the stage to loud applause. I handed her a glass of red wine and took the clown nose of death out of my pocket. One nostril of the clown nose held a fish tube, while the other held a paintbrush. Fishing the tube up the right nostril, pulling it out of my mouth, I pulled the nose closer and closer to my face, until the paintbrush on the other side sunk into my left nostril. I positioned the easel across from Heather and began to artfully eyeball her while unscrewing a tube of paint and squeezing it onto a palette.

Using my nose to dip the brush I said, "Please observe, ladies and gentlemen, as I paint my masterpiece." I painted an awkward circle on the canvas, jumped back and motioned to it with pride. The audience hesitated, then burst out laughing with a round of applause. I proceeded to paint a stick figure portrait which bore a striking resemblance to Heather while draining her glass of wine through the tube in my nose. It was a true work of timeless art. After the painting was complete, I handed her the sword with helium balloons tied to it as if it were a bouquet of flowers and took out my old leather suitcase.

"Inside this suitcase is something more dangerous than bullets and HIV. Ladies and gentlemen, you have heard of the bed of nails. You have heard of the bed of blades." I opened the suitcase with great trepidation. "This is the bed of chickens. The Henrietta Sisters, retired Las Vegas show chickens, plucked and defeathered for your viewing pleasure. They have the sharpest squawks known to tear eardrums, and I'm laying them down one by one, the way they want to be laid. The way they've been laying eggs all their lives for you. And God said, 'Thou shall not commit adultery with the poultry, and bestiality is not a victimless crime.' Get your minds out of the gutter! I know they look good in their matching polka dot bikinis, but it's not that kind of a show."

When the chickens were all in a row, I laid down on them, making them scream. I instructed Heather to step up on me, squishing me into the bed of chickens with one foot on my waist and one foot on my chest. She stepped up to a thrilled audience who really got the joke. I stood up after she stepped down to reveal my back, unscathed by the razor-sharp squawks of the Henrietta Sisters.

I traded the sword for a pair of scissors I pulled out of a pocket in my jacket. I told Heather that after the sword was swallowed, she was to cut the balloons off the handle and pull the sword smoothly and straightly out of me. I stabbed my neck with the super serum syringe that was going to give me the ability to swallow the sword, squirted the serum out and said, "It looks like I missed the vein. Sometimes you have to take a shortcut to enlightenment." I dropped the sword down and gestured to Heather. She cut the strings, and cartoon balloons sailed to the rafters of the Roseland Ballroom. I bowed before Heather Holliday with a wink and a motion to remove the sword. She pulled it out slowly, held it up in the air triumphantly, and handed it back, smiling as I cleaned the blade under my armpit: it's always important to sanitize and sterilize the implement after it has been down in your digestive system. "One more round of applause for the volunteer, and thank you, ladies and gentlemen! Remember, I am Jellyboy the Clown. Goodnight!"

Afterwards, I thanked Heather for being in the show. We were talking about backbends, and I fell down backwards trying to do one by walking my hands down a wall. Heather and her friend thought it was funny. They asked if I wanted to go to a diner to get some French fries, but I couldn't leave. Cobweb Jon was somewhere in the convention.

He had lost his cell phone, and I didn't want to leave without letting him know. Plus, all my props were still backstage.

While wandering the floor looking for Cobweb Jon, I ran into Tyler Fyre. We struck up a conversation about torches on the handle of swords. I was working out an idea for a double act where a person breathes fire off the handle of a sword after it has been swallowed. Not long after that, I saw a photo of Tyler holding a sword with a lit torch on the handle.

"Have you had people breathe fire off the handle of your sword?" I asked.

"Oh definitely, I had Slymenstra Hymen breathe huge fireballs off my sword in the Brothers Grimm." As usual, Tyler was excited, with his animated blue eyes seemingly selling something you didn't know you needed. "It seems like an obvious combination," he said. "I thought I was the first to do it. Then a while back I saw a picture of it in an old circus book. Nobody owns these stunts—it's the presentation that should be different. That's what makes a performer stand out above the rest." Then he was off, that seed of wisdom planted in my brain.

I finally found Cobweb Jon at the bar drinking with two beautiful Asian vampire girls, talking about fire spinning. He made introductions and ordered me a drink. We were chatting and having a good time until their boyfriend came over. That's right: the two girls shared a boyfriend. He was also a fire performing vampire, with long blond hair and leather clothes. Vlad the vampire looked to be in his early forties and was immediately jealous and rude. It was obvious that Cobweb Jon was hitting it off with the girls, and it was humorously uncomfortable how much it bothered the vampire. He ruffled his feathers, puffed his chest like a peacock, said a few things about how important he was in the vampire world, and then ushered the girls off. Cobweb Jon kept his cool; people at the convention knew who he was as an artist, but he wasn't throwing his weight around.

We missed the last bus back to Philly. Someone had invited Cobweb Jon to an afterparty at a place called the Red Dragon Tattoo Shop. We walked around for a long time late into the night carrying all my props. After an hour or so, it became obvious that we were hopelessly lost. Our feet hurt and we were tired with nowhere to go, so we walked to the pedestrian path above the traffic on the Brooklyn Bridge, and went to sleep, leaning our backs on an old stone pillar until the sun came up over the water. As the city was waking up, we found our way through a park where hopelessly dirty people with wild hair were smoking crack. We made it back on the Chinatown bus to Philly where Matterz, Barry Silver, and Red were waiting to take me to Washington, D.C.

There was a show that night at the Palace of Wonders on H Street in the Atlas District, an art and nightlife neighborhood bubble in the middle of a rundown section of the city. Among all the excitement of crowds, bars, museums and motorcycles, the Palace stood out! Rising up out of a brick facade, it had a colorful carnival banner line front, with a lightbulb-covered marquee. There was a circus bar with an old-time oddity museum featuring sideshow memorabilia and oddities. There were monkey-faced medallion lights that lit up the first floor behind the bar with an amber glow. The whole room was decorated with circus banners. Overlooking the stage was a balcony where the oddity museum was displayed. The artifacts were all contained in glass cases with a Halloween orange light illuminating them.

Front of Palace of Wonders, Washington, D.C., 2008 (Strange Eye)

The collection was vast and well-labeled with photos to back up the stories. There were costumes that had been worn by Percilla the Monkey Girl, Melvin Burkhart the Original Human Blockhead, and the wedding dress of Jeanie Tomaini, the World's Only Living Half Girl. There was an eight-legged goat taxidermy named Billy the Spider Kid, a giant rat, an assortment of shrunken heads, a couple of Feejee Mermaids, and the Flesh-Eating Toad of Madagascar. One thing that stood out as particularly odd was the Hairball from the Belly of the Jaipur Ghost, a man-eating tiger from India. It got the name because it had killed many, but was hardly ever seen, until a colonial-era Brit finally shot it and removed the hairball of human remains from its guts.

There were stranger things in the Palace, like Howard the Human Bone Village. Howard was an ill-advised missionary who had all his bones carved into a small village by the people he was trying to convert. On the ceiling hung a sea serpent named Oojee Boo. Fivey the five-legged dog guarded the figure of Joseph Merrick the Elephant Man and the head of the snake that killed Sailer Katzy. To my mind, the greatest treasure of all was the taxidermy Unicorn Goat that traveled with the Ringling Brothers Circus while it was still alive!

I did the show that night with Red and Barry in the same suit, boots, and socks that I had on the night before. It was a special show, because Red was going to swallow a car axle so the writers of *Shocked and Amazed!* magazine could document the act. The collection displayed at the Palace was curated by the magazine's founder, James Taylor, a well-decorated veteran collector of the bizarre. The freakshow dandy historian sported muttonchop sideburns connected by a mustache, and a suit to match his folklore, with many buttons, twists, and turns in the intricacy of his jacket. His well-polished old leather riding boots, his way with words, and his even better polished stories gave him an air of authentic authority.

Over a drink before the show, he explained to me his discomfort with clowns. It all started at the Milwaukee Circus Parade, where he found himself surrounded by a conclave of red-nosed folks in makeup. They were talking seriously about their feelings in a "new age," "self-help," previously wounded type of way. The sentence that haunted him on repeat in his mind to that day was, "There are many kinds of tears. There are happy clowns and there are sad clowns. And there are sad tears and there are happy tears."

Tyler Fyre and his wife Thrill Kill Jill were also at the show. Unexpectedly, two nights in a row, Tyler Fyre was in the same place as I was performing, balancing the line of the tightrope across the flaming pit of modern sideshow history, a small world about to expand into the popular imagination. We all sat together before the show, drinking and trading stories. Red, Tyler Fyre, and James Taylor could all weave some tales. Barry Silver and I were mystified by our situation and the chance to perform with such exalted company.

The show that night was dedicated to the seven torture acts, plus a few more. Fire manipulation, sword swallowing, pincushion, the human blockhead, glass dancing, the bed of nails, and walking on blades. Red would give his classic demonstration of these acts. Barry and I followed up with our own renditions. A duo fire act opened the night, with Red and Barry going back and forth. After Red's blockhead, I did the same painting routine as the night before, only on the flip side of Heather Holliday, I painted a portrait of Barry Silver on the canvas. Red and Barry stabbed themselves with pins in a 'teacher versus student' human pincushion routine. Barry stuck a long needle in between his wrist bones and out the other side, with no bleeding upon the removal of the long needle. Red stepped on Barry, crunching him into the long, foldable nail bed that we made together. The glass walking was a brutal back and forth between Red and Barry, escalating to Red's freefall belly flop and Barry's across the stage tumble, landing on his back, *SMASH!* into the glass.

It was time to try a new one: the "Foot Sundae" food walking stunt. In biblical times, it was customary for people to wash your feet upon entering their house. A tray was filled with water. I took off my shoes and socks that I had been wearing since the day before and placed my bare feet into the water. The same feet that had walked all over New York, slept on the Brooklyn Bridge, and taken the Chinatown bus back to Philadelphia. I asked for the sickest person in the room to come forward and kindly wash my feet. A large, intoxicated man came forward and washed my feet with great enthusiasm. I took out a second tray and a box of mint chocolate cookies. The volunteer carefully toweled my feet dry while I opened the cookies. I tossed a few cookies in the tray and gave the rest to the audience to pass around and devour. The volunteer and I peeled a few bananas and added them to the tray. The final ingredient was whipped cream, added on top of the mint chocolate cookies and bananas. The volunteer made sure I didn't slip as I stepped into the foot sundae. Bananas were mashed nicely in between my toes. My feet evenly squished all the ingredients into a palatable mixture. Then it was the moment of truth.

"Ladies and gentlemen, should this man eat from my feet that he himself has washed in the foot water?" The people in the Palace of Wonders demanded with wild screams that he *EAT!* The man chowed down, licking the sundae out from between my toes. I couldn't tell if it was worse for him or me. But chills went down our spines as laughter built, throwing away all cares into the freedom of the foot sundae. My feet were rinsed and dried again. The volunteer was given proper respect, having eaten his just dessert.

For the finale of the show, James Taylor got on the microphone to talk about Red swallowing broadswords and car axles. The weight of the axle alone was enough to squish his insides like a bug. The axle looked like a giant old-time tent stake, intimidating but no match for Red's callused Adam's apple. Red had recently sold Barry his serpentine blade that curved from side to side to side, moving the throat as it was swallowed. Barry had the honor of ingesting it at the Palace that evening. I swallowed my funhouse sword with a torch lit on the handle while standing on a bed of machetes. Barry Silver perched behind me, balancing on a ladder of swords with a mouth full of fuel. When we were all lined up, he spit the fuel into a mist at the torch, sending a fireball over my head that just missed the people looking down from the balcony.

We invited Tyler Fyre up to the stage. Red, Barry, Tyler, and I stood side by side, held our swords up, let them fall, took a collective bow, and then it was curtains. Kathleen

Kotcher was James Taylor's editor for *Shocked and Amazed!* and she actually bought my blockhead painting of Barry Silver on one side and Heather Holliday on the other from the night before. On the way out, I took one last look at the unicorn goat taxidermy in a glass case on the second floor. When I was a small child, I went with my family to see this very creature alive. It was billed as the last living unicorn. I remember being disappointed, thinking, "*That's not a unicorn; that's a goat with one horn.*" Somehow, frozen under glass, it was more magical dead than when it was alive.

While investigating the internet for performance opportunities, I stumbled upon the Coney Island Rockabilly Festival. They were looking for all kinds of variety performers, burlesque dancers, and circus sideshow acts. The festival would take place on Labor Day weekend. Performances were going to be held up and down the boardwalk, ending up at Cha Cha's bar, "Home of Wild Women and Wise Guys." The whole thing was being put together by an entrepreneur named Ben Wilson. It was the event I had been wishing for, a marathon weekend of entertainment, an opportunity to truly cut my teeth in Coney Island.

Chapter 7
After Dark at the Amusement Park

Removing my boots and socks, smelling them in drunken ecstasy, I lightly placed my bare foot into a pile of spicy barbecue chips by the microphone. Labor Day weekend 2007 opened with a small show on the last Thursday of August at a tiki bar in Manhattan. A three-piece psychobilly band, the Holy Roller Sideshow, were the headliners at Otto's Shrunken Head. Burlesque was also performed. As the emcee and only sideshow performer, I had to fill more time than I had acts for, so I bought a bag of spicy potato chips and did the most dangerous stunt ever attempted by a clown: hot potato chip dancing. The audience went wild with satirical laughter when they heard the crunch of feet on chips. I danced on them and jumped up and down while the audience clapped a rhythm. To end the act, I picked up some of the walked-on chips and ate them the way someone might eat a lightbulb, crunching and grinding into the microphone.

I stepped out onto the subway platform in Coney Island amidst a flurry of swimsuits and beach umbrellas. Ice cream, bumper cars, and food stalls lined the sidewalk. Corn on the cob, potato knishes, breaded shrimp, hot dogs, and pizza sent out savory aromas. Over it all, the scent of the ocean rolled up like a wave, accompanied by hungry seagulls. The Astroland amusement park was only a few steps off the train. Loud music and thrill rides, games of chance with carnival personalities challenging passersby to win stuffed animal prizes. Tarot card readers coaxed the curious to talk about love and fortune.

On the other side of the amusements was the boardwalk, lined with bars and round-bellied people getting tanned, baking in the sun. Further down the boardwalk were amazing tacos and fruit smoothies. Folks were flying kites, lounging under beach umbrellas, running and splashing in the Brooklyn waves. On the pier, men were crabbing, fishing, and playing drums.

In search of the sideshow, I walked past Cha Cha's Club Atlantis and wandered up to "Shoot the Freak." There was a freak in a pit with a helmet and shield that people would line up to shoot. "It's no fun to watch," dared the talker on a distorted microphone. "Have some fun with a paintball gun," he yelled. "Shoot the freaking freak in the freaking head and the freak don't shoot back." Paint was fired and splattered on the freak all day long in between Cha Cha's and Ruby's bar on the boardwalk.

I made my way around the outskirts of Astroland to Sideshows by the Seashore. The old theater was covered in colorful hand-painted banners advertising the acts inside. There were paintings of Serpentina the snake charmer, Eak the Geek who tattooed his face like outer space, Donny Vomit the human blockhead, Heather Holliday the sword swallower, and Insectavora the fire eater.

It was Insectavora's birthday. Since I knew I was going to be in Coney Island that weekend, I brought her a present. I had commissioned an artist friend to make a colorful cartoon of her face on a giant spider body holding a roach with my face saying, "Please don't eat me." She loved it and showed it to all the people in the sideshow. I told them what we were doing that weekend and said if they wanted to check it out, we would put them on the guest list at Cha Cha's.

It was going to be a big night across the boardwalk. Bands all day, and at night, fireworks! I wanted to see everything, and help be the fire in the fireworks, to feed that growing monster-birth. Feeling like every moment lasted forever, still leading into the next, and not wanting to be anywhere else. Like being the impossible possible personified, floating in a storm cloud over Coney Island, I jumped into a twister and rode the ride. Suddenly, I was a part of the place I had been daydreaming about on the outside, haunting history in a crowd of living people, among the ghosts on the boardwalk.

In preparation for the weekend, a sideshow friend named Lenore gave me a haircut I had drawn in a sketchbook. The Big Malerkus mop-top had been shaved into a three-sided clown 'hawk, dyed bright orange in the center with the hair sticking out around the ears left dark. Now the canvas of my head had expanded, making room for a white face with long, black eyebrows to curve up the forehead around the temples to the back of the skull. Heather Holliday said I looked like I should be in a John Waters movie and that my eyebrows looked like a shadow of the banana Andy Warhol painted for the Velvet Underground's first album.

No one had been hired to emcee the events on the boardwalk, so a young vaudevillian sideshow magician named Nelson Lugo and I volunteered for the job. We stepped up to present the acts, introduce the bands, and assist with the transition of props, microphones, and crowd control. It didn't seem like an extra responsibility: it was natural, like breathing. The day went by without a visible hitch.

The night was refreshing as it cooled down, and the fireworks screamed over Deno's Wonder Wheel. That meant it was time for Burlesque at the Beach. The Great Fredini, Julie Atlas Muz, and Bambi the Mermaid hosted a game show "This or That."

Volunteers were called for. I was selected by Julie Atlas Muz, the beautiful co-host comedian with the most vibrant eyes and eyelashes like wings. None of us had any idea what we had just volunteered for. They were trying to choose three contestants out of the six of us pulled up on stage by seeing who could fake the best orgasm. I mimicked sex with the microphone and collapsed. Some of the others were rather convincing, but the awkward orgasms were the real crowd pleasers. In the end, I'm glad I was not chosen to go to the next round. The people who won the orgasm contest moved on to face absurd stupid human challenges, rewarded by getting to choose between what might come out of two doors.

Insectavora came out of "This" door and ate fire while straddling a chair. Bambi the Mermaid came out of "That" door, strutting her stuff smoking a cigarette while wearing a camel mask and a too-tight bikini that gave her a "camel toe." My gut hurt from laughing, but I had to leave during intermission to get to Cha Cha's for the night of rockabilly music. I found out later that the guy who won looked like a mixture of the smiling Coney Island Tillie mascot face and Alfred E. Neuman from *MAD* magazine.

Cha Cha's Club Atlantis was jumping with psychobilly freaks, but the biggest freak of them all was managing the place. Past the boardwalk and the clam bar, past the doorman and the main bar, seated with an old-time mob of professional drinkers was the beginning of a wild bash. Standing room only with a stage where music happened, decorated year-round for Halloween with fake spider webs and cardboard monsters hanging from the ceiling. Posters of *Scarface*, *The Sopranos*, and John Dillinger lined the wise guy walls, all leading to a door that said *Private: Keep Out*.

That night the office was also backstage. I walked in with what I thought was caution but turned out to be a bang of an entrance. The weight of the metal door slammed shut behind me, making a deafening crash. I was confronted by the wild words, "Don't slam the fucking door!" from an old Italian man with white, greased back hair, clenched teeth, and bizarre blue eyes that were open wide with the shock of intoxication.

"People who slam doors around here end up in the basement, and that's not a place you want to be." Spit flew from his lips as he spoke.

"It won't happen again," I said.

"Oh, it won't happen again because Machine Gun Johnny is going to put you in the basement with the rest of them! That's me, by the way, Machine Gun Johnny," he said, reaching for a knife.

"I'm Jellyboy the Clown. I'm with the freakshow," I said apologetically, reaching out to shake his hand.

"Jellyboy, you're a real fucking wise guy barging in here like you own the joint. I'm the freakshow around here. My finger looks like a penis." He held it out for me to see. On his pointer finger just below the cuticle was a raised ridge of skin that went all the way around. He used the knife to cut the most delicious looking pie. Instead of shaking my hand, he handed me a slice of pie and offered me a shot of whiskey from the arsenal of baked goods and alcohol on his desk in the corner of the long rectangular office lined with couches, mirrors, and stacks of beer cases.

The festival was sponsored by Coney Island Lager from Schmaltz Brewery. Big glass bottles of sideshow-themed beers were free for performers that weekend. Diamond Donny Vomit graced the label of Human Blockhead Ale, Heather Holliday was on a bottle called the Sword Swallower, and Serpentina the snake charmer had her own brew called Albino Python Lager. My favorite was the Mermaid Pilsner with Insectavora's tattoos on the smiling face of Coney Island's mascot, Tillie. The night disappeared into rockabilly music and drunken sideshow clowning.

On Saturday, the bands started on the boardwalk and the beer garden in the early afternoon, leading up to the nighttime burlesque blowout at Cha Cha's. The room was lined with round tables and curtained off from the bar to accommodate those who were just there to drink instead of paying the twenty-dollar cover to see the show. The backstage was packed with naked burlesque dancers from all over the country. My job was to get all their names and titles to introduce the marathon of over thirty striptease artists. The festival organizer, Ben, was holding down the door, allowing me to hold down the stage and help him talk to wild-man manager, Machine Gun Johnny, who was very emotional and better known as J.T., or John Thomas. He was in heaven backstage with the dancers, but his mind was racing and fuming, thinking out loud about the bar's owner, Cha Cha, trying to move in on his cut of the weekend's profits.

As a clown, I somehow had license to bridge communication between the entertainers, organizers, bartenders, sound, lights, and mobsters. The trick was to pace myself with the free drinks and stay focused. I was trying to stay a few steps ahead of the game. I made the rounds from backstage to the microphone, to the bar, and the door. The clown with the upside-down frown had found his calling that weekend in Coney Island.

No performances happened inside the bar in the daytime. It was just a magnet for heat, despite the open window with a high-powered fan in the crow's nest that overlooked the stage where the equipment was stored. When the sun went down, the cool air came off the ocean and made the interior less like soup and more like a place for people to pack together for the nighttime spectacle.

We introduced a few bands before it was time for the Sick-A-Billys to take the stage supporting their new album, *Storming the Gates*. It took them longer than anticipated to get set up and to get the sound where they wanted. Sasquatch, otherwise known as King Sickabilly, was a large, intimidating greaser with mean, well-groomed sideburns. His band was a long-haired, stand-up bass player with a lazy yet aggressive lean, and a sharp looking lady behind a striped drum kit. While they tweaked their amplifiers, Nelson Lugo and I did acts and told jokes until we ran out of ammo.

We had the audience screaming and counting while I ran up and down the stage inflating a balloon until it popped. As soon as it burst, Sasquatch kicked into his first song. It was like being at a heavy metal concert with a rockabilly beat. The audience was swept up in a slam dance tornado of jitterbugs. Sweat and spit were flying off the band and the whole room lost control. As they played, King Sickabilly literally transformed into a creature. While he was in full shapeshifter mode, word was passed to me that the bar had to close, and someone needed to tell him they only had two songs left. Well…that someone was me. They had been playing for an hour, but it only felt like ten minutes. Sasquatch was in rare form when I crept up onto the stage and whispered the news into his ear. He spat and addressed the audience. "Alright people, the show is almost over, so this next song is dedicated to the freaks, the clowns, and the circus misfits of Coney Island."

The Sick-A-Billys launched into a song that picked me up and set me swinging, and the room ignited. The band had been drinking heavily the whole show, with people bringing offerings of whiskey to them while they played. During the last song, the bass player puked. I found myself dancing and sliding around in his vomit while dancing onstage with the band. When the show ended, a woman spit on Sasquatch and got in his face for a reason I didn't understand. It escalated to him jumping off the stage. They were both screaming in each other's faces with a tense crowd around them. I managed to climb a wall and perch above the argument like a gargoyle, somehow keeping the peace. After all that drama, we went backstage. Another wild woman followed us and threw the drunk bass player in the bathroom and locked the door to have her way with him.

After everyone was paid and went home, I stayed with Ben and J.T. to count the rest of the profits. Ben paid me what he originally promised, plus a big stack of cash as a bonus for helping to hold the whole chaotic festival together. Ben and I got on the subway at about five in the morning to go to Manhattan; we fell asleep and ended up in Queens. He bought me breakfast and we jumped in a cab. At that point it was Monday morning, officially Labor Day, 2007. I caught the Chinatown bus past the vegetable market under the Manhattan Bridge back to Philadelphia.

With the combination of painting houses full time and the money from shows, I was doing better than I ever had. Matterz Squidling was able to quit his job at the Philadelphia Flower Market, where he had been grinding his wheels making deliveries. This allowed him to focus all his time on editing and creating the sound for the horror movie. It really was a full-time job, and ultimately what Matterz was meant to do. A lot of effort had been put into the movie and it just needed a final push. The master plan was to combine all the things we were doing with music, film, and circus in a traveling show. The road was calling like a message written in the sky, but the work needed to be completed.

After long hours painting houses in the autumn sun, I got a big break and landed a job performing sideshow every weekend of October at the Six Flags Great Adventure theme park for their Halloween event, Fright Fest. Our group was called the Cavalcade of the Odd. Bubbles Corvelay, "the world's 15th greatest daredevil," was the man in charge of the show. Bubbles and I had been introduced by a mutual friend on the internet. We jumped right into making shows, hiring a girl named Rita Riggs from Carnivolution to be a green-skinned alien hula hooper.

We each got our own trailer behind the amusement park, three hundred dollars a day, and free rein to ride any roller coaster in the park. I had grown up coming to Six Flags with my family and always was a roller coaster enthusiast. We had to do five forty-five minute shows a day, three days a week. It was a dream with the loop-de-loop Great American Scream Machine in the center. I stood up on the Batman roller coaster, laid down on the

Superman, traveled two hundred miles an hour up a corkscrew into the sky on the Kingda Ka, feeling like skin would tear off my face, covered in clown makeup.

Fright Fest's stage was in the Wild West section of the park. The Cavalcade of the Odd entered the stage from the other side of a saloon's swinging doors. I walked out of a fog machine mist into the company of zombies while frightening families, and I was getting paid to do it. For the most part, I had my own trailer. There was only one night I had to share it with the Skullduggery & Skin Show of Albert Cadabra, Gal Friday, and Ruby the Wonder Dog. Ruby was a super smart poodle with mountains of charm, always right there in the conversation with you. The dog would run up Albert Cadabra, perch on his shoulder, and do whatever he instructed with a gesture. Gal Friday was like a red-headed damsel in distress from a detective novel. She was straight-faced, full of humor, and focused intently on the patter leading to the punchline. Albert was cleanly bald with big red sideburns and wore a tailored suit. I asked them if they minded if I smoked. They asked if I minded if they turned on the TV. I did not normally watch TV, and they did not smoke. In the end, they did not mind the wacky tobacco smell and I did not mind the sound of the TV.

I showed Albert some of my props. He liked the slapstick best, so I slapped myself on the head with it a few times. Albert was cracking up. He tried it on his shiny bald head.

"Ouch, that really hurts," he said.

"Come on, Albert, give me your very best shot, right in the noggin," I coaxed. Hesitantly, he cracked me on the head, then a bit harder. Ruby was barking. Gal Friday was smiling, half watching the little trailer TV set, and half watching us. We stayed up late talking about shows and New York. They knew many things I did not, and I had the feeling by the end of the night that Albert the sideshow magician and Jellyboy the sideshow clown would be friends for a very long time.

Albert was doing one-man shows in a different section of the park, but we were able to slip away and watch each other's performances. The Cavalcade of the Odd was an onslaught of clockwork weirdness. The times for our shows were posted on a wooden sign by the sideshow saloon. Every show was packed before it started. People sat on benches made of logs and stood up behind them after the seats were full. Bubbles Corvelay opened the show on the microphone while hidden behind swinging doors.

"This show is brought to you by Dr. Scholl's. I would like to invite everyone to take off their shoes because this show is going to knock your socks straight through them!"

Bubbles warmed up the audience, getting them in the mood to make a lot of noise. He was excellent at balancing large objects on his chin and building tension before a stunt.

He wouldn't release me from backstage until the audience was screaming as if being murdered. I would come running out onstage wearing an evil clown Halloween mask, beating myself over the head with my slapstick, falling down and getting back up until the mask was removed by my trembling hand. Out of my pockets came the danger that people were screaming to see. It was a mousetrap and a nail for the sound of the wood against metal. The slap of the trap on a fleshy tongue. Swallowing the cane sword got easier and easier. The bow with the sword down into my stomach became deeper and deeper, bending at the hip until I realized I could lay on my stomach and do a push up with the sword in me. It was spontaneous insanity, but that wasn't the craziest part of our Cavalcade of the Odd.

Bubbles Corvelay balanced a six-foot ladder on his chin in front of a tarp full of broken glass. Every show he gave a large audience member a piggyback ride over the glass. After safely putting down the person, he climbed to the top of the six-foot ladder that he had just balanced on his chin. The suspense rose up like the pitch of a boiling tea kettle as Bubbles climbed, pausing at each step to face the audience, confronting them to dare him to jump. When just about to step up to the top, he stopped and looked down at what was written on the step.

"Sorry ladies and gentlemen, I can't go any higher. It says, 'Do not stand or step on the top of the ladder.'" He sat on the step instead, looking down at the broken glass and back at the audience. Then, at the height of the tension, Bubbles "the world's 15th greatest daredevil" made a leap of faith off the top of the ladder into the broken glass with his bare feet.

It worked out for the most part, with no cuts or bruises until one unfortunate rainy day. It had just started raining in the middle of the show and the audience all took out umbrellas and put on raincoats. We kept the show rolling with unstoppable momentum. After piggybacking a large man through the wet broken glass, the question popped up in our minds: should we cut the ladder jump? Was it really worth it? We communicated this to each other in a way that the audience was unaware. Feeling the mania of sideshow momentum coursing through his veins, Bubbles decided to pull down the safety goggles on his aviator hat over his eyes and take a chance, jumping six feet into the broken glass of doom. When he landed, he slipped forward a little and fell on his backside, causing his feet to slide across the wet glass instead of coming straight down. He played it off as if he was miraculously okay. He left the stage with a triumphant limp, leaving behind bloody footprints with each step. I took the show on to the end. Bubbles did not return to the stage that day: he was taken away in an ambulance with a cut so deep he needed stitches. According to Bubbles, it looked like there was a bloody vagina on the bottom of his foot...but even with the stitched-up foot, Bubbles was back for the next day of shows. He breathed fire off the torch on my sword so many times that by Halloween, the handle of encrusted plastic skulls was melted. For the show's finale, he balanced a flaming charcoal grill on his chin, which was the greatest balancing act I had ever seen. Teetering on the edge of disaster, appearing drunk on the ledge of a window to the weird.

Albert Cadabra and Gal Friday were being picked up by their friend Big Heath and his teenage daughter and missed our last show by a fraction. They were sideshow enthusiasts on a level that I could relate to. Albert introduced us as we were packing up and asked me to show them the slapstick. A few cracks on the head later they were laughing. Almost instantly, we had a crowd of people as an audience to a show that was meant for the private amusement of two people. Albert Cadabra watched as Big Heath and his daughter watched me. The rest of the audience was also watching them, watching me going through the human blockhead routine and sword swallowing antics, intoxicated by the end of the night at the roller coasters' last run on the tracks.

A science in sensation. The first few times I rode a ride, it was a thrill, with screaming, flinching, and the feeling that we might fly off the tracks was very real. Heart racing, the spirit outside trying to catch up to my body on the first drop down. After a while, I got to memorize the twists and turns, the loops and the jumps, to the point where I could relax into them, letting go of all fear and tension. High speeds with a low pulse were a euphoric out of body experience, all alone in the thundering afterlife of roller coaster mania. The relaxing sounds of screams in careless wonder.

Keith Bindlestiff, who was famous to us, visited our show one day when he was hired to do a one-man act at the park. He was a sword swallower who had been traveling with his own Bindlestiff Family Cirkus since the 1990s. He was in the book *Freaks and Fire* where I had first read about the Enigma. A sharply dressed showman with black hair tied back under a fedora, Keith looked like a private detective from the Order of Mystery.

Rita Riggs and I were on to him. He was there to see what we were made of. We trailed him for a bit, then the green skin hyperactive alien and I jumped out of a smoke machine to try and scare him. We introduced ourselves excitedly, but he did not seem impressed by our clownish entrance. Keith's alter ego's name was Mister Pennygaff, so he was part clown himself. He gave a half-amused stare and said, "You better not suck."

We laughed an understanding chuckle. We realized how many new acts were emerging all the time on the trail that the Bindlestiff Family Cirkus had helped blaze. "You won't be disappointed, Mr. Bindlestiff," I said, tipping my top hat.

Nothing like having a veteran sword swallower around to test your nerve. Feeling a bit intimidated, I ran out onto the stage in the horror clown mask with two orange mats of hair hanging off the sides of an otherwise bald head. I cracked with the slapstick to the murderous screams and laughter among the animated audience. There stood the stoic Keith Bindlestiff, unmoving and undecided in the back of the crowd. I always scan the eyes of the audience to see the mixed emotions and play them off of each other. As the momentum of the act unfolded, Keith began to warm up. He was watching the audience as much as the show.

After our show, I snuck out to watch him perform on the midway. He gathered an audience quickly by standing with a lit torch as if he was just about to eat the fire. When he noticed I was there, Keith Bindlestiff saluted and gave me an approving nod.

Chapter 8
Traveling with the Show

Our big old pirate ship of a house on 4811 Chester Avenue was built in 1880. The roof was a bit leaky, so we patched it here and there and set buckets in the attic when it rained. The Green Line trolley stopped right on the corner, just before the bridge, over the train tracks for the regional railroad. The property owner did not want to be bothered with repairs to her house on the wrong side of the tracks. The house was heated by an expensive oil furnace in the basement where our band rehearsed before it started leaking, making us move all the gear up to the living room. The house was taking water from the top and the bottom but still stood despite years of neglect. It had a strong foundation.

With the end of the season came the realization that our house would not last the winter if something was not done about the roof. We had an elaborate bucket system and a tarp over the hole that had developed through the old slate shingles. There was a trapdoor in the attic that allowed me to climb up on the roof when a storm was coming to weigh down the tarp with cinder blocks on top and water jugs hanging off the bottom.

After inspecting the roof, our landlord realized something had to be done, so she called a roofer. The roof was only seriously damaged in one spot, but they told her she would need a new roof. They offered a cheap price, and she was sold, but you get what you pay for! Before the sun came up, we found that our roof was being attacked by a gang of whisky-drinking pirates, like a horde of giant squirrels with crowbars. They tore off the beautiful old slate roof from the 1800s. The heavy slate crashed down all around the house, crushing the gardens that Matterz had cared for through the summer into fall. They replaced the old roof with cheap shingles. The next time it rained, it rained inside the house worse than before. Upon inspection, the roofers never attached the metal flashing. Their boss was a criminal who didn't pay them properly and took off with most of the loot. We were left with a totally sinking ship and no choice but to think of an exit plan.

Nothing could be done right away, so we fought the elements and waited it out, allowing the momentum of what we had been building to come to pass. Things didn't go down without a fight.

In the midst of all this, I received a message on *MySpace* from someone I had never met before. Her name was Bubblegum Betty and the message read, "*Let's play!*" According to her profile, Bubblegum Betty was a belly dancer and yoga teacher. She was truly beautiful, with big, blue eyes and long, black hair; skinny, but full-figured with a long, strong torso. To my imagination she resembled a spy, or an assassin from the 007 movies. In a state of disbelief, I responded, "*Where and when?*"

We decided to meet at the Satellite Cafe on 50th and Baltimore Ave. She asked how she would recognize me, since I was wearing clown makeup in all my profile pictures. "Is a clown still a clown with no makeup?" was my wiseass way of saying, "Don't worry, you'll know me when you see me." We sat all the way in the back of the punk rock coffee shop with art all over the walls and a bike shop above. Coffee mugs hung on the bike wheel over the sink behind the counter. There was a gray cat named Luna on a little purple couch that we claimed as the spot for the first of many conversations.

Betty had many questions about sword swallowing and fire. I had questions about yoga. Her voice had a wise, raspy quality with something funny behind it that made me want to know more. We talked for a long time and decided to get together again as soon as we could. Betty came to my house the following week and I snuck her upstairs, not wanting to share her with my housemates. She learned to feed me the sword while standing over me on a table. We wrestled and played, but she wouldn't let me kiss her. It turned out that Bubblegum Betty had a boyfriend, ironically named Red, whom she lived with. The chemistry was there, so rather than screwing things up by fooling around, we decided to be show partners. She helped me with yoga, and I showed her what I knew about clown makeup and some basic things about the nature of sideshow secrets.

Most everyone in the house went home to see their families for Thanksgiving. Matterz and I stayed with our parents in Lancaster for the whole weekend. When we returned the following Monday, no one was around, but the kitchen window and back door were open. Upon further inspection of the house, we realized that we had been robbed! Creepy feelings lurked up our spines as we tried to recreate the break-in. My older brother's black and white Stratocaster guitar was gone, as well as some cash and an Xbox video game system.

Lucky for us, the burglar didn't open the sliding door to the Hydrogen Jukebox's practice space, because we were all set up in there to jam and make recordings. In fact, we were in the middle of recording an album called *Fingerprint Land*, which was a collection of new and old songs by our current arrangement of the time. We had made a few other albums: *Cosmic When You Ride* in 2001, *Birth of the Squid* in 2004, and *Eat Your TV Watch Your Meat* in 2005.

It was starting to get ice cold again as December approached, so we filled the oil furnace in the basement, stapled plastic and blankets on all the windows, and bled the radiators on the second and third floors so the heat could rise up to the upper reaches of the house. The frost of the first snow actually came into the attic through the missing flashing on the corners of the roof.

Despite all the problems with our sinking ship of a house, there were happier happenings on the horizon. The band was focused, the sideshow was inspired, and the movie was finished. We had a projector, a screen, a full band with a PA system, a few beds of nails, and a black and silver short bus to carry us where we needed to go.

The Enigma joined us on a small tour to promote the movie throughout December, leading up to the New Year at a show in Brooklyn we called the Danger Party. With big plans for a road show, we printed one thousand DVD copies. The tour focused on Philly, DC, Baltimore, and most of all, New York City. All of us knew we wouldn't be staying at 4811 Chester Avenue much longer, however; the focus was staying afloat to take the show on the road leading to New Year's, 2008.

Our big show and movie screening was on December 14 at the Trocadero, a huge old, haunted theater in Philly's Chinatown with a history going back to the heyday of burlesque and vaudeville. Joe Tiberino's son Raphael organized the date for us. He and his sister Ellen worked there as bartenders. The screening would start the night and lead to an epic onslaught of live entertainment.

The destination for the next screening would be our headquarters for the week: the House of Yes at 19-49 Troutman Street on the border of Brooklyn and Queens. Next to a gas station, among the old factories and houses, overlooking a graveyard of junked cars, was the home of our New York family, the Lady Circus. We stripped the group down to the band plus a skeleton crew sideshow and screened the movie. It became one experience. The House of Yes was too friendly a place for my psychedelic meanderings.

After the show, the time went so fast that the next morning arrived before I knew it, and sleep crept up, causing me to miss a tattoo appointment in Staten Island with the artist I met at Dottie Lux's birthday party. Magie Serpica was going to help me become the Living Cartoon by tattooing a circus train traveling up my ribs, but I had slept through the appointment. It was dark again by the time I woke up, and she wouldn't answer the phone.

The Hydrogen Jukebox took off back to Philadelphia, leaving Matterz and me behind at the House of Yes with our mysterious circus strongman housemate, the Duke of Flies. He was from down south and had recently become a part of our group as a pierced weightlifter, with his super strong stretched ears. We had almost every day booked for our three-person sideshow and movie screening tour.

That Monday we went to work, meeting up with our friend Sean Kershaw the Coney Island Cowboy at his regular gig at Hank's Saloon in the East Village. Fire was painted on the walls and our movie played on all the TV screens, a little honky-tonk horror and sideshow comedy. We sold some DVDs, made a little money, got drunk on whiskey, and carried a bucket of glass and an anvil on a cart through the New York City subways to sleep on the stage at the House of Yes. That Tuesday we woke up fairly early, surprisingly motivated with no real hangover. I found the number for Magie's tattoo shop, which was, oddly enough, called Studio Enigma. A Russian woman answered the phone and said that Magie would be there in about two hours.

Matterz, the Duke, and I headed to the Staten Island Ferry, which was a lot like a giant floating subway. As it sailed past the Statue of Liberty, tourists from all over the world were snapping pictures while New Yorkers tried to ignore the spectacle for a brief moment of rest. After we landed in Staten Island, we walked with the herd of people onto the dock; after a few stops on the train, it was just a short stroll to Studio Enigma. The old Staten Island native who greeted us had qualities of showbiz and organized crime. He got an instant kick out of the three of us. It was a song, a dance, a stunt with a nail in the head and a sword in the stomach, close to the heart of tattoo culture. The Russian piercer from the phone call looked like a rockstar. She was instantly inviting with her witch-like black hair, and we realized that Matterz and the Duke would soon be victims of her art.

Magie watched from the back, still angry about the missed appointment two days ago. I apologized and tried to explain the situation. She had come in special to tattoo me and wasted her day. Well, not wasted completely—she drew an evil comic about me as a sword swallower clown in jail being sexually assaulted by inmates and writing love letters to Heather Holliday.

"Any attention is good," I said, and laughed at the amazing darkness of her humor. "Will you please tattoo me?" I asked, trying to keep a straight face.

"I'm going to torture you," she said, fighting off a fit of giggles.

Matterz wanted a chaos star tattooed on his arm. The Duke of Flies wanted his nipples pierced to add to his pierced weightlifting act. Stretched holes in his earlobes filled with big jewelry were capable of lifting an anvil! Magie Serpica and I went to the local library to look up pictures of steam trains and ships. We hit the books and the photocopy machine. Then it was back to the shop to make the sketches and find the right placement on my rib cage. I wanted a stick figure operating the train and another stick figure in the crow's nest of the ship holding a spyglass.

The plan was to tattoo the entire right side of my body from finger to toe. Therefore, we figured it best to start in the middle and work out from there over the course of many sessions. When Magie finished the sketch, I gave my approval, and we placed it in the mirror. The nose of the train was on the outside of my armpit going down past the nipple, stopping in the middle of the ribcage. This connected with the ship, ending in line with the navel to pay tribute to the Navy. The image was copied to a piece of wax paper that was wet down and placed on my body. The outline stuck to the skin as if Magie had drawn it there with a marker. She set up her ink and put fresh needles in her tattoo machine, pushed down on the foot switch, and listened to the buzz.

It was very cold in the room even with the space heater at Magie's station. Horizontal and half naked on the table, I waited for the first bite and sting of the ink-laying needles. The nerves in the side ribs are unbelievably sensitive. My job was to remain still and be a good canvas with no recoil as she carved the cartoon into my skin. After every buzzing cut, the ink and blood were wiped away to make room for the next. The pain changed as my body quivered in a strange, numbing shock. I focused on the music, the cracks in the ceiling, my breathing; anything but the jarring needle grinding against my bones until that was all I wanted to feel.

The tattoo grew and I tried to meet the sensation instead of ignoring it, until the line of the train was about to cut over my nipple. "Could we go around the nipple and make it part of the roof of the train?" I asked. My nipple was spared, but the edges were blended into the train with a sharp pull that will stay with me as long as I live.

Pain can make five minutes feel like an hour, and an hour felt like it was never going to end. How much pain is a person capable of feeling before they are no longer conscious? I accepted the sensation but couldn't stop my body from shaking when it was all done and burning raw, open to the air. Magie cleaned me up and wrapped the tattoo in plastic so the fresh wounds wouldn't stick to my shirt on the way back to the House of Yes.

The Russian piercer asked if we wanted a gig the following night at a Russian club called the Downhouse off the Avenue X stop on the Coney Island train. How could we refuse? We didn't want a night off anyway, even though we had plans to modify and enhance my carnival sword. The Duke and I had been conspiring to make a new handle for the sword that was in fact a flamethrower.

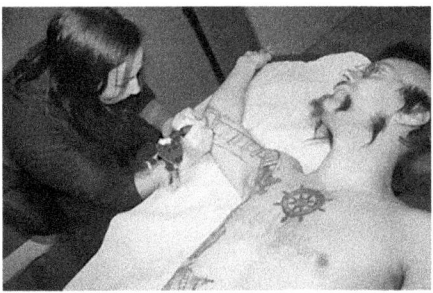

Magie Serpica tattooing Jellyboy, Staten Island, 2010 (Matt Broomfield)

This was something that I could operate alone with a trigger on a can of butane gas, built into the hollow handle, shot at an open flame.

The same night after getting work done at Studio Enigma, I called the Enigma and told him of the strange coincidence on our way to screen the movie at the Bowery Poetry Club in Manhattan. He would be joining us in a few days when our big show reunited to go to Baltimore and Washington, D.C.

The next afternoon, the Duke of Flies and I got to work on the flamethrower sword handle. We cut a PVC pipe to the size of a can of butane gas with a metal trigger. It had a hole just big enough for the plastic nozzle to poke through the metal of the trigger, sticking out like a T which went up the handle as a finger guard. When it was squeezed, the gas would shoot out in a jet horizontally, not vertically as expected. We added a hand guard and cemented the whole thing together using Bondo, a stinky mixture of chemicals normally used to fix dents in cars. We used it as filler to repair windowsills when painting houses. The flamethrower sword was created at the House of Yes in the afternoon with the door open for ventilation. There were still a few kinks to work out, but that day a reality came to life out of the sketchbook of a clown.

Having just got his nipples pierced at Studio Enigma, the Duke needed a night of rest. Matterz and I ventured out with our bucket of broken glass and sideshow stunts to join the Russians and Magie Serpica in a hilarious evening of good food, live music, and way too much to drink. The sideshow was a ridiculously over the top hit. The room of drunken Russians were just nice enough and mean enough to truly laugh from the gut at the painful and the impossible.

At the end of the show, they wanted one more stunt. The only thing I had was a staple gun. The husband of the Russian piecer was very enthusiastic in his intoxication, so much so that he inspired all the others. He declared that no less than a twenty-dollar bill be stapled to me. I took off my shirt to reveal a huge fresh tattoo and said, "Staple me anywhere but the tattoo…within reason."

I had talked the staple gun act but never performed it, and suddenly I found myself surrounded by happy, drunk Russians holding twenty-, fifty-, and one-hundred-dollar bills. The T50 carpenter-grade staple gun was pushed hard against paper money into the side of my ribs where I wasn't tattooed. I waited for the snap of the gun and the kick of pain from the staple bang. The gun snapped and everyone in the room recoiled with bloodlust excitement. The money fell off of me onto the floor and we quickly realized there were no staples left in the gun. It was like a game of Russian roulette with no bullets, and a shockingly disappointing way to end the show, as we watched all the money go back in the pockets. Nothing really to do but laugh, have a few more drinks, and get back on the train to the House of Yes. A tough lesson learned: never assume you have ammo in your gun, and always make sure there is something to reload it with.

Matterz and I arrived back at the House of Yes around 3:30 in the morning to find most of the house and a few other friends seated around the kitchen table with the Duke. I saw a little lady, somewhere between four and five feet tall, running toward me. She attacked me with an assault of hugs, saying, "Oh Jellyboy I've heard so much about you and your show! We are going to be great friends." Everyone around the table was laughing. Matterz and I were quite disoriented from Russian vodka and the New York subway, but it was hard not to join in the laughter, even if I wasn't sure if Nati Amos was real or a figment of my imagination.

Nati had a patchwork of scars, and was missing a few fingers on each hand, with a straight, black, classic Beatles haircut. Her brown, watery eyes seemed to be filled with tears of laughter. During her development as a fetus, Nati's face and body never fully formed. The face that I was seeing was the product of a lifetime of surgeries. She told us that she was born without a nose or upper lip, and her eye sockets were uneven. With eyes now even, and her upper lip joined to make one, the most marvelous part of all was that she had been given a nose with just one functioning nostril.

She had experienced a life in and out of hospitals in a relatively constant state of healing without pain medication due to her opiate allergy. With her tolerance for discomfort and sense of humor, she found the sideshow very attractive. Fingers that felt like suction cups hugged me and wouldn't let go. At that point, having money stapled to her and dancing with a feather boa were her acts. "Hello, my darlings," Nati would say, hopping from lap to lap in the audience.

The Duke had shown Nati some transfer maneuvers from torch to torch with fire contact. She climbed his shoulders, lit up and showed me the flame passed to her tongue, over to an unlit torch. I told her that we would be performing and screening the movie the following night at the tiki bar called Otto's Shrunken Head. We had no choice but to have her in the show.

Enigma and Angel arrived the next afternoon. I hadn't seen Enigma since he escaped Philadelphia, and Angel had been in Maine since she showed me how to breathe fire. Neither of them had a chance to watch the movie yet. Enigma drove us and all our props with his Jeep into Manhattan. Spliff and Ji Ji the Carnie Girl from Disgraceland joined us at Otto's Shrunken Head for our eight-person sideshow horror extravaganza.

The room filled up quickly with people. Enigma put an apple in Nati's mouth and carved an X in it with his chainsaw, making applesauce splatter across the people seated in the front. Spliff and Ji Ji came out of semi-retirement to do some sideshow acts. The rest of the Disgraceland crew had scattered. Roc Roc-It had fallen off the stage at Coney Island, knocked out his front teeth, and burned his face breathing fire at a party. He had overstayed his visa for three years, so he decided to turn himself in and get a free flight back to Germany. GanJeesh and M.C. A.K.A. had a baby and moved to the west coast.

The Disgraceland Family Freakshow had become the Disgraceland Hook Squad. They had been focusing mostly on flesh suspension, hanging from their skin with big meat hooks. Ji Ji lifted a small bucket of paint with chains attached to coins in her eyes and Spliff the Amazing Amazonian Affliction did some pierced weightlifting.

The Duke was thrilled to meet Disgraceland. Seeing photos of them in a tattoo magazine was the inspiration for starting his path as a sideshow strongman. We were all together, one photogenic freakshow family, ready to take on the world. Good fun with the staple gun ended the show with the Disgraceland tradition of choosing which freak you wanted to staple. The Duke, Spliff, Ji Ji, and Nati were lined up and ready to go, each with their own gun and their own line of people ready to staple them.

The Palace of Wonders in D.C. was the next stop. They had a small stage with a high ceiling and a balcony for an extra layer of audience. We had been there before with Red and Barry Silver, in the show dedicated to the seven torture acts. This time it was a convergence, our own little sideshow gathering of the Unholy Sideshow, Red Stuart,

Enigma, Angel from the End of the World, and the Squidling Brothers Circus Sideshow. An advanced variation on classic stunts never before attempted by human marvels or clowns alike! With so many sideshow performers and only so many stunts to go around, we had to coordinate who was doing what and be creative in our presentations.

It was sad to see the movie tour come to an end, but we hoped it would be the first of many. Christmas was the following day with New Year's right around the corner. Angel got into Enigma's Jeep, and he drove her to celebrate Christmas with her friends in Ohio. He was off to bring gifts to his daughter in the Midwest.

On December 27, I went back to New York City for the screening of another independent movie, a documentary about the Coney Island Rockabilly Festival, shown at a little burlesque club on the Lower East Side called the Slipper Room. I decided to stay at the House of Yes and help get things ready for the Danger Party that we would all be a part of on New Year's Eve. Just before New Year's, I got a message online from a vampire. He wanted me to host a party in the basement of a Chinese restaurant turned drag queen joint, called Lucky Cheng's. Earlier that day, I was with Kae and Anya helping design the Danger Party at an enormously huge warehouse in Brooklyn. We were using heavy-duty staple guns to hang ribbons on the ceiling, and test driving a spring-loaded harness for a human piñata. I wondered why vampires would want a clown to host their party.

Chinese dragons guarded the outside of Lucky Cheng's with drag queens singing and dancing on the inside and vampires in the basement. Who would have thought people would look at me strangely in this environment? But they did, and I loved it. The vampires were squeamish about a needle in my neck: clown blood would only make them laugh. I tightened a wrench as much as possible and let it dangle from my septum. I took a goth Barbie doll with a noose around her neck and a strap-on dildo between her legs out of my pocket and hung her off the wrench attached to my nose. The vampires cracked up laughing, showing their fangs in the dark nightclub basement.

This time I made sure the staple gun was loaded before the show. The vamps went nuts. Out came their money and *bang, bang, bang*: I was tacked up before I knew it by the bloodthirsty suckers. It was hard to move with the staples in my ribs, and I didn't know why until I decided to remove them. It was like a bad dream; the staples just kept coming out. I had used the wrong gun! It was the one the Lady Circus was using to hang up party decorations. It looked like mine, but mine was filled with shorter staples: these were way longer than they needed to be. They left big welts and I bled nicely for the vampires.

Some scary-looking beautiful girls came up to me and asked where my pack was. I didn't understand. They said they were werewolves and figured that I must be a werewolf, too, because of the things I did, even though I was a clown. "Don't worry," said their were-chic leader, "A lone wolf always finds its pack." That night I slept on the stage at the House of Yes, as they had given me a key. The staple wounds hurt, but I had found my pack of shapeshifters; a sideshow circus clown on the stage of the underground.

When I woke up the next day at the House of Yes, a guy I had never met before said, "Good morning; please stick out your tongue." For some reason, I did as he asked. He took out a vial. My senses were heightened; awareness went through the roof. I cleaned every inch of the House of Yes, hallucinating like a werewolf on New Year's Eve.

The Danger Party was true madness that only Brooklyn can provide. It was set up like a carnival of chaos, with all kinds of bizarre prizes on an absurd drunken midway of the psycho-normal. Anya was in the center of the room, dangling from the ceiling on two silk fabrics. She commanded the crowd, tied herself up in all kinds of knots, then climbed to the top and let herself fall inches from the floor. She created a safe perimeter by spinning in a circle with her long legs stretched out like helicopter blades which could behead anyone who got in her sphere. Dangerously beautiful in the party lights wearing a body-hugging unitard, the definition of her muscles stood out in the contrast of shadow. Black shoulder-length hair whipped upside-down in a momentum of erotic violence.

Yes; we said yes to danger, and danced disintegration. People were spinning fire on the roof with kerosene on staves and chains. The Duke of Flies had recently learned to breathe fire, and he was getting carried away, going through bottles of lamp oil. It was windy on the roof that night. The gusts were carrying his fireballs higher than seemed possible until the wind shifted against his favor: it lit up his face with a mouth half full of fuel still inside him.

Meanwhile, I hid backstage, watching out the window at the fire whipping around while waiting for the set with the Hydrogen Jukebox. It was getting a bit hot and smoky in the room we were in. "Man, those fire spinners are using a lot of fuel; you can smell it in here!" I said out loud.

Lenore came running through the door. The Duke's face was burned, and he was poisoned from all the fuel, but he was still with it and seemed to be handling himself alright. At that moment, we realized the smoke was not coming from outside! Matterz's five string bass was in its case, resting on a heater. While we were backstage smoking weed, having a good time, the case had melted. The guitar was a bit melted too. Hot as hell! We took the smoky, smelly instrument outside past our scorched strongman to cool off and let the toxic fumes waft into the winter air.

Luckily for us, our friend Aaron Goldsmith, who had introduced us to the whole scene in the first place, was a bass player, so we were able to borrow his instrument. Anya was unstoppable! She knew exactly where the bass was, and only she could have gotten through the party quick enough to save the show, arriving with the bass in the nick of time. The elemental fire licked its lips, and 2007 became 2008. Just like that, the Hydrogen Jukebox rocked the New Year with flames to a sold-out crowd.

Chapter 9
The Unicorn Goat

Upon returning to Philadelphia, I found that Bubblegum Betty had added Bloomerz to her name and removed the Bubblegum. She surprised me with a video of her in clown makeup, effortlessly swallowing a wire coat hanger and bending it with the muscles of her neck, revealing a smile matching the shape of the hanger. A smile or a frown, however you look at it, Betty had already figured it out with a creative spin. We planned to continue our showbiz partnership.

All the activity leading up to the New Year was like being launched out of a cannon into the illumination of the night sky to the unknown realm of nonstop adventure. January was slow motion, flying through the mental circus air, catching future shows in the arch of the cannon's fire, leaving trails of sparks on the way to February and March.

Making clown magic of the sideshow variety, Betty learned the mental floss and we performed an act called the Tunnel of Love, where our heads were connected by the fish tube.

We added jump roping, tug of war, and acrobatic balancing to make it an exciting routine. Betty would climb all over me with a wine glass in her hand. I provided surfaces for her to stand on while she drank the wine through a straw, woven through both our heads. On February 2, we performed at a house party for Betty's best friend's birthday. It was our first show as a duo with no one else to back us up, for a mostly queer audience of

Jellyboy and Betty Bloomerz drinking wine through a nose tube, Palace of Wonders, Washington, D.C., 2008 (Strange Eye)

pleasantly drunk women in their twenties. Playfulness prevailed! We developed our acts on and off the stage, allowing things to happen in the moment as we danced. Jokes flew through the air to amuse and confuse, daze and amaze, confound and astound.

The following week, I went alone on a Greyhound bus to the Baltimore tattoo convention. Enigma had invited me to join up for the weekend with his new group, the Electric Acid Theater. As an experiment I decided to do the show as a clown with no makeup. The bus station was just outside the city. I walked the slippery streets toward distant skyscrapers, past cranes, under roads, and over snowy grass-patched mounds. When I finally reached the hotel, the familiar buzz of tattoo machines filled the convention floor as the usual modified suspects scanned the scene. I searched for the Enigma, but he was nowhere to be found. He wasn't answering his phone either.

By the stage area, I stumbled upon an illustrated man who stood four feet, three inches tall, with hands where his arms should be. He had large, stretched earlobes with nice, heavy stone jewelry and a mohawk. I approached him shyly and asked if he had seen the Enigma. He looked at me a bit suspiciously.

Jason Brott the Illustrated Penguin Boy, pierced weightlifting, Palace of Wonders, Washington, D.C., 2008 (Strange Eye)

I introduced myself: "The name is Jellyboy the Clown. I'm a sideshow performer."

"I'm Penguin," he said, leaning in to shake my hand with his, which had no arm attached, only a shoulder. "I'm doing a weightlifting act tonight with my ears. I want to use a bucket of ice but can't carry it because my hands only have so much gripping power." He had knees that could not bend. One leg was a bit longer than the other in braces. This meant that he had to walk with his hips, throwing the legs forward with each step, all core muscles and attitude. I liked him right away and ran off to get a bucket of ice from the bar.

When I returned, Enigma was there with his new girlfriend, Serana Rose, a young woman raised on a goat farm in Iowa. She knew how to hypnotize chickens, which fascinated me. We quickly decided to be BFFs (best friends forever). Since Penguin, also known as Jason Brott, was performing solo, the four of us thought it made sense to do the show together. It was Enigma's standard formula, but Serana joined in with some poetry, playing bass guitar and performing stunts.

"Enigma is worldwide adored because he can swallow a sword. This ancient art rests the blade on his heart, I hope he's not punctured...or gored."

Serana Rose and the Enigma's kiss of death (Kali Miles)

After the show, we sold our horror movie in the lobby while Enigma made a lot of tattoo appointments. I agreed to meet up again for more shows in the future with Penguin, and I took a bus back to Philadelphia from Baltimore.

The next weekend it was *Bam!* Off to D.C. with the Hellcat Girls to a sold-out show at the Palace of Wonders. One of the dancers, Candy Mayhem, had taken me under her wing (or boob) and I was fast becoming one of the girls. Betty had given me a polka dot dress, pink bloomers, and stockings for my clown burlesque with a fish tube in my panties. Lil' Steph showed me how to properly take off a dress: hands crossed, back to the audience, with a booty bounce.

Jellyboy with Candy Mayhem, Palace of Wonders, Washington, D.C., 2007 (Strange Eye)

Experience with burlesque performers inspired me to want to do it too. My burlesque disguise was a dress, pink fishnets, combat boots, a feather boa, and a devil mask, with a pair of red polka dot pants on my head like a babushka. My fish tube and power drill were ready to bore into my face when the mask was tossed aside to the song "He's So Unusual" by Helen Kane, a high-pitched singer of the 1920s who was the inspiration for Betty Boop. The song was about a gay man who drives her wild with love and is out of her reach. The staple gun was once again a very profitable hit: all of us went home with extra loot in our boots.

It wasn't hard to get me out of the door—all I wanted was to run cross country to the nearest circus or cabaret. February ended with a wham-bam-thank-you-ma'am; I joined the Hellcat Girls at a roadside circus bar in Delaware called MoJo 13. The entrance was a clown's face that looked a lot like me. Another full house, a raunchy rumpus. The Hellcat Girls had just launched a campaign to recruit new talent. They held auditions for junior Hellcat Girls, or "Hell Kittens." Their new star was Miss Rose, "the flower that everyone wants to pluck," a flexible intellectual with long, dark hair and an old pistol tattooed on her leg. The show also featured the bizarro burlesque stylings of sweet, red-headed dominatrix Darcy Deluxe; short, cute, big-butted pit bull enthusiast Lil' Darlin; South Philly vintage movie starlet Lil' Steph; and Athena Onatopp as the crass, take-no-shit hostess.

At the end of the show, there was a fifty-dollar bill stapled to my head that really hit a main vein. Once again, I had a bit too much alcohol in me and wanted to bleed to end the show. When I pulled out the staples of my body before the bugged eyes of the audience, a few left nice trickles. But when I pulled the staple out of my forehead, blood started to run down. Instead of stopping, it picked up momentum and started to pour into my eyes, under my glasses. It cried down one tear duct like red wine.

I was still in character, clowning about the bleeding, but I started to feel lightheaded. I grabbed my magic polyester red and white clown shirt covered in stripes with polka dots and used it to apply direct pressure, but the blood soaked through the shirt. I wrapped it around my head like a pirate, bowed to the audience with prayer hands, and ran backstage to find a mirror to see how bad it really was.

Miss Rose was right there with me. "That shirt is important to you right?" she said, looking at my blood-soaked, most favorite flammable polyester garment.

"Yes," I said with red splattered all over my face, cleaning my eyeglasses in the sink.

"Let me get the blood out of it for you," she said and took the shirt out of my hands. "Cold water gets fresh blood out of clothes before it dries and stains."

I was so grateful I almost cried. That night I vowed to remove the staples backstage with proper clean medical supplies to avoid being a bloody mess, even though the photos were exciting. Too much blood spilled is overdoing a good thing.

Not only was February filled with shows and adventure, but it was also filled with the enormous job of leaving our old house. If I had my way, we would still live there. I might like to be a ghost haunting the place. Our time was up, no way around it, so we weighed the options of getting another group house, versus Matterz and I getting a place just for us with a separate rehearsal space for the Hydrogen Jukebox. In that little window of time, a space opened up at the Tiberino Museum where we did the Carnivolution shows. Two rooms on the third floor. The second floor was Joe Tiberino's private space for painting, and the first floor was part of the museum with a kitchen. We could store things in the basement which could be reached through a secret trapdoor in the kitchen floor.

Everyone else was already gone, so it was the obvious choice to move to the art compound. The band found a rehearsal space in Upper Darby just up the tracks from Philly, but there was a fire in the building shortly after we arrived. This forced us to move all our equipment to a vacant house in the Tiberino compound that was being renovated to rent to other artists. Eventually we got a space to practice and record—a room in the lower level of a parking garage on 47th and Pine. It was nice to play loud music in the equivalent of a fallout shelter.

Carnivolution, The Ellen Powell Tiberino Museum, Philadelphia, 2008 (Lunchbox)

Momentum led us to the Palace of Wonders in Washington, D.C. once again. This time it was the Squidling Brothers and the Lady Circus. Something about that name must have struck a chord at that moment in time, because it was beyond sold out. There was hardly room to move. We made more money that night than we had ever made from a show before. It was fitting that Betty Bloomerz would be joining us that night for her first time onstage as a sword swallower. Also joining us was Kae Burke from the House of Yes, as the pregnant bearded lady with antics on stilts and aerial silks. It was March 14, 2008, and somehow, in the midst of this chaos, our lives had worked out.

Betty had said she would never kiss me unless there was a unicorn in the room. One thing I knew that she didn't, was that there was a unicorn in the Palace of Wonders, on the second floor where James Taylor's oddity collection was kept. It was the unicorn goat taxidermy from the Ringling Brothers Circus in a glass case. We went upstairs after the show and had no choice but to kiss. It was like a bite from the forbidden fruit of knowledge. That clown makeup kiss by the unicorn goat sent me spinning.

Nothing like a crying, baby-monster to get you out and looking for work. Good thing I had a job, and the season to work outside was upon us. Betty and I started borrowing her father's car and shooting off to do shows in Washington, D.C. and New York City. We worked with the Hellcat Girls and the Skullduggery & Skin Show with Albert Cadabra and Gal Friday. Betty started incorporating trapeze into our crazy sideshow dances with a homemade one from Carnivolution that we hung in the backyard of the art garden. Swallowing swords on the trapeze upside-down became her obsession.

Jellyboy and Betty Bloomerz, upside-down hanger swallow on trapeze, Palace of Wonders, Washington, D.C., 2008 (Strange Eye)

On April 22, just a week before my birthday, I got a phone call with some very bad news. The House of Yes had burned down! Everyone escaped unharmed, but they lost the life of their orange cat Pilgrim and everything that they owned. The whole thing was triggered by a greasy toaster in the kitchen. It caught fire right under a giant puppet head hanging on the wall. The puppet was furry and made of some surprisingly flammable synthetic materials. It went up quickly and flames spread faster than anyone could fight. Before they knew it, the fire was crawling on the ceiling and there was nothing to do but run for their lives. By the time the fire department arrived it was too late: everything was lost. Benefit shows followed. We all came together to help raise money for a new House of Yes that was even bigger and better. Burned birthplace of my flamethrower sword, only a few months after its construction. It's a good thing the spirit of the House of Yes was indestructible by any natural means.

On April 30, Frank Walsh the Masked Perfesser told me something I had never heard before. "Happy Walpurgisnacht, Jellyboy. This is the night of the witches, the polar opposite of Halloween, where the veil between the living and the dead is thinnest. On Walpurgisnacht, the witches have the most power! People all over Europe are having huge celebrations to ring in the first of May, lighting fires and dancing around maypoles. Fertility rituals, planting, the promise of a new life; happy birthday, you trickster." Then he danced around like a pop-eyed loony tune and let out cackling laughter of cartoon joy, spinning in a circle. Twiddling his fingers, Frank pretended to cast a spell for the mercy of the Misfit Mother, pregnant with protection from the danger we were in.

The outdoor amusement season had started again, rumored to be the last year of Coney Island. A huge real estate company was buying everything up and was going to put condos and a mall on the boardwalk. It was in all the papers and people were overwhelmed with nostalgia. They were ready to fight to keep Coney Island from being turned into typical beachfront luxury property. History was huge in the public imagination.

When the annual Mermaid Parade came around in June, I had to attend and make the most of it. I brought my sword cane with the torch handle, a flask of fire breathing liquid, and money to have a good time. We had a big show that night at the Kimmel Center in Philly; however, the parade was in the afternoon. I went to Coney Island by bus and by train, all with my clown makeup on.

When I got there, I drank a lot of Coney Island Lager and watched the sideshow about six times in a row, as it was on a continuous repeat; a grind show. I loved the blade box, a long, wooden box on wheels that was pierced by solid metal blades. A performer would get locked inside, and twist around the blades as they fell through zigzagging slots and slits, until it seemed impossible for them to be inside without being in a tangled, mangled position. The audience was invited onstage to look down inside the box and learn its secret. For a minimum of one dollar, they could see "Madame Twisto" tangled around the blades, like a snake or an octopus would wrap around its dinner.

The sixth time I watched the blade box, I went up to see Heather Holliday wrapped around all of the blades and put a tip in Donny Vomit's tip bucket. Before putting a dollar in the collection bucket, I put in a broken mousetrap, a needle in a plastic cover, and a small rubber chicken. As soon as the show began again, a security guard came up with one of the managers to escort me out of the building. They were furious at the objects I had drunkenly placed in the tip bucket on their busiest day of the year. The angriest person was a performer named Remy Vicious who was working the ticket counter and had also worked the door at the New York tattoo convention. We exchanged heated words as I was being escorted out of the sideshow. "I'll remember this," I yelled, waving my cane sword at her. "You haven't seen the last of me!"

Just as I was being kicked out, the biggest art parade I had ever seen started coming down the street. Huge floats carried musicians and dancing sea goddesses with pink and green hair. Mermaids and marching bands rocked down the streets. I jumped uninvited into the parade, past the barricade. The mermaid captain kept kicking me out and I kept jumping back in at different sections. I breathed huge illegal fireballs, swallowed the cane sword, and did pushups in the middle of the street to the extreme approval of all the spectators. I was even on TV, interviewed by the History Channel!

After that, I went over to the Coney Island bally stage and was about to breathe my last big fireball when Donny Vomit came running over and made me spit out the fuel. I went home to Philly drunk, angry, and blacklisted from the Coney Island Sideshow. The shame of it was, I had a gig there the following week with Albert Cadabra. That night we did our show in Philly to a big audience, but I just couldn't stop thinking and complaining about being kicked out of Coney Island.

Banner line by Marie Roberts, Sideshows by the Seashore, Coney Island, 2011 (Norman Blake)

It took a lot for Albert to patch things up and make it so I could perform in his Burlesque at the Beach show. Dick Zigun, the unofficial mayor of Coney Island, agreed to let me perform out of respect for Albert. However, he wanted to give me a lecture when I showed up.

I showed up to Coney Island ready to face the music and show them my act, for better or worse. I wasn't allowed inside until Dick Zigun was ready to see me. I'd never met him before and was starting to sweat—the smelly kind of sweat that made me shake a bit in my hands. I knew what I had done at the Mermaid Parade was more than a little off color. I had already exchanged emails with Donny Vomit about it. I needed to accept responsibility and redeem myself with a big response from acts full of jokes and danger.

After they had me wait outside for a while, Dick Zigun sat me down at a table in the Freak Bar at Sideshows by the Seashore. He was an older intellectual carnival character with an amused smirk, tattooed sleeves, and a bowler hat. He attempted to hide his smile with a stern warning. "In the carnival, you are with it, for it, never against it, Jellyboy. You have entered a larger world of which you are not the center. That being said, welcome to Coney Island! Don't screw up!"

We shook hands and I told him he wouldn't be disappointed. I thanked him for giving me a chance and he showed me backstage. Albert grinned as Dick Zigun escorted me into the room. Albert Cadabra introduced me that night as the hideous, the horrible, the unpredictable Jellyboy the Clown. I emerged from backstage to the warmest welcome ever known to a clown dancing in a devil mask.

"I'm the clown with the upside-down frown turned upside-down, the Living Cartoon and a natural born weirdo. People usually clap when I say that, but no, it's okay: do you want to see something dangerous?"

They yelled a loud "YEAH!" into my ears, lighting up all eyes to my syringe of super serum and flamethrower sword. After missing the veins in my neck, through the skin in front of my Adam's apple, there were explosions when Albert threw firecrackers in the path of the flamethrower sword. I laid down on my belly and slithered like a snake, stood up and released the sword with a long, thick line of drool, which I ate after dangling it over my face. Somehow the chaos magic had flipped, from my being thrown out to being embraced in celebration.

Only inspiration followed as the summer went on, and we expanded our show with many innovations. For Carnivolution, we built a seesaw for Betty and me to ride in Matterz's bed of nails act. We balanced a red and black plank of wood across his torso, with a metal bar in the center that was attached to the base with handles on either side. Betty and I jumped up and down on either side of the board, squishing Matterz deeper into the spikes. "When the first person goes down, I want you to yell SEE. When the second person goes down, I want you to yell SAW." Betty went down and I jumped. "SEE!" I went down and Betty jumped. "SAW!" "SEE-SAW, SEE-SAW, SEE-SAW!" The audience repeated it over and over again, until we both stopped at the same time, landing our feet on the floor.

Jellyboy and Betty Bloomerz riding a seesaw on top of Matterz Squidling at Carnivolution, The Ellen Powell Tiberino Museum, Philadelphia, 2011 (Lunchbox)

We also made a red coffin with a plexiglass viewing window and completely buried Matterz in broken glass. He wore a gas mask and shorts while someone would walk on him, and then jump up and down. He emerged from under the live burial like a zombie from the grave, without so much as a scratch.

Enigma wanted Betty and me to join him for the Las Vegas tattoo convention. We flew in for an exciting sideshow getaway and were picked up at the airport by our local freaky comrades, the Swingshift Sideshow. Enigma asked me to write all the acts into his existing formula from the combined forces of Swingshift, the Squidlings, Electric Acid Theater, and the former inside talker of the Coney Island sideshow, Frank the Fire God! We all bought little laser pointer revolvers, prank pistols that sent out an electric shock when the trigger was pulled but released a laser when you put your thumb down on the hammer.

Andrew S. and Kelvikta the Blade from SwingShift had a sideshow house off the Vegas strip with other members of their troupe: Sleazo the Clown, and his partner in crime named Pirate. Andrew S. was the most impressive and daring sword swallower I had ever encountered, a creative powerhouse who took everything to the threshold. He could swallow a 28-inch sword to the hilt past his stomach, to somewhere around his hip bone, and with a little alignment adjustment of the pelvis, to the left. He did deep muscle piercings using long solid needles, shish kebabbing his bicep to Kelvikta the Blade's bicep. On the menu was heart relocation and balancing on the single point of a spear, with his arms and legs off the ground. With large hooks in his eye sockets attached to chains, Andrew S. could lift a person off the ground.

His most iconic stunt was an act called ScrewFace, where two metal coils attached to power drills were put up his nostrils and came out of his mouth, from the back of the throat, in a solid mental floss. Kelvikta was also a sword swallower who could queef darts through a blow gun using her Kegel muscles while on roller skates! Alive and deadly with wicked accuracy. Sleazo was a pain sponge who soaked it up on a gnarly bed of nails that had spikes that were far apart, for maximum suffering. He blockheaded a turkey-basting syringe full of Pirate's pee and spit it back into her mouth after shooting it through his nose! These freaks were on a different page, but at least they were all on the same one.

They had a nice backyard with a bondage swing set up for flesh suspensions. The last night after the convention was over, under a billion desert stars, Betty Bloomerz wanted to try a flesh hang. First, they tried piercing four hooks in her back, up by her shoulder blades. Sleazo, Pirate, Kelvikta, and I stabilized the legs of the swing. Andrew stood tall and thin, with an orange-red wizard beard swaying in the cool night breeze of the desert. Half of his hair was shaved, and the other half was long. His strong hands ran the rope and pulley system to hoist Betty off the ground with the graceful, healing intention of a modern mystic.

While in the air, Betty suddenly turned white as a ghost and her body went limp. Andrew let her down immediately. Kelvikta's motherly instincts kicked in. She threw back her shoulder-length fluorescent red hair and ran from her leg of the swing to stabilize the situation. Betty awoke while talking about being visited by her dead grandmother, crying in the embrace of Kelvikta's arms, all inked black with large, solid tattoos.

I didn't want to go up on hooks until I saw Betty Bloomerz crying. It broke my heart so I said, "Please pierce me with two big hooks in the back, and we will have some fun!" I breathed in deep before they pierced me, while sitting backwards in a chair. On an exhale, the hook went through my skin with a pinch and came out the other side with a pop. I felt lightheaded as the piercings heated up around the hooks, and I found my center with deep breaths while Andrew S. tugged softly. Betty took a minute to get in better spirits and watched closely.

When I went up under the stars, Sleazo was on the ropes. We were both in multi-day-old clown makeup. I imagined that the hooks were part of my body, not foreign objects. Up, up, and away I went. Enigma yelled, "How does it feel to fly, Jellyboy the Clown?" I wiggled my fingers and toes, dancing in the air, waiting for the ride. Andrew said, "Try moving your legs to swing yourself and spin." Freedom was mine, confined to the tug of hooks like a puppy in the mouth of the Misfit Mother, held by the scruff of my neck.

What I really wanted to do was attempt to swallow a sword in the air while suspended, so I asked them to hand me my cane sword. It was difficult to raise my arm enough to get the sword at the right angle to fit inside me, the way a key goes into a lock. Another challenge was aligning my body while I was dangling from ropes attached to hooks in my upper back. With a shift in my legs, I was able to straighten my body at an odd angle and slide the sword down. A feeling of transcendence overwhelmed me with light in pixelated particles. Looking up into the night, I saw the stars spinning while feeling I was part of the sky; the hooks and the sword, as well as my own molecules, all held together by mysterious plasma.

The ride was so much fun that Betty was inspired to give it another try. This time pierced in the lower back, she went up beautifully right away, and giggled flexibly in the air. The next day we flew home sore, but happy. On the airplane, "Rice Krispies" were in our backs from air bubbles that entered the hook wounds when our skin was stretched. We massaged each other and fell asleep a mile high in the sky.

Chapter 10
Coney Island Clown

Our pendulum swung so high on an upswing, it went over the top and around again. The Coney Island Rockabilly Festival was happening again on Labor Day weekend. As a reward for stepping forward to emcee the year before, I was allowed to hire all the sideshow performers and host the event with my face on the poster and the T-shirts. It said, *"Jellyboy and Weirdee Girl hosting the festival."* Weirdee Girl had started a burlesque troupe of New York all-star dancers called the Merkinettes with great names like Lil' Miss Lixx, Stormy Leather, and FemAppeal. We were billed for the Friday night Burlesque at the Beach event at Sideshows by the Seashore, after the fireworks display that happened every week during the season.

I still had to wait outside until Remy Vicious was finished working before I was allowed in to set up the show, but I was hopeful to get the chance to redeem myself. Matterz, Betty, Duke, and I had all our intense props waiting on the sidewalk. Quite a spectacle indeed with several beds of nails, six five-gallon buckets of broken glass, a coffin for Matterz Squidling's glass burial, an anvil, a sledgehammer, and a seesaw. We were also going to hang a trapeze for Betty Bloomerz's upside-down sword swallowing.

It turned out to be the most well attended Burlesque at the Beach of the season, with all the seats filled and many crammed into the wings, standing room only to see the show. The audience was loud, drunk, and ready to rock and roll. Weirdee Girl and I shared the microphone. She was a red-haired sprite with fine freckles on her skin and a devilish grin; tall and thin, she invited them in. The audience went berserk as we gave them more than they had bargained for.

Directly after the show, I booked it over to Cha Cha's bar just in time for the band to end. Matterz, Betty, and the Duke cleaned up the stage. My job was to keep the action going between bands. I had to think of something fast, so I called for an arm-wrestling match of carnivore versus vegetarian. The thrill-thirsty psychobilly greasers and postmodern pinup girls ate it up. The largest vegetarian I had ever seen was victorious. The next band was still setting up when the contest was over. I had no choice but to make a speech about the evolution of brain surgery from primitive times through Egypt and modern-day science, all as a windup for the human blockhead with Enigma's giant flooring spike.

I chugged a Coney Island Lager, which got people chanting while I pretended to knock the nail into my forehead. "So, you are just gonna let me do this?" I asked, echoing the Enigma, and lined up the nail against my nostril. The glass on metal sound rang out loud across the room.

When the nail was all the way in, I said, "Okay, who wants to make out with me?" Scanning the room for a willing volunteer, "Women, men, anyone?"

Out of the blue, Betty Bloomerz emerged, running up to the stage. She jumped on me and stuck her tongue in my mouth. Clown makeup collided and the crowd erupted with screams of laughter. When the screams died down, Betty bit the end of the nail and slowly pulled it out and in, in and out of my nose. When it was out, she held it between her teeth. I bit the sharp snotty end, took it from her mouth to mine and licked it clean

"That tastes funny," I said.

"Like a clown?" Betty replied.

The band was ready to go, and the people were ready to dance in the swinging jitterbug psychobilly mosh pit of sweat. Betty and I joined them and danced, danced, danced until our legs hurt, out of breath and smiling. I was kicked in the head by a crowd surfer. Pain, problems, and the world disintegrated, as we were drunk in a wise guy bar at the end of the boardwalk in Coney Island.

That night, J.T., the manager of the bar, was in a great mood. The owner Cha Cha wasn't there, and that was part of it. When it was time to kick everyone out, he let Ben, the event producer and all of us sideshow folk stick around with the bar staff. They brought in the oyster bar from the boardwalk and closed the metal sliding gate. J.T. gave us all tequila and took us up to the roof through a scary side staircase.

Boardwalk, Coney Island, 2012 (Lunchbox)

MEMOIRS OF A CONEY ISLAND CLOWN

J.T., manager of Cha Cha's Club Atlantis, Coney Island, 2011 (Lunchbox)

On the roof, we smoked a joint and looked at the ocean over the Coney Island skyline. That night they let us sleep on the floor of the bar, giving Betty and me a sheet and a fan to help keep the mosquitoes away. The Coney Island mosquitoes are huge, mutant monsters that could suck the blood of drunken thrill-seekers and stagger away on intoxicated wings. I became an expert at hunting and killing them as they pressed their stinging lips to my veins.

It was nice to wake up as the amusement park was opening, and watch the boardwalk come to life on Labor Day weekend. The Squidling Brothers didn't have to perform until that night, so Betty and I had all day to enjoy Coney Island: ride the rides, kiss on the Wonder Wheel, and watch the sideshow grind the afternoon away.

When night fell, our job was to keep the show flowing in between bands with our acts. Our props were kept in a crow's nest to the side of the stage. Behind the stage was the office and burlesque changing room. Hearing of the previous night's success, the owner of the bar showed up and sat in the office to flirt with the burlesque girls while they changed.

Cha Cha was fat and funny; not like a clown, but like a real wise guy. He had a spot in Little Italy as well and had been in a lot of gangster movies. He was not a guy to be messed with, but armored in my clown makeup I was able to cross lines and make everyone feel comfortable. My bag of magic beans was being a stage gargoyle, watcher at the door, psychiatrist, and keeper of the peace.

Saturday was even more packed than Friday had been. Tension was high behind the scenes because of all the money being made. J.T. had produced the event with Ben as a partner, and Cha Cha was keeping a close eye.

While Sasquatch and the Sick-A-Billys were tearing up the room with whirlwinds of dust-devil sound, I got a tap on the shoulder and a whisper in my ear. J.T and Cha Cha wanted to see me in the office. I wondered if I had done something wrong. At the height of the show, I sat in a big leather chair, face to face with Cha Cha behind his desk, and J.T. sitting on the couch on the side of the room. They were both in a strangely good mood, and seemed to be getting along amazingly, as if they had been conspiring on a grand scheme they wanted to bring me in on. I thought they were about to make me an offer I couldn't refuse.

Cha Cha spoke first, matter of factly. "Jellyboy, do you think we could make this happen every weekend next season?" J.T. smiled a madman John Dillinger grin. "How much money do you think it would cost to do this once a week?" I was shocked and stared back at them in silence for a long moment.

Cha Cha broke the silence. "Every Friday night after the fireworks, we could have a circus sideshow with the burlesque girls. I don't care about the bands."

I looked back and forth between the two of them and said, "It could be done. The only thing is…Sideshows by the Seashore has Burlesque at the Beach after the fireworks on Fridays. Nothing at all is happening in Coney Island on Saturday night. If you can guarantee me a thousand dollars, I can get you the best performers in New York City: we can have sideshow, burlesque, and aerial. It could work."

J.T. looked at Cha Cha and said, "Next summer I see big things for Coney Island…big things. I feel it!"

Cha Cha seemed to think what I had offered was reasonable. We had a deal!

Then they invited Ben in. We counted the money together and cut up jackpots. Ben gave me what he said he would, plus a bonus for the success of the weekend. It was a long time before I walked out of the office with the money to pay Matterz, Betty, and the Duke. The Sick-A-Billys had finished, and everyone was cleaning the stage. It was the end of the festival.

Most people who were left in the bar were either staggering drunks who didn't want to go home, or performers gathering their gear and selling last-minute souvenirs to people who had had too much fun.

Matterz said, "We were worried about you, brother; what went on in there?" He was standing with the Duke, both curious to hear what I had to say.

"Well, we got paid more than we thought we would, for one, and they want us to do a weekly show next summer." They both smiled with relief.

"Where is Betty Bloomerz?" Matterz pointed to her, talking and laughing with two drunk guys who appeared to be her new best friends. I walked over to them to say hello and to tell Betty we were about to start packing up.

"Jellyboy!" she yelled and threw her arms around me. "These are my new friends from Holland, Pim and Richard; we met on the roof." The two Dutch men smiled sheepishly as if they had consumed too much of a love potion. They shook my hand and kissed me three times each on both cheeks.

"We want to help you," said Pim.

"Okay," I said, "We are going to start carrying all of our props to our car." Staggering, Pim picked up our anvil. "Careful, watch your toes," I said. Giggling like children, we walked in a line that was more like a zigzag down the boardwalk to the parking lot.

When Betty met Pim and Richard on the roof, they hadn't realized at first that she was in the show, but when they did, Pim showed her a funny act, sticking his tongue through a newspaper, making it come out of the lips of the picture on the front page. As it turned out, Pim and Richard held festivals in Amsterdam. They had flown to Coney Island on a whim after a crazy party, forgetting about a large amount of ecstasy in their luggage and accidentally smuggling it into the USA. When they realized what they had done, they ate all of it and rolled through the Coney Island Rockabilly Festival, only to be hypnotized by the beauty and humor of Miss Betty Bloomerz. They wanted to hire us for a party at their club for New Year's in Amsterdam.

Pim and Richard didn't want to leave us, but we had to get back to Philadelphia. Betty had to teach yoga in the morning and return the station wagon to her father. Somehow, as wasted as they were, I believed we would see each other again. We exchanged emails, pointed them in the direction of a hotel, waved goodbye, and watched them stagger off into the Coney Island night.

In November, we got an email from Pim saying he wanted to fly us to Amsterdam for their New Year's show. I immediately contacted Roc Roc-It from the Disgraceland Family Freakshow. He had moved back to Germany and suggested that we stay in Europe for a little while to make a tour out of it. We rushed to get our passports processed. Meanwhile, Betty had made friends with the leader of the Wanderlust Circus in Portland, Oregon.

We decided to plan a grand adventure. We'd fly out to Portland, take a train to San Francisco to make shows with friends, and be home in time for Christmas. After that, we would fly to Amsterdam and travel with Roc Roc-It for six weeks in Europe. Roc said he could sort out shows and places to stay all over.

A lot had to be done in a short amount of time. Betty and I decided that she should move in with me to consolidate our rent. We researched size and weight allowances for flying with luggage. How could we put all our props on an airplane and carry them all over without a car?

Our first thought was, "How do we make the bed of nails weigh less? Then it came to me: aluminum! We ordered eight hundred eight-inch gutter spikes. They were menacing, hardly weighed anything, and didn't rust. Our friend Lance had a machine that laid out a grid with lasers and pre-drilled all the holes on the board perfectly. Everything else could fit in a duffle bag. We asked people to start collecting glass bottles for us to break in the faraway places we were going. Betty left a couple of weeks ahead of time to make money for the trip, working as a dancer in a club she knew in Arizona. Matterz and I would meet her in Portland.

The night before we got on the plane, we were still building the bed of nails in our living room. The Duke hammered the spikes into the holes of the board. They fit nice and snug. Loudly hammering eight hundred nails in the middle of the night woke up a few of our neighbors, but we made it happen. There was a wooden protective case made for the nail bed that we screwed together. Matterz and I *just* made the weight limit for what two people could take aboard a plane: it was science!

We got to the airport with a bed of aluminum gutter spikes in a wooden box on wheels, alongside swords and machetes wrapped neatly in a blanket, placed in a duffle bag full of important props. We flew from New York to Portland, to stay and perform with the Wanderlust Circus ringmaster William Batty, the center of the hub of the underground circus, the welcomer of wanderers with a voice that could fill a room without a microphone.

We took a train ride to San Francisco down the beautiful coast of southern Oregon and northern California. The double-decker sleeping train rocked along rolling waves, on a voyage to nowhere on the edge of the world. Huge, ancient mountains shaped by earthquakes stretched out in shockwaves. Carved out of these rolling mountains was a treeless stretch of hills filled with black cows, packed in so tightly they could hardly move. The stink overwhelmed the train. We called it "Cowschwitz" because it looked like a giant bovine concentration camp. After that, the beauty of the Redwood Forest appeared with trees as tall as towers, leading the way into the vineyards of wine country.

After a nap, we awoke in the San Francisco Bay. An old friend that we used to live with at 4811 Chester Avenue met us at the station. Back at his house, the dogs from the old Hydrogen headquarters jumped up and licked our faces. He was living in a house with a woodshop. In preparation for Europe, he and a friend helped us improve the bed of nails travel box with a design from my sketchbook. It was a combination machete ladder, sword cabinet, and bed of nails on wheels, all connected with hitch pins and hinges. It fit in a taxi and met the weight restriction of airlines. It was now easy to wheel around all of our swords, machetes, the trapeze, and a sledgehammer for smashing cinder blocks. We had set up some shows in Oakland and San Francisco to try out our new multifunction prop. We rolled a big, fat, funny cigarette and smoked it to celebrate!

Isotope was a true cartoon of a human being who owned a comic book shop in San Francisco. He had seen us perform at the Palace of Wonders in Washington, D.C. and invited us to SantaCon with him. He bought Matterz, Betty, our old friend, and me Santa Claus costumes, plus all the alcohol we could drink for a fifteen-hour bar crawl through San Francisco. We went from bar to bar with over a thousand Santas, perverted elves, gingerbread generals, and sexy reindeer getting sillier as we marched. The alcohol made us invincible as we engaged in a snowball fight using artificial snow dumped into a park just for this demented holiday occasion. Snowballs went down the back and in the face under a bright, sunny California afternoon.

We kept pace with the SantaCon horde until nighttime. Betty Bloomerz's feet were worn out, so we drunkenly wheeled her in a shopping cart to a sushi joint and feasted. Being loud and ferocious, white-bearded beasts of holiday cheer, we were seated outside so as not to annoy the customers on the inside. Isotope removed his Santa hat and pulled the fake beard down around his neck, revealing a well-kept beard of his own underneath.

He threw back a shot of sake, looked around the table and said, "I do believe I have drank myself sober."

At that moment I realized he was right. We had been drinking since the afternoon and it was now late at night. Somehow, consistently drinking throughout the day had heightened our tolerance. Drunken cackles radiated from our table in various pitches. No one who looked at us could keep a straight face. Jolly old elves who laughed in spite of themselves.

My old friend from the Hydrogen house rubbed his belly and leaned back in his chair, letting out a guttural moan of delight. "I'm going to feel wonderful in my unitard at trapeze class tomorrow." He belched, wiggled, and slapped himself in the face. The circus spark had led him to start dating his trapeze teacher, who was whipping him into shape, outside the comfort zone of the good things in life that he enjoyed so well. There was a thrill to the trapeze that made the pain of learning it more acceptable than other kinds of pain. We all had a final toast of sake: "To SantaCon!"

Back on the east coast, there was a Christmas show in Brooklyn at the new House of Yes!!! The speakeasy underground circus setting now had thirty-foot ceilings for aerial acrobatics, and three different floors. The second floor was called "Make Fun" and was dedicated to costumes, their brightly colored collections hung on the walls next to worktables and sewing machines. The third floor was living space and offices. After losing everything in the fire, the House of Yes had reformed into a fortress.

Anya the aerial daredevil painted herself gold and jumped out of the second story doorway leading to the sky box, and the House of Yes sky box was born! The silk fabrics grazed the audience below as she swung into place over the stage, whipping around like a spider on a webbed thread over Matterz' bed of nails. There was live music as well as circus stunts. We brought the Carnivolution and our giant perverted puppet, the great Grandma Madoodi, the green-skinned goddess with four arms, four breasts, and infinite nipples. The Hydrogen Jukebox brought the strange sounds to turn the sit-down performance into a raucous dance party.

The realm of possibilities accepted us with the open arms of the Misfit Mother. Our passports were in order, and everything seemed perfect. However, nothing is ever truly perfect. Lack of perfection is sometimes responsible for making something memorable.

We got all our bags and the bed of nails screwed into its protective box to the JFK airport in New York, en route to London. In London, we transferred our luggage to the plane for Amsterdam. However, our luggage was mistimed, and we missed the flight. Tremors of fear scrambled through our minds: *Are we going to miss the New Year's show?*

I guarded the baggage, holding a cup of coffee. I was thinking about geography, having just looked out the window while flying over the Atlantic Ocean for the first time. Where we came from was where we were going, even though we had never been there before. Betty Bloomerz ran off to an internet cafe, trying to contact Pim in Amsterdam. Matterz and his girlfriend Sharleen were enquiring about alternate ways to get there. After being hit with waves of paranoia and frustration, we got standby tickets not too far off from our original flight.

Landing in Amsterdam was wonderful. English had not completely vanished from the signage, but Dutch was all around us. Finally, we were somewhere so unfamiliar that even using the phone was a challenge. International codes and voices we could not comprehend held us captive in the frosty, numbing air for well over an hour before Pim showed up.

We took a taxi to the venue, Pacific Parc, which was an old factory converted into a restaurant and nightclub. After dropping off our gear, we enjoyed some fine dinner at the attached restaurant. The kitchen was in plain view with aromas that jumped up our nostrils into our watering mouths. Pim made sure we had plenty of beer, ravioli, and crispy potatoes.

The warehouse behind the restaurant was going through the final stages of preparation for the New Year's trailer trash carnival bash. While wondering what happened to Roc Roc-It, Pim's cell phone began to vibrate. Pim threw us in the back of a truck with a bunch of bedding and drove to the airport again. Roc was traveling with four people and Larz Vagas, who had been traveling with Roc when we met in New York at the Disgraceland Fun House. Everyone jumped in the back of the truck, and we made excited introductions.

Pim had a two-story, two-room house that he let us take over for a week while he stayed in an apartment closer to the center of town. We left our collective brain stuck to Pim's ceiling long after we were gone.

We got right to work at Pacific Parc, smashing bottles for Matterz's glass routine and setting up the stage. We were to breathe fire from the cars of an indoor Ferris wheel to get the party started. In the meantime, I swallowed a sword on the nightly news, inviting the city of Amsterdam to join us at the Trailer Trash Carnival New Year's Bash. We received a warm welcome from a place we had never been.

When our preparation was done, we walked down the road past the tents of Circus Zanzibar, who lent us a sledgehammer to hit an empty beer keg on top of Matterz as he lay on a bed of nails. There was outdoor skating with hot wine to drink. The spell was binding. The snow had frozen as we planned our first of many shows. It was the calm before the storm. An empty warehouse, full of disco lights and a cardboard carnival midway; a trailer trash Luna Park of the mind, about to be overflowing with faces. Everyone was getting in makeup, dressed up for the big change. One year gone, slipped away with no point in grasping. Too many memories to catch onto with a golden glow in sight, deeper into the time-tunnel dark ride.

Betty Bloomerz looked out of this world. Her clown makeup made her ice-blue eyes reflect the cool fire of the lights. White face, red nose and lips with her black hair up, she was wearing little under a sheer black evening gown that I had bought her for Christmas. We walked onto the dance floor before people started streaming through the doors.

Clown face to clown face, I said in the tone of a serious joke, "Will you marry me?" We both laughed.

Betty said, "No, but if this is a dream, I don't ever want to wake up."

We held on tight, swayed, then let go and danced, swinging and jumping into a full body rhythm, eye to eye with a spin and a dip.

It was time to get on with the show. We climbed aboard the Ferris wheel in our separate cars with torches and flasks of fuel for fire breathing. Carnival music filled the room, joining with the loud, electronic beats from the dance floor on the other side of the warehouse. The Ferris wheel was the centerpiece of the midway, between the games and happenings set to the back of the stage. We went around the wheel a few times, letting out synchronized fireballs. An orange glow flashed and summoned the party goers closer with the gleam reflecting off their eyes. When the people got assembled, we came off the Ferris wheel one at a time to start the show in the face of 2009.

Roc Roc-It and Betty Bloomerz became a hypnotic human banner line making us seem larger from far away than we seemed up close. Matterz played the keyboard and manned the soundscape as I approached the microphone. Shouting over the disco noise from the dance floor in the back of the warehouse, I wove the spell in English. The calliope music crept around and fused with the heavy bass distorting the cardboard midway. Spectators strained their Dutch ears to understand through the noise and their New Year intoxication. I was translating the feeling of a Coney Island stunt show, American slapstick comedy, in the dimension beyond the language barrier where all are inappropriate children, heckling the lecturer in disbelief.

A woman was pulled up to the stage to verify the authenticity of the first swallowed sword.

"Is it real?" I asked.

After close inspection she said, "Echt, de werkelijke!" Words full of whistles, phlegm, and heartfelt humor erupted like fascination suspended in disbelief. The mysticism of the tentacled jester was embraced by the growing crowd, who encroached closer and closer in mind and body.

I felt harsh and funny in Amsterdam's tribute to Luna Park, with a miniature Wonder Wheel behind us. People were lined up to watch the show from the air for a couple of go-arounds on the wheel. Being on stage with Matterz, Bloomerz, and Roc-It was a waking, walking daydream come true; touched by all kinds of spirits channeled from the whirlwind that carried us across the ocean. Betty Bloomerz turned on like a plasma globe when she moved. Her eyes danced us into the hearts of enthusiastic observers. The alchemy of our experiment bubbled in the invisible beaker. Lead was made into gold!

We stayed a few nights after the show in Pim's little house, which was walking distance from the ferry that took us across the water to the city center and the red-light district. Following a night of drinking, everybody went to bed but me and Roc-It. He declared we could not sleep until we had consumed everything in the house. The last of the alcohol was a bit of brandy from a glass jug with a crystal top. There were too many things to talk about, to catch up on, to reminisce, and one big secret. When we were on the last glass of brandy, I revealed what had not been mentioned: the real reason we came all the way to Europe to join forces.

"I've got to show you something, Roc-It," I said. A sleight-of-hand gesture revealed a glass jar, the same size as the one we were drinking brandy from. An incubator for the monster. I removed a red cloth draped over the jar and told him of the Misfit Mother of Death and the bridge between worlds. Roc's eyes fully focused when he saw the creature.

"It's...a Squicken," he said, "A real live Squicken!" There was immediate affection between Roc and the monster-birth. It had grown a bit from the performance the night before. When it saw Roc, the little Squicken's eyes grew more human. Two of its tentacles grew the toes of a chicken. A beak sprouted from its face. Its pupils sharpened from human eyes to the shape of a cat's. Only we would be able to see this miniature mutant kraken chicken, but everyone who saw our show could feel it. The child lived and was nourished by the roar of the crowd. In that moment, the Misfit Mother of Death stood just far enough away to keep us warm without setting us on fire, illuminating unseen emotions. The following morning, I woke up with chills and a high fever that took a day to sweat out before a long, drunken train ride to Berlin.

Roc, Larz, Betty, Sharleen, Matterz, and I stood on the Amsterdam train platform, watching our icy breath and dancing to keep warm. Ahead lay a maze of train transfers that Roc had mapped out to save us money. Larz had a lightweight, futuristic pocket speaker, some rum and chocolate milk. We ate the rest of the hash we bought in Amsterdam, swallowing it like pills, and piled onto the first train, the aftermath of the New Year's party that refused to end.

Larz cranked his little speaker to the extreme annoyance of many on the train. He smiled, passed around the rum and chocolate milk, and enjoyed the tension our presence was causing as only a punk who grew up in East Germany in the '80s could do. Larz was covered in spikes in more ways than one, with a sly, wise look in his crow's feet-framed eyes. He felt it was his duty to make a bit of a performance out of civil disobedience.

As we drank, we became louder until a few of the passengers spoke up. Some college students were the first to ask him to turn the music off.

Larz responded with an aggressively comedic statement: "I wish your parents had given you souls," he said, loud enough for all to hear. "In the '80s, we carried our music around and no one cared. Now everyone must be quiet. Fucking fascist, fucking Europe!" he yelled.

The college students told him to fuck off and returned to their seats, grumbling. Next, a businesswoman approached Larz and screamed at him, demanding that he shut his music off. He offered her some chocolate milk and they shouted at each other in English on the Dutch train.

Roc poked Larz saying, "Hey man, you're going to get us kicked off the train or arrested."

Larz looked at him and said, "I see your performance all the time. This is my performance. I know what I do. I walk the line. I'm straight, people. This is my country." Technically it wasn't his country because we hadn't reached Germany yet, but Larz believed we had.

The train conductor approached to politely ask Larz to lower the volume. He lowered it and said, "I'm good, I'm straight, people, no worries." When the conductor left, Larz turned the music back up again.

The businesswoman jumped out of her seat and started screaming, "You are really fucking me off!" Larz only laughed with a sarcastic grin. "You are an asshole!" she yelled. She snatched his speaker and ran back to her seat, followed by Larz who tried to convince her to give it back. The conductor reappeared and kicked us off the train, where we were met by the police who checked our passports and put us on another train bound for Germany.

Larz passed out drunk in the middle of the floor of the train as soon as we got to Germany. People were laughing, stepping over him as they were coming on and off the train. He woke up out of the blue, not knowing where he was, and stumbled off smiling to the next train car. Roc-It giggled and said, "I think I should follow him and give him his ticket."

We finally ended up in Berlin at the Ostbahnhof station in Kreuzberg, which was covered in snow. The big river that ran through the city was littered with chunks of floating ice. The neighborhood was half broken, with graffiti on the buildings from a bygone era. New buildings were springing up in between. Cars zoomed fast on the slippery streets. People walked with bottles of beer in their hands. As soon as we got off the train, Roc bought everyone a round of Sternburg Export beer, 80 cents a bottle. We all felt a bit rich having been paid quite well for the New Year's show, but we were going to be in Europe for five more weeks and had nothing else booked.

Roc and Larz had ideas for shows we could set up quickly. We got right to work, carrying all our gear through the snow to the Køpi, a punk rock squat stronghold, an old hotel that had been bombed in World War II on the border between East and West Germany. Graffiti and huge sculptures decorated the tall building, surrounded by a trailer park and a huge, spiked fence. We were home.

We walked up five flights of stairs to Roc and Larz's apartment. The first thing we did was light a fire in the oven, heat up some wine, cook some pasta, and pack a chillum with hash and tobacco. As we passed the chillum, I became lightheaded and faded off into the music and conversation. There was much to be done. Riding high on the inspiration of New Year's and the new Squidling Brothers Circus Sideshow, we hit the streets and talked the talk to wild bar owners and landed several gigs. When time was of the essence and it was cold outside, we huddled around the burning oven after splitting wood and buying coal. A balanced intoxication formed us a solid plan from fire and ice.

Chapter 11
Other Side of the Pond

Roc and Larz's kitchen became our office and the meeting place for many interesting minds. Posters and flyers were created around the warmth of the wood burning stove by Roc's artistic friends. Sev, from Holland, who made freak bikes and did graphic design, helped us with an image for one show. Pete Missing, an expatriate rabble-rouser from the States, sat and weaved tales of the '80s, rolled joints and laughed about the state of the planet's war of the minds. He was an industrial musician, an artist full of layers of graffiti color. Niccoli and his girlfriend from Italy were filmmakers and amazing cooks. They gave us pasta, weed, and lines of super speed unlike anything I had ever tried. Roc's girlfriend Vesna drew a picture of the Squicken that we turned into a silkscreen t-shirt design and a poster for one of the shows.

A guy named Thomas ran a street festival in the spring. He and his girlfriend had access to a warehouse called the RAW Tempel that we could use to put on a show, if we were willing to put in some sweat and transform it into a circus over the course of a few days. The Køpi, where we were staying, also had a bar in the basement. Behind the bar was an old, burnt-up theater where many legendary shows had happened. There was also a bar full of mechanical monsters in the center of Berlin by Alexanderplatz, called Eschloraque, or "the dead chicken bar." To top off our list of venues, there was a heavy metal pub down the road called Trinkteufel, which means "drink devil" or "drink with the devil." We had our hands full making four shows over a week and a half.

The snow was heavy in the city that winter, but no one seemed to mind. People were alive on the street at night, and so were we. Betty, Matterz, Roc, and I walked along the remaining ruins of the Berlin Wall one night, hanging posters with a wheat paste mixture to put the circus up like wallpaper into the minds of passersby.

Everywhere we went we had beer, with Jägermeister, and miniature bottles of Boonekamp liqueur. In Germany, it was legal to drink on the street and on the train, so we exercised our freedom and took full advantage of our rights. I felt freer in Germany than I did in the United States of America.

So full of beer and booze, we followed Roc's example and emptied our bladders wherever we could find a little nook, turning the snow a steaming yellow. One night, Betty and I left an internet cafe giggling and full of beer. I was telling people my name was Shizah Minnelli. Betty and I urinated together by a chain-link fence lined with trees. We looked in each other's eyes and let it flow onto the snow. Between her legs we made a cross stream, laughed, and held hands, feeling the warmth of our alcohol-infused urine rise up from the frost. It was the closest to love I had ever felt. A clown romance far away from home.

Home by the wood burning stove in the old stronghold of the punks, work was pleasure, a game that we were winning with beginner's luck on our side. The task of rearranging the RAW Tempel space wasn't easy. We had plenty of help, but we needed to clear a year's worth of stage props from countless shows. We hung a parachute on the ceiling and lined the room with wooden cutouts of clowns and imaginary animals. The stage was made of wooden pallets.

When it came time to launch, we had a nice, small crowd of around fifty people at the RAW Tempel. The German audience was a bit more difficult to break the ice with. Once we took down the wall of silence, it was highly emotional, full of chills and laughter. The show was like hot chocolate with rum, and floating eyeballs in the shadows of a spotlight.

Even though Roc could speak German, he said sideshow jokes only worked in English. In the opening speech to warm up the audience he asked, "How many people understand English, raise your hands. How many do not understand English, hands up." Then Roc said to the people that did not speak English, "If you do not understand what I am saying, just laugh when everybody else laughs, okay?" Somehow this joke always cleared the air wherever we performed. People really did laugh whether they understood or not. The stunts, the dancing, and the rhythm of the words was all that we needed.

The weekend came and, by that time, word of our RAW Tempel show had spread. All the Køpi knew we would be performing in the old theater behind the basement bar. More than a hundred enthusiastic punks packed into the stone bleachers, ready to see the sideshow. Free dinner was served to everyone at the bar. The price of admission was a roll of dice and the chance to staple money to me at the end. We didn't expect much from the audience, but they stapled large euro notes to strange parts of my body and put way more money into the hat than any of us thought possible.

The next night we loaded all our equipment onto cargo bikes. Some pedaled and others took the subway to get to the Dead Chicken Bar, which was full of mechanical monsters. The Squicken felt at home with these other creatures. The bar was set up as a lounge with dark red lights illuminating the moving metal monster sculptures. Some looked like metallic sea creatures, some like human-bird hybrids. Others were in jars of liquid with bubbles flowing through them. There was a nice stage in the back with an office next to it that we used as a dressing room to prepare as the room filled with people. There was hardly any room once the show got started. People were huddled around on couches, on bar stools, and sitting on the floor all the way from the edge of the stage to the front of the room where the drinks were served.

We had our own stash of beer, Jägermeister, and weed in the little office. After everyone was good and ready to start, Roc took a piss and smoked a cigarette, as was his custom before any show. He opened with his fire-eating rubber chicken and introduced my burlesque act as "the hottest act we could find." I came out wearing a polka dot dress, Betty Bloomerz's fishnets and panties, and a devil mask with a red polka dot bonnet. There was a white balloon in my underwear inflated in the shape of a giant sperm made to swim. At the end of the striptease, I snorted the tail of the balloon up my nose, coughed it out and stretched it around like a demonic, boyish femme fatale.

The show was snappy like popcorn over a fire, with movements to match the art of the monsters who called the Dead Chicken Bar their home. These monsters meant no harm to any creatures including ourselves. What we were doing was coming from a place of love, to love a monster. Being a clown is not so much about being funny; it's about telling the truth, though it's much easier to forgive funny people. Some truth is in the mirror, and some is in the wine. The divine spark inside the mortal shell.

A page in my sketchbook read, *"Betty Bloomerz, misty maiden of the German train. Soon we curl up in a squat, wrap around and sleep in the country of our old people. We will travel a long time through the thrill of wanderlust. I'll kiss your eye tonight in the snow."*

The snow fell in slow motion, and time in rapid fire, darting to the next day, the next show. The heavy metal dive bar Trinkteufel let us take over the kicker table room to use as a backstage and set up a table in the doorway as a platform for us "living marionettes" with invisible strings. What strings we had that night were being pulled by the drink devil, raising glasses to our lips into the first hours of the morning.

The idea was to stay up all night and catch our flight to England. After a raucous, intimate show and a wild afterparty when the bar closed down, we drunkenly packed our gear. Swords and machetes wrapped in a blanket in a rolling duffel bag, the bed of nails screwed into its protective wooden box. Just before washing my makeup off, I rested my eyes for what seemed like a moment. Waking up was quick and startled, everybody running around like headless chickens. "Everyone fell asleep! We're going to miss the plane!" We all reacted fast, still as drunk as we were when we closed our eyes. We muscled all our gear onto the train across the river a few blocks away. We ran through the doors without buying tickets, just in time. The ticket collector checked us, and then gave us a fine for not getting passes before boarding.

I staggered into the airport with clown makeup half on and half off my face. We dropped our bags off and ran to get through the line to the X-ray machine. Passport missing, I frantically emptied my pockets and backpack. Finally, I saw it in the suitcase with the rubber chickens. The buzzer went off when the luggage went through the conveyor belt. I was called aside by a luggage inspector. We tried not to laugh as I said, "Yes, those are rubber chickens." She reached inside the suitcase and pulled out a meat cleaver.

"How did this get in here?" she said with a German accent.

"I must have forgotten I put it in there," I said, thinking she was going to call the police. Instead, she made a motion with her fingers, like shaving meat off the bone, as if she was saying, "No, no, no; bad little boy." She put the cleaver in a plastic bag for confiscated items, and let me pass, laughing at the melted-face drunken clown with a suitcase full of rubber chickens.

When I got to the other side, the guard looked up and said something like, "*Habbin shlabbin?*" which in my half-asleep drunk mind meant "Have you slept?" in German. I just smiled, and he managed to smile back. We made it to the plane just as it was boarding. I don't remember taking off; I sat down, buckled the seatbelt, and I was gone. I woke up just as we landed in London.

Crusted with sleep and leftover particles from Berlin, we staggered off the plane to retrieve our luggage. We put the red box back together, packed it with a sledgehammer, a homemade trapeze, and all of our blades, wheeling it onto the airport train. The cobblestone streets caused our box to rattle and vibrate like a little train.

We made our way to Crouch End in North London to a squat that Roc had lived in called the Krankenhaus. The place used to be an old age home in the urban suburb. The residents were a mixture of Italian and English squatters. They got enough recently expired food from the dumpster of a nearby supermarket to sustain a house of about fifteen people. In America, we called it dumpster diving, but in England it was called skipping. They were not eating garbage: they were eating well, off of the waste of perfectly good food, and cooked so nicely.

We walked in off the street, dirty from the nights before in Berlin, our props dragged in bags and boxes. We took our bags up into the rafter bedroom that had recently been constructed for guests and traveling bands. It was covered all over in graffiti written in markers, and was just tall enough to sit down in. The idea was to set up a few shows with some street performing in between. Our red box was parked next to a wild collection of bicycles that led up to a few levels of hallways lined with rooms. There was a kitchen on each floor and a common area at the top of the stairs, brightly painted with graffiti art and full of windows where the people who lived there gathered to smoke, drink, and watch TV.

For the most part, the squatters were employed in various jobs like cooks, baristas, bike messengers, drug dealers, and street performers. The real passion that united everyone was squatting, skipping for food, and living for free to fight against the system in their own way. They were always looking for abandoned buildings to break into and set up housing projects for other punks. Why waste perfectly good living spaces? They had a bit of a deal with the owner of the former old age home, trying to legally turn it into a community art space. There was a great united social scene among the people of the house and the other squats around London. Party planners plotted a big event for which the Squidling Brothers Circus Sideshow would be the entertainment!

The house came to life with hundreds of people beyond capacity. At a certain point, they had to start turning people away since the house was far too crowded for people to comfortably move about. In one of the rooms, a large television played our *Unholy Sideshow* movie on repeat all night long. We had a little dressing room set up behind a makeshift stage in the practice room. This was for the different bands that rehearsed in the house.

We were all set to go in our costumes when a rock from outside shattered a window in our dressing room. Outside, armed with knives and chains, there were around ten hooligans who had been turned away, attempting to break into the party. Immediately, a legion of Krankenhaus residents assembled to fight them off. A lot of shouting and skirmishing started to break out. In my clown face, under a dress in fishnet stockings, I held a sledgehammer, just in case I would be needed for the fight. Matterz and Roc were nearby holding machetes. Not too much time went by before other people in the house gathered. They outnumbered the hooligans and drove them off.

Shortly after that, it was show time. Some audience members began to heckle us and try to get attention for themselves. Roc-It and I returned the heckling with shots of our own, turning the rest of the audience against the hecklers. Roc even invited one giant intoxicated joker onstage so he could do his crude performance of interpretive dance until the audience booed him off.

Roc said, "Hey, if you want to be funny, get *yourself* a show."

At that point the audience was completely ours, and we launched into a roller coaster show, the crowd rolling on the floor with laughter. They shouted loudly together, united by the spirit of wonder like sparks from a lightning generator.

Leaving England, we took a ferry from the White Cliffs of Dover across the water to Belgium. The cliffs were flat white rocks, rising high out of the sea with gun slots and doors cut into the rock for defense at a time before our birth, when England was under threat of attack from mainland Europe. We went straight away to the duty-free shop on the giant boat and bought a tax-free bottle of whiskey, drinking it above deck in the frosty sea air while Roc rolled spliff after spliff. It was amazing to see land vanish and be surrounded by water, then to see land emerge again in the distance. When the ship docked, we took our gear and loaded onto a bus from Belgium, through France, and into Holland.

In a frozen and slippery Amsterdam, it was difficult to muscle our gear through the snow to meet our friends from the Carnival of Hellucinations. Roc made sure we stayed drunk enough not to be bothered by the cold, and while staggering through the ice, I fell and smashed the handle of our beloved red box. Matterz also slipped on the way up the ramp of the Dochouse, the venue where we would be performing and sleeping. He smashed the side of his head on the corner of the box and was knocked unconscious. An Australian clown with a mop of curly hair named Ewan came to the rescue. A bag of ice on his head, Matterz revived with a drunken cackle, quickly moving inside to the cozy warmth for a smoke and a cup of tea.

Ewan's building had a guest room below the bar. After a night's sleep, we got straight to work on a show. Ewan called it "Circus My Ass." He was a brilliant clown with a long nose and a massive collection of costumes and props to tell his high-paced stories of madness. His girlfriend Erin was a beautiful expatriate from New Jersey, much younger than him but a perfect match. She played multiple characters in his surreal dancing-clown plays, and illustrated wild circus banners that framed his rapid-fire action. For one of his gags, Ewan, also known as Smelly the Clown, poured lighter fluid in his shoe, lit it on fire, and extinguished the flame by shoving his foot in the shoe. He hopped around with smoke shooting out of his feet.

A nice backstage was created for us behind circus banners. The trapeze was hung over the balcony of the upstairs bar and restaurant. Erin made the most delicious food. Her cakes were like heaven and came with the price of admission to the show. There was a little smoking room made of plastic with an air vent by the window.

The show happened in the basement where we slept. It was a huge relief and different from the defensive feeling we had in London. Betty swallowed a sword upside-down on her trapeze. Something about the sparkle of her eyes turned on the entire room. People sat huddled together on the basement floor in awe.

Pim greeted us back at Pacific Parc with a lovely meal and plenty of beer. We did a dinner theater show there with the Carnival of Hellucinations that ended with a great dance party of retro soul music. The people of Amsterdam knew how to party, dancing all night long, having all kinds of interesting conversations.

We walked the streets over bricks, frozen waterways, and fast-paced bicycle lanes of ringing bells to the red-light district, where sex workers leered from windows in their underwear. During a visit to the Bluebird Coffee Shop, we sampled all kinds of hash and marijuana, and then it was back on the bus to the ferry across the water to London.

It was Chinese New Year, and the streets of London's Chinatown were alive. Fireworks, drums, banners of Chinese characters, and long lines of acrobats in costumes made serpentine dragons with long tentacle-like whiskers in street party celebrations. We had come back to perform at the birthday party of one of Roc-It's favorite squats, the Cheese Factory. It was bigger than the Krankenhaus, more of a warehouse and former factory that had been abandoned and brought back to life by the same extended punk family of Italian and English squatters.

We would only be staying for a week before returning to Berlin. Our main mission while there was to learn the ropes of street performing and watch as many performers as we could to see how the formula could be put together. Early in the morning, Roc took us to Covent Garden where all the professional, licensed street performers drew straws in a lottery for the order they would go on, to try to make their fat hats of money from the many families of tourists who flocked there. It was an open marketplace, layered with old cobblestones surrounded by cafes with balconies overlooking the pitch. A virtual goldmine for street performers, even in the middle of winter: it was an all-day affair, and the cold didn't seem to matter.

There were acrobats from Africa, slackline walkers, jugglers, tall unicyclists, sideshow performers, musicians, and escapologists. The hat was not passed around at the end of the performance. People walked forward to place their money while the performer winked, smiled, and thanked them, standing in place. In Covent Garden, hat-passers were often hired to skim the back of the crowd of people sitting in the balconies for donations.

The fattest hats were earned by those who could end their shows high above the crowd and be seen from beyond the circle. Throughout the course of each show, the idea of tipping money at the end was artfully inserted so people didn't just walk away after the whole thing was over. This was how the buskers made their living.

Gathering the crowd was the most difficult part. Performers would ask the first few curious onlookers to help them out as they arranged their props and turned on the music. Most of them had portable sound systems with headset microphones. People scattered about were asked to walk up to a rope or a line of chalk. They were encouraged to clap and cheer before anything actually happened. When others passed by a group of people enjoying what they saw, an undertow magnetized them to the gravity of the spectacle.

The best of all the performers that day was a guy by the name of Sparky Mark. He started the motor on his juggling chainsaw and placed it on the ground, then kicked a soccer ball out into the crowd. Instantly, his charming little dog retrieved it. Every time the dog brought it back, he sent the ball out again. Putting out the rest of his props, he gestured for people to come closer and sit by his rope. A ridiculously tall unicycle lay on the street beside him. In no time at all, there was a crowd.

The whole show was a build up to the idea that he would be juggling a chainsaw while riding the tall unicycle. After the crowd was formed, he got people stomping and clapping to a rhythm while showing off some of his juggling skills. To demonstrate the authenticity of his chainsaw, he got a cute, adventurous little girl as his volunteer. She held it while he chopped aluminum cans with the blade, throwing off sparks. She had an endearing, serious expression of concentration on her face that won the hearts of the audience.

When the demonstration was done, he gave the little girl a ten-pound note for her bravery, telling the crowd with a wink, "What you give comes back to you," as they screamed and clapped for the little girl whose smile looked like a crescent moon glowing on her face.

Next, he called for three strong men to help him. He climbed one man while another two held his unicycle upright. Sparky Mark stripped off his clothes, making it look accidental, and ended up in a little white speedo. When he finally got to the top, brilliantly clumsy as if he might fall at any moment, the volunteers passed him his dangerous juggling equipment. Suspense was thick when he launched off the volley of knife, torch, and chainsaw. It was quick and powerful, with everyone completely hypnotized.

When he successfully caught all the objects, the crowd went insane with noise. He allowed himself to fall with the unicycle, landing on his feet with a bow. His hat overflowed with large notes and heavy coins. Roc introduced us and we spoke about the psychology behind it all. Sparky Mark had become quite wealthy over the years and had been able to buy property, as well as travel the world.

When we got back to the snowy streets of Berlin, Larz Vegas was waiting for us on the top of the stairs of the Køpi stronghold with a packed chillum and some beer. The oven was full of wood and coal, making the apartment cozy in the comfort and sophistication of anarchic crust. The foundation of the cracked Køpi felt solid and strong, even though the beams holding the place up were getting weak with age, freezing, and thawing. Magic held the building up. The art and sculptures and years of patching made the old hotel look just like the punks that lived there: living art with spray paint holding it all together.

Larz had gotten us a show at a place called White Trash Fast Food. Looking like a Chinese restaurant that served American food, it was elegant in its trashiness as a fashion statement. It was run by American expatriates and always full of wealthy people eating fancy "white trash burgers" and "freedom fries." Chinese dragons and paper lamps hung beautifully from the ceiling. The Squidling Brothers fit into the high class, trailer trash European trend of slumming in the rough-and-tumble rubbish. Amsterdam had flown us to Europe for a recreation of Coney Island, and now White Trash was feeding us, getting us drunk on good German beer, and paying us very well to freak out their customers at a hamburger dinner party for Europeans with cash. We brought Pete Missing and some other punks to walk around the restaurant like jesters, picking leftovers off the people's plates.

We did miniature sets of sideshow in between a rock 'n' roll DJ. People loved it, with the exception of a few tables who took their food and walked to the other section of the restaurant, but that was all part of the experience. Hired to entertain on the edge of acceptability so people would have stories to tell, and we almost had way too much fun doing it.

We were called back to Eschloraque (the Dead Chicken Bar) for another round because of our previous success. Matterz and Sharleen had just returned from Spain and were ready to do one last show together in Europe before we headed back to Philadelphia. The owner of the Dead Chicken Bar was a small man with a high voice, who only spoke German and always had a different, tall, beautiful woman on his arm. He was enthusiastic about making the monsters for the show and took all of us Squidlings into the basement where he was working on his new art project.

There was a room of mirrors and an entire mechanical monster band with different instruments for heads. It was a long-term project with a way to go. There were work materials and unfinished creatures all around. All the monsters would be able to dance and play music when it was done. He was extremely generous with alcohol and seemed thrilled to have us back. It was like we were imaginary friends from a dream reality, who had come in the flesh for a short visit to entertain the living, the dead, and his monsters hiding in the corners of the bar.

Once again, the cabinet of curiosities filled up to capacity. A nice way to say goodbye to the hauntingly beautiful, frozen city of Berlin. It was over just the way it started: fast, fast, fast. We promised to return and have more adventures as soon as we could.

Hugs and drinks and a smoke before we hit the road, dragging our stuff through the streets, across the river to the train station, to the airport in Berlin, to the airport in London, to the airport in New York City. We got all our luggage with no problem, filled out the customs forms, and got a few more stamps on our passports. So much was waiting at home. Six weeks was the longest I'd ever been away before. Now it was a lifestyle in my DNA. Our drops of the blood we spilled in every town made us part of all the places along the way. A feeling like we had been there before and would be there again. Here was there, and the point of no return was taking us home again.

We came home with a bit of money to pay our bills and hold us over to the next job and the next show. Life would never be the same. The Squicken had grown and was getting too large for the old jar. In the middle of February, with spring on our minds, we began to plan for the next session of Carnivolution. In the museum where we lived, Betty and I wrapped ourselves around each other and breathed deeply in our little room on the third floor, with Matterz just down the hall. We could finally rest, but not for long.

Chapter 12
Wild Women and Wise Guys

Living on the road meant making do, but in Philadelphia, everything I needed was right outside the door. The Tiberino Museum was my home and the home for Carnivolution. Lots of work to be done in the neighborhood with plenty of old houses to paint just down the sidewalk from us on Spring Garden Street. Before I knew it, Walpurgisnacht returned on April 30, and I turned thirty-two. I cast a spell and rolled the dice of chaos magic, breathing it into the space-traveling perverted puppets of Grandma Maddoodi's nipple-shaped ship. We formed a circle around a cauldron of thought, tossing ingredients into the bubbling brew. Banners were painted; puppets were stitched.

Our house in the museum was backstage where everyone could put on costumes and makeup for the show. Anticipating possible rain, we climbed the trees in the garden and hung an elaborate tent system of tarps over the stages and the bar. All the work paid off when the night arrived, and we packed the yard to the point where it was difficult to walk from one end to the other. It rained like crazy, making people huddle together under the tent to watch the show.

Along with Carnivolution, we began the first of the summer shows on Memorial Day weekend at Cha Cha's on the boardwalk. It was the second official 'last year' of Coney Island. A corporate real estate company was still trying to buy the amusement district and modernize it with condos on the beach. John Strong's sideshow set up across the street from Sideshows by the Seashore. The Ringling Brothers Circus set up at the other end of the boardwalk. To avoid competition with the Burlesque at the Beach Friday night series and fireworks display, on Saturdays the Squidling Brothers set up camp at Cha Cha's, home for wild women and wise guys.

Life is better when you are laughing at the amusement park behind the scenes. There is no next time; it's now or never, as the clock ticks you into history; don't quit your daydream. In the carnival, life is but a job that isn't really working, just rowing down the stream of consciousness, and it rowed us right into John Strong's human sideshow and freak animal tents.

We received a warm welcome from a true Coney Island character. Such life forms have existed which are so unique in their incarnation as to make you question the very nature of the Misfit Mother's rhyme and reason. Is life a poet at the source, springing forth mutations to breed never-to-be-seen-again flashes in the pan? With minds to take in the world through more than two eyes, wishing to walk in more directions at once than a body can choose to travel? All given rise by the spark of sex; that mistaken, purposeful division of cells which causes those gifted with reason to wonder, why? Why did those twins conjoin, and not continue to become two separate beings? Two animals, incomplete by the standards of the others in their family. Two animals that as one creature become more than they started out to be in the embryonic state of conception, altered by fate and circumstance, a chance to see deeper into the forces behind this world. That is what John Strong was offering for two dollars a ticket, whether he knew exactly what he was doing or not.

Matterz, Betty Bloomerz, the Illustrated Penguin, and I went to Coney Island early one day to walk the park and meet the other show people. We brought with us a spirit of noncompetition and an invitation of inclusion, with a rebellious twinkle in our eyes, unwilling to flinch at the sight of magic or mayhem.

John Strong's sideshow was lined with classic banners that looked like modern recreations of the ones I'd seen in books. When he received word that the Squidlings had come to say hello, he came from his trailer in the back to meet us right away. John Strong was a large, husky man with a baseball hat and a big mustache. He shook our hands with delight. In meeting Penguin, he was so enthusiastic that it made us a bit uncomfortable. It was as if John Strong was eyeing up the Penguin with a kind of lustful desire to turn him into a taxidermy exhibit.

He was exuberant and kind as he invited us to see his living freak animal display. There was a two-faced cow named Mosey Rosy, the second face being an undeveloped parasitic twin; a bow-legged dwarf horse named Tiny Tim; a five-legged, two-headed turtle; a pair of walnut turtles connected at the shell; an alligator snapping turtle with two heads; a five-legged gecko; and a spider girl illusion where a lady would appear on a web with a human face and a spider's body.

The tent had a strong smell in the heat of the summer, like a barn and the reptile section of a pet store. John took us behind the tent to his trailer to meet his organ-grinding monkey, Jocko. The monkey was tiny with big fangs and a whistling voice like a bird. John said if we ever needed jobs, he would love to hire us, especially Penguin, who was received as royalty in this setting.

We were introduced to the people who worked for John Strong from the tent next door, at the entrance of the new Dreamland Park. There was the outside talker who had a magnetic, midway-criminal-carnie aura about him. There was also Kima the Elephant Woman, who was African American, with thick, dry, cracked skin; she danced and conversed happily with people in her Bronx accent. A crust punk couple named Jackie and Johnny Bizarro worked the blade box. Jackie was pretty and flamboyantly dressed in neon colors. They both seemed high and were naturally funny characters.

Headlining the sideshow was Mystic Marlow, a tall, skinny magician with a mini flamethrower up his sleeve; he worked alongside a modified marvel with a split tongue and face tattoos named Katya Kadavera. We had an immediate connection and I invited them all to our show that night at Cha Cha's. They gratuitously accepted, feeling the comradery of our sideshow situation.

We made our way over to see Dick Zigun at Sideshows by the Seashore with sawdust in our shoes. Dick seemed a bit put off by the idea of so many shows coming to Coney Island, where he had been basically the only show in town since the early '80s. We went to see the grind show and invited him along with his crew to our first Saturday show of the year. I told him I chose Saturday as to not compete with his Friday nighttime shows, and that Cha Cha had asked me to put the show together. In other words, it wasn't my idea, nor was it part of some strange conspiracy.

Dick had a copy of the New York *Metro* newspaper which talked about all the groups converging on Coney Island, with many quotes from J.T., the manager of Cha Cha's. Dick was amused, shocked, astounded, and confused. He was split four ways down the middle of his feelings, but he showed up to see us that night with a curious crew. So did John Strong and his people. And so did the Ringling Brothers band! Along with all the show people, there were a bunch of drunken Coney Island regulars as well as a few tables of mob-type guys with suits. One wise guy stapled a hundred-dollar bill to my scrotum to end the show in a very strange display of respect.

After our show, I met with J.T. in the back office about getting paid our guaranteed amount. He seemed troubled. He was holding a bottle of tequila, there was white powder on his nose, and he was crying. He said, "We can't give you the guarantee; we didn't make enough at the door."

I felt bad for him, but I said, "I guaranteed the performers money. I have to pay them or I'm not a man of my word. If I don't have my word, I have nothing, and my reputation goes out the window. If you can't make good on the guarantee, then this is my first and last show this summer."

He understood. We both had tears in our eyes. J.T. said, "Alright, I'll pay you the rest of the guarantee out of my pocket because I believe in you, and I believe there are big things in store for Coney Island." Then we did a shot of tequila and shook hands.

J.T. yelled out, "What are we doing this for!?" Then he answered his own question: "For the spirit of Coney Island!"

We both smiled through our tears, and I said, "I'll drink to that, J.T." As the next few weeks went on, the show got better and better.

Albert Cadabra asked me to work for him on the weekends doing shows outside of the Ripley's Believe It or Not Museum in Times Square. We were on the same street as Madame Tussaud's wax museum and the *Mary Poppins* Broadway musical, across the street from B.B. King's and *Spiderman: Turn off the Dark*.

All kinds of costumed characters walked up and down the sidewalk posing for pictures with tourists: Mickey Mouse, Elmo, SpongeBob, Batman, even people dressed like the characters from *Alien vs. Predator*. Street performers were all competing for attention but, most of all, money. There was a man who had a collection of trained rats: "Rat Man" dyed his rats different colors and trained them to crawl up his body. The rats would hang out on his shoulder. People who walked by would scream and then want a picture. All the performers made five bucks a photo and were barraged by people all day long.

In front of Ripley's, Albert and I had our own bally box to stand on with red ropes around it. We had an amp with a headset microphone that made us bigger and louder than the other performers. Every half hour we made a five-minute show, where we stopped sidewalk traffic and got an overwhelming crowd that spilled over into the street. The game was to get them to stop, to watch, to call and respond, to make noise, and then hit them with the sales pitch just before the finale.

"The lobby is free to see. After the show, come into the lobby and see the free attractions. We got Sexy Sadie, the singing, bearded fat lady; the six-foot vortex; the world's smallest taxidermy tea party, featuring sipping squirrels, dressed like royalty. Check out my personal favorite, the two-headed lamb, born with two heads, one body. Come in right after the show and we will be handing out these VIP discounted passes, five dollars off each ticket, and good for up to eight people." After our big finale, we would get people flooding into the lobby where the greeters inside would sell them on the museum itself.

The pitch was down to a science, and Albert trained me to do the same. He helped me write a sword swallowing act with a wire hanger and the flamethrower sword. At first, he would talk it for me. After a while, I knew the pitch and would present it myself.

I stepped out onto the box and asked, "Anyone know what time it is? It's showtime! Showtime, anything goes time. Step right up to the red rope, the free show is about to begin outside Ripley's Believe It or Not. What you are about to witness is the ancient and honorable art of sword swallowing. A lot of people think sword swallowing is fake. This wire hanger bent into the shape of a sword is what we like to call the Convincer. It's a solid piece of metal." I banged it against the Ripley's sign overhead.

"What I'm going to do is swallow it all the way into my stomach. Then I will hook onto something and pull up an egg or a donut!" I held the hooked end of the hanger sword towards my mouth, then stopped and said, "I may be crazy, but I'm not stupid. I'm going to swallow it the other way, for some of you more squeamish people. You want to see it, let me hear you say, 'Yeah!' Alright, you asked for it, so don't look away. In fact, take out your cameras because nobody is going to believe you." I swallowed the hanger halfway, gave it a flick, then put it down the rest of the way, bowed, smiled, and removed it. I stared at it and said, "Wow, does anybody want to smell it? I don't recommend it, but it's the only way to get the egg or the donut. If you look closely, you'll notice they are both there, just mostly digested."

At that point, I had a large, enthusiastic crowd who were ready for fire. "That was just the beginning. Ladies and gentlemen, this is the world's most dangerous sword. Come a little closer and I'll tell you why." I crouched down to invite the audience to come closer to the red rope. When they slowly moved in close enough, I said, "It is the world's most dangerous sword because it's got a flamethrower built into the handle, but don't worry no one is going to get set on fire! What I'm going to do, I'm going to light this torch and see which way the wind is blowing. If you are standing in the direction of the wind, we will move you safely out of the way and I will swallow the sword, take a bow, and shoot the flamethrower in that direction. When you see the fire, all I ask you to do is scream. Okay, let's practice."

I'd light the lighter and say, "Come on somebody, scream." The audience would all let out a large, funny, amusement park-style scream. "Isn't that fun? If anything should go wrong, remember to stop, drop, and..."

I'd pause for the audience to finish the sentence as they yelled, '*ROLL!*' "And then come running into the lobby here at Ripley's Believe It or Not. The lobby is free to see, and I'll be handing out these VIP discount passes..."

After the pitch describing the attractions in the lobby, I'd light the torch on the sword, check the wind, move the people out of the way, line the sword up, let the blade fall slowly, take a bow, pull the trigger, and shoot a huge jet of flame while the sidewalk crowd screamed. After the sword was removed, I said, "Delicious and nutritious real steel, brought to you by Ripley's Believe It or Not!"

I stepped down from the box and greeted people with discount cards as they flooded into the lobby. The job was fun, but the street was alive with insanity, and you never knew when a heckler or a drunk would confront you in the middle of the spiel. It was all part of the show and sometimes got a little ugly. There was a 1980s Michael Jackson impersonator who did street shows and photos right next to me, in between Ripley's and Madame Tussauds. His performances would occasionally overlap with mine. He played *Thriller* on a big boombox and gathered a crowd doing the moonwalk. One day Michael Jackson and I had some serious words. I was going into my flamethrower bit, and he was completely unaware. I shouted in the headset microphone to get his attention and the attention of his audience that I was about to shoot a flamethrower in their direction, and they should move out of the way.

Michael Jackson did not budge. He kept dancing like a zombie android. I got a bit louder and more serious, attempting a joke to help them understand the danger they were in. "Yo, Michael Jackson," I yelled, "You don't want to end up like that Pepsi commercial?" referring to the time the real Michael Jackson's hair went up in flames due to his hair products mixing with pyrotechnics on the set of a Pepsi commercial. It was a famous happening at the time, and I figured it would be a reference that any Michael Jackson impersonator would understand.

The audience moved aside with the encouragement of lobby greeters from Ripley's who were acting as my fire safety security guards. It's a crowded street for a flamethrower to go off once every half hour. Michael Jackson was not happy, and I could see through the jet of the flamethrower that he was not quite right in the head.

After the show, we confronted each other. I don't remember exactly how it happened, whether I came at him, or he came at me, but we were both heated and ready to fight. I remember sitting in the office behind the gift shop fuming with anger and frustration, and I imagine Michael Jackson must have been outside on his sidewalk office doing the same. There had to be some sort of code among performers. With so many distractions in Times Square, it was hard enough to get the undivided attention of passersby with different schedules in mind, without another show starting just as yours was about to finish. The hardest part of all was bringing the crowd into the lobby without them rushing off when the show came to a close. It's equivalent to a street performer getting people to put money in the hat before sneaking away.

I stepped into the lobby, wearing my headset microphone, carrying a mini amplifier, my sword, and a coat hanger to see Michael Jackson waiting for me. We had a small crowd forming to watch our clash of alter egos; a sideshow clown versus a pop star impersonator. It sounds funny, but we didn't see it that way. Just before things got ugly, the peace-keeping voice of the manager of the lobby greeters intervened and allowed us to listen to each other's frustrations.

My point was that I had a dangerous job to do that required the cooperation and respect of the people on the street. Ripley's was paying me to bring in a crowd, and him starting a show when mine was at its most dangerous and crucial point prevented me from doing what I was hired to do. We vented our anger to the point where we could see the other's point of view. He agreed to wait for me to finish before he started his show, and I agreed to do the same, with no jokes about Michael Jackson on the microphone. We shook hands. After the air was cleared, we actually got along alright.

With a certain sixth sense, the Misfit Mother smiled down like a ghost hunter around the museum of the strange. I was on the verge of understanding the public in Times Square, giving them what they didn't realize they wanted to see, and welcoming them to the world of the weird.

One day I showed up for work and "Cat Man" was standing on the bally box; Stalking Cat was their name. A surprise special guest for Ripley's Sideshow Wonders, they held the world record for the most permanent body modifications to look like an animal, with fourteen surgical procedures to make their face look like a female tiger.

Stalking Cat was clearly transgender and trans-species, an explorer in the realm of body modification to fit physically in the spirit of their totem animal. The first thing I noticed about Stalking Cat was the odd shape of their face and body, as well as the striking orange, black, and white pattern tattooed across their face. Tiger stripes across their cheeks and blackened lower lip perfectly framed the sacred geometrical design that was marked on their forehead. Long hair hung over pointed ears with a purposefully receding hairline. Implants were under the skin to change the shape of their cheeks, with silicone injections in the lips and chin to make them larger. Stalking Cat's upper lip was split to mimic the cleft palate of a great cat. Long whiskers were sticking out of their face, attached to transdermal piercings on the top of the forehead and through the upper lip. Their nose had been flattened by a septum relocation.

The teeth in Stalking Cat's mouth were ferociously filed to points. Large fangs were added to the canines in the upper and lower rows to produce a fascinating, frightening smile. They had green eyes with feline slits. Oddly, their arms and hands were tattooed with blue and green fish scales. Out of the tips of their fingers sprung dagger-like nails, painted like barbershop poles. Their clothes were shockingly normal compared to the rest of their body. They wore jeans and a Ripley's Believe It or Not T-shirt.

A crowd had already formed to gawk and take photos. I snuck past through the lobby and gift shop, still wearing clown makeup from the night before. Albert Cadabra was in the back room waiting for me.

"J.B.!" He greeted me enthusiastically. "Did you get a load of 'Cat Man Don't' out there?"

I replied, "I don't think I could help but notice. Why do you call them 'Cat Man Don't'?"

Albert replied, "Because Cat Man Don't got no act. Just stands there and gets a crowd."

"I wonder why Cat Man doesn't have an act," I said.

"Probably doesn't need to. That's our job. You and I are going to switch off shows every half hour like we always do, and Cat Man will be on the bally box in between. Come on, J.B., let's go get a coffee and a classic coffee cake across the street. It's on me today."

On the way back from the coffee shop, Albert introduced us. We shook hands and I realized Stalking Cat was quite heavy. It appeared like they had six breast implants hidden under a baggy t-shirt. On the tip of my tongue was a question that I was too shy to ask. While Albert and I did our shows, Stalking Cat stood to the side and watched with great interest. On a break, we took a few moments in the back room to talk.

"You've got a good gimmick in your sword act with that flamethrower, Jellyboy."

"Thank you. Why don't you do any acts?"

Cat Man seemed happy to answer the question. "I've thought a lot about it, but I don't really want to do any of the classic sideshow acts. I'd rather do an act with a real tiger, but to tame a great cat I would have to own one. They are just so expensive. Even if I could afford one, they eat so much raw meat, I'd never be able to pay that much money. A friend of mine had a tiger he would let me play with. I just loved that cat. He stopped letting me come around because I wanted to wrestle with her. He said it was too dangerous. She was the sweetest pussycat, just didn't know her own strength. She struck me one day with one of her claws. It was bloody, but she didn't mean it. That cat and I had a connection. It was a very romantic relationship for me," they said.

Going out on a conversational limb, I asked, "Are you sexually attracted to cats?"

"I love all cats. Yes, I guess you could say I'd like to have sex with a great cat. However, sex for me isn't about penetration; it's about playful, gentle wrestling and the spirit of the animal itself." Stalking Cat was very free with their answers, so I asked the question that was on the tip of my tongue the moment we met.

"I was wondering…you resemble a female tiger, and I couldn't help but notice you seem to have breasts; I mean, more than two. Do you have six breast implants?"

Fangs came out as they smiled. "No, it's nothing like that. I feel both male and female. It's just that I'm developing breasts and I've gained a lot of weight. I got started in my transformation when I was diagnosed with cancer, and I had to get my genitals removed. Now I'm basically sexless and, without the testosterone from my testicles, I've developed breasts. It was a painful time; I thought I wouldn't make it, so I went on a vision quest with a medicine man from my tribe. The vision made me realize I was an aquatic female tiger. When I survived, I dedicated my life to becoming the likeness of my totem animal."

"That is amazing, I mean truly fantastic," I said, drinking coffee and breaking off a piece of the coffee cake that Albert got me earlier. "Are you hungry? Do you want some coffee cake?"

"I am a little hungry," said the Stalking Cat, "but I only eat raw meat. It's the only thing I crave. I'll have to eat in private after work when I get back to my hotel room." Cat Man started laughing.

"What's so funny?" I asked.

"Oh, I was just thinking about that Michael Jackson impersonator out there. With me there, he wasn't getting any attention, so he got angry and left for the day."

"I got into an argument with him the other day. He is very sensitive. To him, Michael Jackson is his totem. The guy really feels connected to the spirit of Michael Jackson."

Stalking Cat started loudly laughing. "That reminds me of a joke. Michael Jackson is dead. When he died, they did an autopsy on his body to find the cause of death. They found out at his time of death, he was eighty percent made of plastic! So, they melted him down and turned him into Legos so little kids could play with *him* for a change." We both started cracking up.

"Oh man," I said, "the Michael Jackson impersonator would not like that one! But me, I'll remember that one as long as I live."

"It's a body modification joke," they said, "I've got a million of them. We should never take our lives too seriously. If we can't laugh at ourselves, who can we laugh at? I better get back to work!" And off went Stalking Cat with a fanged smile and a green gleam in their contact lenses.

The official, unofficial Mermaid Ball happened almost by accident as a going away party for Betty Bloomerz.

Betty Bloomerz as a mermaid, 2010 (Clayton Ryder)

Jellyboy as a Tillie face, 2010 (Clayton Ryder)

*Gal Friday and Albert Cadabra backstage,
Cha Cha's Club Atlantis, Coney Island, 2009
(Lunchbox)*

Betty and Insectavora had been asked to join the famous human pincushion, Zamora the Torture King, in a show called the Hellzapoppin Circus Sideshow. The show was originally going to tour with Slayer. Insectavora had always dreamed of a heavy metal life on the road with a band of such legendary proportions. Shortly before the tour, though, it was revealed that they would not be joining Slayer on the road.

Feeling disappointed and lied to, Insectavora dropped out of the Hellzapoppin tour. She had already told Coney Island that she would be taking a season off, so she was without a job. Albert Cadabra asked if she would join us at Ripley's. I asked if she would help me host the weekly show at Cha Cha's, starting with the Mermaid Parade! They weren't having their usual Mermaid Ball that year, so we jumped on it, in a "spoofing pirate" way with the wise guys of Cha Cha's.

We recruited some famous Coney Island freaks and weirdos, including Miss Coney Island herself, Gal Friday. We had the Illustrated Penguin, Remy Vicious (who had me kicked out of the sideshow during the Mermaid Parade the year before), Albert Cadabra, Insectavora, Bopsy the Clown from Carnivolution, and Matterz Squidling. After the ball, Betty Bloomerz was set to go on the road for two months with Hellzapoppin.

We were excited but also quite nervous. Betty and I braced for the separation and stared into the great unknown of the summer with open eyes. Raised eyebrows stared back through open windows within windows to the worlds of circus and sideshow. The Ringling Brothers Circus band came out to revel with us in the presence of King Neptune. A little window found Dick Zigun peeking in and wondering, "Who are these clowns?"

We wanted to see it all, do it all, before we died and keep our souls. Not merely keep them but advance where they reached to. Why not make ripples and waves, as long as it was all in the spirit of the amusement park, and the old guard was on our side. We were new but knew that one day we would be the old guard, with our eyebrows raised like Dick Zigun. Staring through a little window, past a series of other little windows.

It was a Halloween dive bar ball. The smell of oysters and salt water mixed with tequila and beer in the heat of June; a party where everyone was invited. We filled the room with curious faces: J.T. with his John Dillinger bank robber smile, Cha Cha with his wise guy calm, John Strong with his red, sunburned neck, and the carnival mischievery of Dick Zigun peering through the academic showman's lens.

It all summoned the Ringling Brothers, the Squidling Brothers, assorted weirdos, drunks, honky-tonkers, and the spirits of the sea. All of us wished Betty a fond farewell onto the rock 'n' roll road, sad and happy, enjoying the confusion. With bands like Gogol Bordello and Marilyn Manson, huge crowds were waiting for her to perform. I gave Betty Bloomerz my sword cane as she was whisked away to Sweden.

Chapter 13
Children of the Sword

The abundance of opportunities in that freaky summer were out of control. I jumped into working seven days a week, painting houses in West Philadelphia Monday through Friday; working with Albert at Ripley's Saturday and Sunday from 12:00 to 7:00 p.m.; and Saturday nights with the Squidling Brothers at Cha Cha's in Coney Island. Insectavora and I hosted the show while Matterz held down the sonic atmosphere as the Impenetrable Music Man.

The Mighty Lunchbox had become a regular in our show. He went by such titles as "The Tutu-ed Man of Long Island" and "The Condiment King of Nassau County." Lunchbox did eating acts with bizarre combinations of food, not always fit for human consumption, wearing nothing but a tutu with his gloriously hairy, tattooed Buddha belly oozing out over the sides. He drank bottles of hot sauce, A-1 steak sauce, and chocolate syrup, eating dog food and angel hair pasta with pickles and sardines. In Carnivolution, he painted his face red and performed as the devil, also performing as Prince Lunchbox, the lazy husband of our glorious, perverted puppet, Grandma Madoodi. Matterz and I stayed at Lunchbox's house in Long Island on Saturdays with his mother, Kathy, and his girlfriend, Joy Nightingale. Not much time for rest causes time to fly by, and at moments also feel endless.

Our Saturday show at Cha Cha's lined up with the Fourth of July holiday. I invited my friend Spliff and his crew to join us in a mock sideshow competition, where everyone would be a loser. The Disgraceland Family Freakshow versus the Squidling Brothers went down on Independence Day, 2009. Led by Spliff the Amazing Amazonian Affliction, the crowd chanted as if they were about to charge on the battlefield: "*D-I-S-G-R-ACE-**LAND**! D-I-S-G-R-ACE-**LAND**! If you don't know, you better ask somebody!*"

As the battle cry sounded to start the show, a new member of Disgraceland named the Big Tobacco was hoisted up to the ceiling in a seated position by a pulley system, hooks pierced into his skin. He sat relaxed, reading a magazine, drinking a Coca-Cola, while a slight, clever smile crept across his face. Disgraceland had set the tone with their opening statement.

It was time for the battle of the bed of nails seesaw! We wheeled our three-section hinged bed of spikes onto the stage. Matterz stepped out from behind his keyboard to demonstrate why he was the Impenetrable Music Man. He moved his hair out of the way, which stretched the full length of his back, and laid across twelve hundred spikes. Insectavora brought the base of the seesaw over and placed it on Matterz's stomach.

Spliff said in mock mockery, "Insectavora, it wasn't long ago that you were a member of Disgraceland."

Insectavora replied, "I've been a member of *every* sideshow."

I told the audience we were going to ride the seesaw on top of Matterz Squidling, pushing him deep into the spikes. "Who should go down first?"

The audience yelled, "Insectavora!"

I said, "To set a good example for all the men in the room, I will go down first." Insectavora jumped, and I went down. "SEE!" Insectavora went down and I jumped. "SAW!" "SEE-SAW, SEE-SAW, SEE-SAW!" We stopped and removed the plank, and then the base of the seesaw.

"Now the moment of truth! Is Matterz Squidling alive? How are you doing, Matterz?" I pointed the microphone towards him to speak.

"I'm stuck," he said in a crunched voice.

"Ladies and gentlemen," I said, "He needs to hear you scream." As the audience screamed, Matterz sprang to his feet and turned around to show them his back. "Notice there are deep indentations on his back from the pressure of the spikes, but he is not bleeding. He remains the Impenetrable Music Man!"

Spliff grabbed the mic like a pierced eyebrow berserker and bit his lip. He held the microphone up to his mouth and flexed his forearm to pop out the implants under his skin that made it look like his forearm had a rib cage. "Not bad, not bad. In fact, pretty freaking impressive, Squidling Brothers. Now, get ready for the Disgraceland seesaw of nails!"

To lay on a bed of nails with someone standing on you is a strong feeling of discomfort. Stepping on a bed of nails is an even more intense sensation. Ji Ji the Carnie Girl not only stepped on the nails, but she also walked across them at an uphill angle and leveled the bed out straight on top of Spliff. She then tilted the nails downhill, and walked the rest of the way, turned around, and walked back in the other direction.

In the spirit of comradery, to take things one step further, we joined our beds of spikes. Spliff was on the bottom, face down. The bed was placed on him, with Killah Words face down in the opposite direction. A third bed was added with Matterz on his back. Then a fourth, where I lay on my back. To top it off, a fifth bed was perched on the pile. Ji Ji quickly climbed a chair to the top of the stack, a twisted smile across her face.

The stack was a bit shaky, so to prevent it from falling we had two friends on either side as safeties. Spliff was on the bottom being crushed into the spikes by the weight of four people and four beds of nails! The stack had to be taken down just as fast as it was put up. As soon as Ji Ji reached the top, she smiled, winked at the audience, and began to climb down. The two safeties removed the bed she was on and supported me as I got off. I supported Matterz after the safeties removed my bed. Matterz's bed was taken off Killah Words, who pushed himself up and off Spliff. When the last of the nails was taken off, Spliff laid there like a corpse. With a quick jump, he snapped to life, and stood up with a grid of deep indents from the nails on his chest and stomach.

We all held hands and took a bow to an enormous round of applause from the audience. Even Big Tobacco, who hung from the ceiling in his relaxed chair pose, put his magazine down on his lap and applauded. Disgraceland let him down from the ceiling. There were no "winners" in this sideshow battle. In fact, Disgraceland and the Squidling Brothers were proud that we were *all* losers.

The Big Tobacco hooked to the ceiling, Cha Cha's Club Atlantis, Coney Island, 2009 (Lunchbox)

Spliff and Jellyboy tug of war, Cha Cha's Club Atlantis, Coney Island, 2009 (Lunchbox)

Spliff, Matterz, and Jellyboy, Cha Cha's Club Atlantis, Coney Island, 2009 (Lunchbox)

Ji Ji the Carnie Girl, Spliff, and Killah Wordz with the Disgraceland bed of nails seesaw, Cha Cha's Club Atlantis, Coney Island, 2009 (Lunchbox)

Ji Ji the Carnie Girl, Jellyboy, Matterz, Killah Wordz, and Spliff on the bed of nails stack, Cha Cha's Club Atlantis, Coney Island, 2009 (Lunchbox)

Insectavora, Ji Ji the Carnie Girl, Killah Wordz, Spliff, and Jellyboy, Cha Cha's Club Atlantis, Coney Island, 2009 (Lunchbox)

Times Square and Coney Island phased in and out, from long workdays on ladders in the sun, to the ocean where J.T. 's wild tequila eyes invited Insectavora and me to perform at a wedding at Cha Cha's one Friday night. The Halloween oyster bar looked out over the boardwalk with a new Astroturf on the roof as fireworks lit up the sky. A red-hot ember melted a hole in my show pants while I was drinking with J.T. and Insectavora. Everyone at the wise guy's wedding was dressed in suits, ties, and dresses, except for a friend of Cha Cha's named Skinny Vinny who showed up in shorts and flip-flops. Skinny Vinny was told to show some respect and get lost with his beachwear. This made Insectavora happy, because Vinny was always creeping on the burlesquers while they changed in the back office. The wedding party were delighted with our performance and handed Insectavora and me an envelope of cash. We said goodbye to the wedding, and J.T. shook our hands, smiling like a madman on all the right medications.

We got into a taxi and rushed to our second performance of the night. It was on an old ferry boat docked on the East River in an obscure industrial corner of Brooklyn. Our fire show was set up on the roof of the dance party that happened all over the deck of the ship. Insectavora danced with flaming fans, while I breathed fireballs to get the attention of the party below for a short rest in the sea of movement.

A profitable night of adventures led us to Greenpoint, Brooklyn, a Polish neighborhood where Insectavora lived with her dog Babo. The little, shaggy black creature began to dance in a circle, rubbed its butt on the floor, and wagged its tail. Insectavora kept him singing and dancing by saying, "Scuttlebutt, scuttlebutt, scuttlebutt." Her room was a lot like mine: shrines and objects lined shelves and tables. A vintage windup toy collection of circus elephants, robots, cars, ducks, chickens, monkeys, and trains was nicely displayed. There was a three-foot, jointed skeleton as well as a tall curio cabinet with skeletons carved into the panels and doors. Collections upon collections were organized with magical intention. That night I thought about Betty Bloomerz while resting on the couch. I wondered where she was and what she was doing, how she was feeling in the show she was traveling with. I wanted her to come home.

September shot itself out of a cannon. The Rockabilly Festival took over the boardwalk. Albert Cadabra helped me host the daytime events at Cha Cha's while I held things down at Ripley's Believe It or Not in Times Square on Labor Day weekend.

As soon as the last show at Ripley's was done, I quickly packed up the stage and amp from the front of the building, gathered my show gear, and ran to the subway, arriving at Coney Island an hour later just in time to see Albert Cadabra's final act of the night before I took over as master of ceremonies. Albert was doing the human blockhead. The nail was pulled out of his nose by the teeth of a beautiful drunken woman. We later found out she was the star of a reality television show called *America's Next Top Model*.

Coney Island was once again teeming with hot rods, pinup girls, psychobilly greasers, sideshow freaks, burlesque beauties, and rock 'n' rollers from all over the country. For three days of the Rockabilly Festival, the Squidling Brothers would entertain between bands late into the night. The only thing that was missing was Betty Bloomerz. Hellzapoppin had convinced her to stay on the tour for another week and a half. I would have to wait until the September Carnivolution show at the Tiberino museum to see her. The summer season of Ripley's and Coney Island ended at the same time. This made way for the Carnivolution script to tie the story together and prepare for fall travel plans, when we would cross-country road trip into Halloween.

Betty Bloomerz's plane landed late, and she got out of a taxi just as our show was coming to an end. While the Hydrogen Jukebox played the David Bowie song "Five Years," Betty ran out of the audience, and we embraced. Finally, together again after two completely separate, intense summertime adventures, we learned that rest was rare and wonderful in the life of a traveling performer, being pulled by the current of momentum.

Shortly after Betty's return that weekend, I was summoned to Little Italy in Manhattan by Cha Cha. He wanted to put together a sideshow on Mulberry Street for the Feast of San Gennaro. It was just a short walk from the Chinatown bus, through a stinky vegetable market, under the Manhattan Bridge. Chinese signs above guarding dragons made way for streets thick with traffic and oily rainbow puddles. Canal Street was filled with shops where merchants stood outside, shouting to everyone who passed by, selling NYC souvenirs of all kinds.

Just past a big, glass sidewalk subway elevator was Mulberry Street. All that remained of Little Italy was a strip of Italian restaurants where Cha Cha sat at an outside table, under a sign with his name on it. He was happy to see me and excited about the coming feast. Parades, bands, food, games, and rides would transform the whole street into a midway, with a taste of Coney Island. I was given a tour of his restaurant, which was full of black and white photos of a young, hopeful Cha Cha with movie stars from the '70s and '80s. He said I could have anything on the menu, so I chose the vegetarian lasagna with three cheeses and tomato sauce. At the front counter were all flavors of gelato and a pizza oven. The smells of good Italian cooking were all around. Families and couples sat at nice tables having lunch.

As I finished my lasagna, Cha Cha came over to introduce me to his business partner in setting up the festival. He looked tough, relaxed, and intimidating, with a face full of gnarled, deep wrinkles and a shaved head. The cold carnie shook my hand and looked in my eyes. Even though he was looking directly at me, he appeared to be looking somewhere else far away. I was invited to sit with them at Cha Cha's table outside and we would talk business. The street was going to be closed off to traffic and there would be a tent in the middle of the street with borrowed banners from the Coney Island sideshow building, painted by Marie Roberts.

We struck a deal about a guarantee for each of the ten days of the festival, as opposed to receiving a cut of what was made.

With a smile on one corner of his face and sharp, freezing-blue eyes he said, "Whatever it takes."

After I came to help with the initial setup of the tent and did the first day of shows, I had to go back to Philadelphia to paint, so I sent some other friends to take over the shows in Little Italy. While working up on a roof, I got a call saying the show wasn't turning the tip and we would need to renegotiate.

I said, "If you want us to continue, it has to be the same deal." Since I wasn't there at the end of the night to get the money myself, he held off on paying everyone, and said he would only give me the money when he saw me on the weekend in person.

I showed up on Friday to do the shows, but the cold carnie who hired us was nowhere to be found. Instead, he sent henchmen to pick up the money we were making throughout the day into the night. At the end of the night, I walked up to the money collector and asked him to pay up. He looked at me and said, "The show didn't make enough money for you guys to get paid."

"A deal is a deal," I said, holding my sheathed ninja sword. "We were promised a guarantee, or we wouldn't have come out here to work in the first place."

The money collector looked me up and down, "You're pretty scary with that clown makeup," he said. "You're holding that sword like you want to cut me with it."

"I'm not interested in violence," I replied. "I've got something more powerful than swords and bullets."

"What's that?" he asked, "Magic?" He opened his hand to reveal a black stone. "I've got protection from black magic; my stone absorbs it."

"A deal is a deal," I repeated.

"Sometimes, kid…you are going to have to take this up with the man himself tomorrow. He took the night off."

The next morning, I showed up early and got breakfast at Cha Cha's. The cold carnie walked in while I was eating and sat at my table. I kept eating breakfast and waited for him to talk first, which he finally did, saying "I worked with Bobby Reynolds for years. Now that was a man who could turn a tip. He could sell you a horn nut or a pen with a ridiculous story. You guys can't do that; you don't have what it takes, you are soft and green."

"Regardless," I said, "we had a deal and you have been avoiding me." His eyes got sharper and bluer.

"You're right though," I said, disarming his glance, "We don't know this pitch. We work different types of shows very well. I wish we had an outside man like Bobby Reynolds. If we have a crowd, we can entertain the hell out of them all day long. Let's call it quits. It's obviously not working out." Feeling that we would get nothing, I offered him a deal. "Give us half of what you owe us now and we will walk. We are taking off for New Orleans this weekend."

Without much thought, he took out a wad of cash, started counting and put the money in my hand. "Be safe in New Orleans, kid," he said, as I put the money in my pocket. Better to have something than nothing.

Leaving town for New Orleans was the best thing we could have done. It was a trip that Betty, Matterz, Insectavora, and I had been planning for a little while. It lightened our spirits to get farther and farther away from home.

We had our adventure down south as the fall was setting in. I left New Orleans with a biting hangover and smeared clown makeup that had been on for three days. We stopped for breakfast at a Cracker Barrel where a waitress gave me an Advil because I couldn't lift my head off the table. New Orleans had made my brain temporarily swollen. Insectavora couldn't stop laughing, so I know it was worth the headache.

Back in Philadelphia, Betty and I were on the front page of the newspaper, swallowing swords side by side. The article was called *Children of the Sword*, and it was all about how Red Stuart had sparked a circus sideshow revival in Philly. A week before Carnivolution, Betty and I ran off to Washington, D.C. to rejoin Albert Cadabra and Gal Friday's Skullduggery & Skin Show at the Palace of Wonders, the first place we kissed by the unicorn goat.

Coming from a summer of heavy metal touring to a nonstop string of shows, Betty Bloomerz was moving fast, and things were getting a bit out of control. In a little more than a year's time, Betty had gone from being a belly dancer to one of the most magnificent sword swallowers one could witness at any point in history. She was a natural performer with a hypnotic charm in her eyes, and a stunning vocabulary for movement who had just discovered her medium as an artist. She swallowed swords to the hilt upside-down, on a trapeze over a bed of nails, past the bottom of her ribcage nearly to her hip bone with a 27-inch serpentine sword on a regular basis. Work and recognition came out of it, but she was truly doing it for the spirit of the artform, living very much in the moment.

At the Palace of Wonders, she swallowed the sword halfway, then took a bow. When she stood up again, she allowed the blade to fall down the rest of the way with its own weight. I got the audience to start screaming to make the sword do the impossible with their collective, psychic effort. This time, for some reason, the sword wouldn't go all the way down to the hilt. She waved her finger, took it out and tried it again, readjusting herself to wiggle it down. When it didn't go again, she gave it a little tap, and it went down, but something felt wrong. When we got off the stage, she told me she felt something she couldn't explain, just a great discomfort. There was no blood on the sword, so we thought perhaps it was a bruise, deep inside the valves of the stomach.

Betty sat down and tried to relax but she could not get comfortable. There was no acid reflux, no blood or swelling, just a strange, dark feeling. We didn't want to go to the hospital because neither of us had health insurance. There was no obvious injury because of the depth the sword had traveled.

I called Andrew S. from the Swingshift Sideshow. Andrew advised that if there were no obvious signs of bleeding or swelling, we should get some colloidal silver to act as an antibiotic. It was used by knights in the Crusades before modern medicine made antibiotics to ensure battle wounds would not get infected. He also recommended that she not eat until we were sure she was alright. If there was a deep internal wound that was open and not just a bruise, eating food could lead to peritonitis, which could be deadly.

That night we stayed in Wheaton, Maryland, with my friend Richard Handal, "the master of the obscure." He helped us procure some colloidal silver at an all-night health food store. Richard was one of my all-time favorite travel buddies. I even wrote and recorded a song about him called "Hip to the Wind" with the Hydrogen Jukebox. He was a big, gentle soul who sported a philosopher's beard, an old-fashioned cap, and a button-down shirt with a chest pocket containing pens and a small notebook. He wore thick glasses that magnified his eyes to look like those of a wise, cartoon owl.

His house was a hoarder's haven: bags and boxes of memorabilia lined the walls, with pathways carved out to get from room to room. Richard had worked for years in the audio section of the Library of Congress. He truly knew the most obscure information about all kinds of things, especially music and food. Wherever he went, he took thoughtful, relevant artifacts to back up his stories of historical folklore. We attended Tori Amos concerts all over the country in 2001, ate amazing food together, and would have long conversations on the phone until all hours of the night.

We set up a comfortable spot for Betty to rest and kept a close eye on her while she watched *Alice in Wonderland* on VHS and listened to David Bowie. The next morning, she felt well enough for us to ride the bus back to Philadelphia. She still had discomfort and dreaded the bumpy bus ride, but she badly wanted to go home to the Tiberino Museum. It was strange that all this was happening while we were on the front page of the newspaper advertising Carnivolution.

Over the next few days, Betty got much better and felt well enough to be in the show as a character but decided it would be best not to perform any stunts. It was the end of the season, and the story was about to come full circle. I had been searching all summer for Betty Bloomerz through dimensions, lost in the pits of Hell, and the strange realm of Zombie Zoo Zay, home to the ass-faced nuns who worship the great crawdaddy in a frying pan, trying to find her.

Betty wondered if her sword injury had happened because she was having her period the night of the show. As a result of that, she thought her internal anatomy might have been slightly different. It could have been swollen and tissue-sensitive, blocking the small passage the sword normally followed at the bottom of the stomach before it reached the intestines. Betty started feeling alright by the end of the week after Carnivolution. She even taught a yoga class that Sunday.

On Monday, I was working on the roof of a house in Powelton Village when I got a panicked call from a tearful Betty. She was walking down the street and suddenly doubled over in pain on the sidewalk. After visiting the emergency room, we found out in an X-ray the cause of her discomfort and the result of a week of healing: she had torn her stomach with the sword, but not all the way through. The sword had gotten snagged on a small corner at the bottom that it normally went right past. A few of the thin layers were ripped and had healed into an abscess that looked like an infected blister. It had slowly increased in size over the course of the week, and needed to be drained because if it burst, it would spread the infection in her stomach, which could be life threatening.

Surgery needed to happen fast. We notified Betty's parents. Her mother came right away from Harrisburg, Pennsylvania. Betty asked me to bring her a strange doll that my brother Jason had made for good luck. A creature of Ulana Abadod, it had the head of a clown with a halo. Its body looked like a cat's face with angel wings, with human hands and feet. There were several other creatures he had made like this, but this clown was Betty's guardian. The surgery was scheduled for the next afternoon, just twenty-four hours after she had gone into the emergency room. The idea was to do non-invasive laparoscopic surgery to drain the abscess. A small needle was injected through a tube with a tiny camera on it.

I had to finish up some details on a job down the street from the hospital and meet with Spliff from Disgraceland in New York City. We were going to work at a haunted attraction called Blood Manor, as well as make some business plans. In between all this, Betty had her operation. Her mother was there in the hospital for support. I rushed from my job to the Tiberino Museum to pack some things for New York and ran over to the hospital.

I got there just as Betty was being wheeled off to surgery. She was bravely holding the clown cat-angel creature of Ulana Abadod. I had just enough time to kiss her and wish her well before she went to the operating room. Betty's mother and I sat and talked in the waiting room for a bit before I had to catch a bus. She had a lot of questions about sword swallowing and what it was we did.

I felt horrible leaving for New York, having been the one who brought Betty into the world of sideshow, and I felt guilty in the presence of her mother. I knew Betty would be knocked out for a few hours after the surgery and sitting there waiting would drive me mad. So, I got her mother's phone number and gave her mine. I said I would be back later that night on the next bus after the show.

Betty's mother called me while I was on my way to New York. She told me something had gone wrong in the surgery. They had scratched her on the inside while trying to drain the abscess. They had to do a more invasive surgery, cutting Betty from the belly button to the bottom of the ribs to stitch up the scratch and drain the abscess. This made things a lot more complicated. It would also increase the time she would need to heal, from a few days to a few months.

I breathed fire all night in New York City at Blood Manor and got back on the bus to Philly as soon as the show was over. When I returned to the hospital, Betty was heavily medicated, and her mother was by her side. We cried for a while. Still in clown paint, I stayed there until the sun came up, sleeping sitting down, with my face on her bed.

There was more house painting to be done. I worked and lived so close to the hospital I could visit Betty on my lunch break and come by after work as well. We had been planning a big fall tour across the country with the Enigma, Serana Rose, Insectavora, and Matterz Squidling. We would be starting in Detroit at Theatre Bizarre and travel to the west coast. Now Betty would have to stay home and heal the entire time. It was heartbreaking.

In just a couple of days, Betty was released from the hospital. She came home to our room at the Tiberino Museum to rest a bit while I made preparations for the tour. We were scheduled to leave that weekend. What should have been the start of an exciting trip was quite sad. Even though she could hardly walk up and down the stairs, Betty went with the Enigma to help rent us a minivan for the trip.

We would perform in Detroit as the Show Devils. It was Enigma's idea for combining his group the Electric Acid Theater with the Squidling Brothers into something new that we could take to big events. Betty Bloomerz was going with us in spirit while her body and mind stayed in Harrisburg to heal up beside her mother. It was with a heavy heart, and two full vehicles, that we hit the road to the dark carnival realm of Zombo the Clown, godhead king of the Theatre Bizarre.

Detroit, Motor City, the onetime home of the American dream and heart of manufacturing, had been abandoned by the auto industry and a large part of the population. What was once a mighty jewel of a city and stronghold of the middle class had fallen into an apocalyptic decay. There was a sense of urban pioneering, a resettling of backyard farmers trying to tame a city that grew wild again with nature and a feeling of lawlessness. Many of the major buildings and skyscraper windows were boarded up. Just outside the city limits, entire blocks of houses had been torn down. Many structures remained standing, crumbling after having been set on fire.

The Theatre Bizarre grounds took advantage of this situation to create an alternate reality of art.

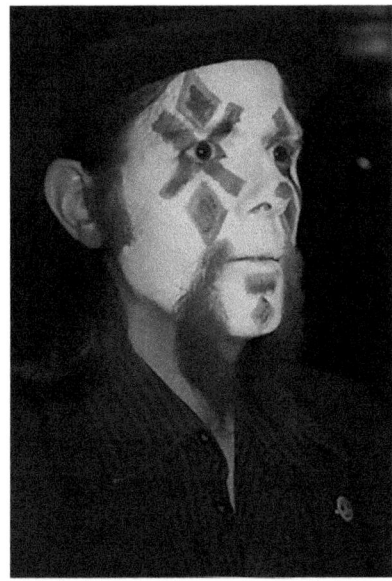

Matterz Squidling in clown makeup, 2011 (Eric Broomfield)

Ten houses with connecting backyards and basements made a thriving funhouse and outdoor theater. To enter the party, people were guided through a haunted house with connected basements. After being frightened half to death, they were led out of a giant monster face into the 3,000-person masquerade, dark-carnival world of Theatre Bizarre. All over the property, there were many stages and roaming performers who resembled the human curiosities on the banner lines. There were people dangling on hooks from the hangman's gallows who shouted at passersby. Flamethrowers illuminated the sky from the roofs. A long line of costumed party goers eagerly awaited their turn to risk their lives riding a homemade, freefall, swinging pendulum roller coaster with flames jetting out of the sides. Dark, twisted trees that had lost their leaves were all over the compound next to the tents and saloons that made up the midway, where all guests walked in the dream of the one undead clown named Zombo.

Each party goer was given an endless orange beer mug with their ticket to this peculiar dimension. As the Show Devils, we performed on the main stage catwalk and inside the sideshow tent. We had some time in between sets to explore other stages and take in the spirit of the party. I had never seen such enthusiasm and merriment in the eyes and minds of people watching our show. The atmosphere created by Theatre Bizarre was more than a mere backdrop: it gave our danger wings.

Clowns, demons, shadows, and freaks danced with creatures of the night. The Enigma, with his chainsaw and blue puzzle tattoos, became a dark deity to drunken carnival eyes. Insectavora was the goddess of gasoline! We were really all too mortal, flirting with divinity, being blessed by the almost forgotten gods of times past. I felt like a wise fool who had just entered a storybook, not knowing that he was a hero.

Zombo, the skull-faced clown with the long nose and orange clothes, came running out of the crowd, and laid his hand on my head. A living dream was over too soon when the sun came up, as we sat around the campfire still holding our endless beer mugs. It was time to sleep at the hotel down the road.

Directly after Theatre Bizarre, we caravanned to Chicago to take part in a steampunk variety show called Carnival Delirium at a rock 'n' roll club. Matterz, Insectavora, and I parted ways with Enigma and Serana Rose to become the Squidling Brothers again, while Enigma and Serana kept the name Show Devils.

A friend of ours came along as a driver. He got in the zone, straight from Chicago to Portland across the northern part of the United States, all without sleeping. From Oregon, the journey took us down the west coast through the redwood forest, past giant sequoia trees that towered overhead. We passed through temperate rainforest fairylands filled with moss, mushrooms, and ferns, right on the edge of the cliffs of the Pacific Ocean. We toured to Oakland and figured out modes of transportation home after returning our rental car. Matterz decided to fly, but Insectavora and I were feeling adventurous. We decided to take the train all the way back across the country.

The journey would take three and a half days. The train followed some of the original route of the transcontinental railroad from California through Nevada, Colorado, Nebraska, and Iowa to Chicago, Illinois. At Chicago, there was a transfer back to Philadelphia. I felt like we were bootleggers because not only did we have some questionable items in our big red box of sideshow props; we also had Insectavora's little dog Babo hidden in a carrier bag. Thankfully, Babo was so quiet and well-trained that no one noticed him.

One of the best parts about touring is the different landscapes and terrains, and America has them all! On our first day of travel, the train passed through some of the most incredible terrain I had ever seen. Outside of the highways, there were wild landscapes. The train tracks were the only sign of humans. We went by Donner Pass, the area in the Sierra Nevada mountains where the pioneers of the infamous Donner Party ate each other while stranded in a winter storm. In Colorado, we saw deep canyons and impossible gravity-defying rock formations on the frosty November ground. At the train stops, Insectavora would go away from the crowd on the platform to let Babo out to relieve himself. She did it enough times that she started getting comfortable and made the mistake of letting him go closer to where the other passengers gathered.

One of the people must have seen Babo and ratted us out. When we got back on the train the conductor said that Insectavora either had to get rid of the dog or get off the train. She cried and pleaded with him to no avail. We gathered her things, and I walked with her to the platform to try and calm her down. I would have left with her, except I had to escort home our big box of sideshow props with a large backpack that couldn't go on a plane. As I talked to her on the platform, the conductor closed the train door. The whistle blew. We were somewhere in the middle of frozen Colorado and all my gear was still on the train. I banged on the doors with both fists and screamed for him to let me in.

An amused conductor opened the door and said, "Alright, get in now or stay with your friend." I got on the train and told Insectavora I would call her, and we would figure out what to do to get her home.

Insectavora had friends all over. It turned out she knew someone an hour away from where the train station was. He picked her up and helped her get a flight from the nearest airport, and she got home before I did.

Alone, I decided to go sit in the viewing car with the glass ceiling and watch the rock formations pass, pretending I was in a time machine. Colorado and Utah felt like a different planet, or prehistoric earth. When the sun set, I went to eat in the dining car. Passengers were randomly seated together at tables of four, which made for good conversation. Generally, I kept to myself on the train and wrote in my book. Meals were the only time I socialized, upset about Insectavora and Babo getting kicked off.

Nebraska and Iowa were flat farmland with rolled hay bales as far as the eye could see. I had a vivid dream while curled up on the double seat of the train. In the dream, it was time for a show with Matterz, Bloomerz, and Roc-It. While I looked through a truck for props, many were missing, including the trigger for my flamethrower. I found out that Matterz threw away most of my rubber chickens because they were too dirty. We argued about it. I said, "Why did you toss them? I was going to give them a bath!" J.T. from Cha Cha's showed up and offered me a chicken circus banner with many mutilated rubber chickens to cheer me up. We all began to sing the rubber chicken anthem. I woke up smiling with a little drool running down the corner of my mouth.

Eventually I got to Chicago and rolled the red box through the train station past canine police who randomly searched people. I just smiled and walked past them towards the Keystone line to Philadelphia. I got back in time for Thanksgiving, thankful I didn't get kicked off the train.

Chapter 14
Holding It Together While Falling Apart

Hot feet hit the ground aimed at distance and speed. Betty Bloomerz was mostly healed and ready for more adventures when we returned from the road. The Squidlings were invited back to Amsterdam for New Year's, 2010. Travel paid its own way, along with enough to afford the bills. Many new songs still raced through our thoughts and fingers with the Hydrogen Jukebox. Ambition ran from Germany to California with a little Coney Island in between. We kept it classic, rough around the edges, and made repairs along the way in an attempt to outrun disaster or dodge the Four Horsemen of the Apocalypse after a letter in the mail from a credit collector named Death.

Dick Zigun invited me to Coney Island to host a weekend of shows in April called the Congress of Curious Peoples. The Enigma was asked to come as well. I moderated the discussion at the podium with a smiley Tillie face on it. To my left was Jason Brott, the Penguin Boy; to my right was Mat Fraser, the Sealboy. Both of them identified as anthropomorphic animals because of their seal-like limbs in the tradition of Sealo the Sealboy, who worked in Coney Island in the mid 1900s.

Jason Brott is four feet, three inches tall with short legs fused at the knees, and an average-sized torso. He has hands but no arms. Mat Fraser stands about six feet tall, with short arms that have four fingers on each hand and no thumbs. His seal-like arms were a result of his mother being given Thalidomide for morning sickness in England during the late 1960s. My job was to ask the two questions in a guided discussion where they would talk about their childhoods. What led them to the sideshow? What were their talents? Betty Bloomerz helped write the questions for the curious people who attended. As a symbol of truth and transcendence, I began with a sword swallow.

"How and when did you get started in performance?" was the first question.

Penguin responded first. "I always liked singing and making rhythms. I was kind of a mascot for the band Wolf Pack and danced at their shows. I didn't think of performing in a sideshow until I was approached by a guy named Bryce Graves at an Ozzfest concert. He had a tent outside the arena and offered me a job."

Mat Fraser picked up after Penguin in his intellectual British rockstar accent. "I've always liked music. I played drums in bands for many years. I found the sideshow in Coney Island when I was making a BBC documentary called *In Search of Sealo*. Sealo the Sealboy looks a lot more like a penguin than myself, but I identified with him because of my seal-like limbs. I recreated many of Sealo's acts and though I was skeptical of the sideshow, I fell in love with Coney Island in the process."

"It's important to have a sense of humor as part of your armor, I would imagine," I said. "Do you know any jokes about penguins or seals?"

"So...a penguin takes his car to the mechanic for an inspection. It's a hot day, so he goes down the street to get some vanilla ice cream. He comes back to the mechanic with the ice cream melted all over his face and asks, 'What's the problem with the car?' The mechanic says, 'Looks like you blew a seal.' The penguin says, 'I swear, it's just ice cream!'"

"A seal walks into a bar and orders a drink. The bartender says, 'What would you like it mixed with?' The seal says, 'Anything but Canadian Club.'"

Both experienced some bullying as children but were also fiercely protected by their friends. I asked about the circumstances of their births. Penguin's condition was a mutation passed down by a recessive gene, while Mat's was the result of side effects from untested medication. Penguin was born with his legs fused in the lotus position; they were broken and set straight when he was about five. His stepfather helped him learn to walk using only his feet and hips without bendable knees. He fell down a lot, and because he had no arms, he could not brace his fall. As a child, he wore a helmet to protect himself from head injuries.

Mat learned martial arts to defend himself with his long, powerful, highly flexible legs. Penguin's form of self-defense was all headbutt attacks. I challenged them to a fight to demonstrate their combat skills and was quickly overwhelmed by Mat's knees to my midsection and high kicks to the chest. Penguin charged like a battering ram, knocked me over, and rode me down the small staircase leading to the stage, as if I was a surfboard.

After that, we had some fun where Penguin breathed fire and Mat kneed a board in half. Penguin expressed an interest in drawing and tattooing. A large part of his body was tattooed, so he went by the tagline "The Illustrated Penguin," tipping his hat to the tattooed people of the old-time sideshows, and the illustrated man of Coney Island.

Mat got on the drum set and played Led Zeppelin, doing his best John Bonham impression. Penguin played noise rock on the electric guitar, laid flat like a lap steel with a glass slide and electric bow that sustained the notes on the strings with a magnet. Betty Bloomerz's laughter could be heard above everyone in the room. The Enigma was in the audience recording the entire thing. The day after, Betty and I joined Enigma in a show on the Coney Island stage. He played a rare set on the piano while I opened the show with firework spark showers off the handle of my sword.

At the end of April, Matterz and I flew to Norway. We intended to meet Roc-It and celebrate my 33rd birthday on the night of the witches, Walpurgisnacht. We were lucky to take off and lucky to land because a volcano in Iceland had just erupted, blowing the top off of a glacier and the ash hit the airstream, causing huge disturbances in travel. As a result, Roc-It was not able to make it from Berlin. When we landed, half of our luggage did not arrive with us. The red box was missing, as well as our black duffle bag. With a show the next day, we crossed our fingers that the luggage would be delivered in time.

In Oslo there was a sideshow troupe called Pain Solution. Their leader greeted us at the airport, a tall man with a bright red mohawk and tattoos on his hands named Håvve Fjell. He was instantly warm and helpful. I could see aspects of my older brother Jason in him. They were the same height and would have been the same age if Jason was still alive.

Norway filled me with a bizarre sense of deja vu. Håvve drove us to his house from the airport through long, rounded tunnels burrowed in the mountains. The countryside leading to the city rolled with snow-capped evergreens. Oslo was by the water, filled with cobblestones. The architecture was a mixture of old brick buildings with stone foundations alongside very modern structures of glass and steel.

Håvve lived in an apartment in an old brick building with a metal gate. There was a huge yard filled with murals. We climbed up a few flights of stairs that led to a wooden door, into Håvve's kitchen. There were many hooks along the wall to hang coats. A collection of shoes lined the floor underneath. He showed us to his guest room that had been prepared and started to cook. "You must be hungry?" he asked, as he gave us bread and tasty cheese.

After a dinner of vegetables that Håvve prepared in a wok, we drank beer and smoked late into the night, talking about how our lives had led us to sideshow. Since the name Håvve translated to "Head," his character was the Headmaster. He had opened a fakir academy to teach a few apprentices how to transform pain into art, after being the only remaining member of various incarnations of his previous troupe. A fakir is traditionally a Sufi Muslim or Hindu holy man who leaves behind all worldly possessions to become a servant of the divine, leading a life of meditation and near passionlessness. In his case, it was the sideshow arts of the fakir that were the focus, minus the religious beliefs. It was about the acceptance of pain to transcend the human form with piercing needles, beds of nails, and other instruments of torture. His students were Morten the Maniac and Marte, the Princess of Scars.

The next day our show was at Blitz, a space in the middle of Oslo for political activists and artists. There was a mural on the front wall of a punk's hand crushing a swastika. Inside was a cafe with affordable vegan food, a concert venue, and places for bands to rehearse. In the upstairs of Blitz, Pain Solution had a storage room full of props and costumes.

A very enthusiastic Morten the Maniac greeted us. He was more than happy to help assemble replacements for our missing props that didn't arrive. He would join us in the show that night since Roc-It had been waylaid because of the Icelandic volcano. Morten was strong, bald, and wiry, with naturally red facial hair. He presented all of Pain Solution's props from within trunks and suitcases. In a little time, we had everything we needed to set the stage.

Morten had a rolla-bolla of machetes. He balanced on two blades, rocking back and forth. This required great concentration and balance because their machetes were *extremely* sharp. Morten's fellow graduate from the Fakir Academy, Marte, was truly the Princess of Scars. Her scars were beautiful, and many lined her body. Some looked to be early experiments in self-inflicted cutting, while others were art pieces in the medium of scarification. Morten and Marte were a well-choreographed sideshow duo.

Håvve presented the acts dressed in a white suit, a graduate's cap, and a crown of long needles pierced into his forehead, wearing spectacles with no lenses. They opened with a few hardcore sideshow stunts presented silently to a musical soundtrack with Håvve in between. Morten the Maniac mixed a drink of gin and tonic in a bucket, with one entire bottle of gin and two bottles of tonic, shaken and exploded on opening. The Headmaster attached a carabiner to his large labret lip piercing and lifted the bucket which drooped his lip as he swung it. Contorted eyes showed over a bubblegum bottom lip smile. After a few good swigs, the Headmaster held the bucket in the air and said, "Shaken, not stirred! In the old days, when we were Vikings, people would pass a bowl around and say, 'Skål,' but now I will pass this bucket around, so we say, 'Bucket.'" The audience all yelled, "*BUCKET!*" in unison as the gin and tonic passed around.

Håvve said a few things in Norwegian to get the crowd going and then switched to English. "I will speak in English for the rest of the show out of respect for our guests, the Squidling Brothers Circus Sideshow!" At the end of Pain Solution's part of the show, the Headmaster asked, "Do you want blood?" The audience was howling and ready. He removed the needles from his forehead and forearm, letting the blood run down while standing on a white lab coat. Those same needles were then pierced through his lips in an X. A bloody smile took over the Headmaster's face, frightening and friendly before we hit the stage.

Matterz Squidling and I took the stage with the props we had. The comedy of the bed of rubber chickens with the bed of nails morphed into our bizarre brand of sword swallowing. Our jokes lit up the Blitz House with fresh enthusiasm, embracing an absurdist's take on sideshow. After a wild show of swords, chickens, flames, games, and staple-gunned money with audience participation, the most absurd thing of all occurred: our lost luggage was delivered by the airport, the best punchline the Icelandic volcano could throw our way in Oslo, Norway.

On Sunday, Blitz was transformed from a theater into the Wings of Desire hook suspension lab, filled with rigging points and tables for piercing and aftercare. Blitz's Suspension Sunday was the perfect place to play with Morten the Maniac as my guide. The piercing of two large, deep sea fishing hooks with no barbs punched right through the skin over my shoulder blades, with a pop and a warm sensation that tingled over my entire body. Imagining that the hook was a part of me, I stood up, stepped off the piercing table to be fastened to the pulley system, and rigged to the metal mesh ceiling.

Matterz and I promised to return for more adventures. Berlin, Roc-It, and Walpurgisnacht were calling. The Night of the Witches in Germany is a time of pagan celebration, with people dressed like wizards and witches in the streets on the eve of the May Day celebrations. It was my 33rd birthday. Healing from the suspension the night before in Oslo, I walked with my brother and Roc Roc-It, a dull ache in the hook wounds and surrounding tissue. I could feel my body working to mend the places where skin had held me strong above the floor of Blitz. The spirits tingled and twitched through my veins.

Mischief and witchcraft levitated like the ghosts of autumn leaves through the warm springtime air. When the sun set, with open bottles of beer, the three of us made our way back to the Køpi, through the armored metal gates decorated in graffiti, garbage and art. Behind a little gate, just off the entrance to the trailer park that surrounded the old tattooed hotel was a girl named Finn with rubber elf ears and brightly colored punk hair, tending a nice little campfire. She invited us over to sit with her. Smoking spliffs, drinking beer, and feeding the fire, we shared in Finn's infectious laughter. A large, floppy black dog named Yashka sat calmly, warming herself near the burning wood.

Finn was curious to hear about the sideshow and raised a toast for my birthday. She especially got a kick out of Roc when he took out his game, Shock-N-Roulette. It was a circle with five finger holes. Everyone put a finger in, and a red light went around. The person who it landed on got a zap in the finger, a jolt from a mini lightning bolt. For some reason, Roc got zapped more than anyone. Finn had a little wagon under a tree just behind the fire pit. She told Roc she wanted a treehouse on top of the wagon, and I could see the wheels spinning behind his eyes imagining building it for her!

We slept upstairs at the Køpi that night in Roc and Larz's apartment, ready to wake up early for the Berlin Lacht street performer festival on May Day. Roc had secured us some good show spots in the festival, walking distance from where he lived, with some guaranteed money, plus whatever we could get in the hat. The friend of Roc's who ran the festival had helped us set up the RAW Tempel into a parachute circus tent the winter before.

Roc gathered a crowd, presenting Matterz's machete ladder and my sword swallowing. He squeezed through a tennis racket and blew up a rubber glove on his head. There was a nice size audience of all ages, families, and fat hats in a circle show on a cobblestone street. We stayed out of trouble by foregoing the punk tradition of burning cars and fighting police on the first of May.

Every time we were in Berlin with Roc-It, the question always came: "When are we going to do this again?" We promised to return the following spring. We would meet up for a proper tour of Scandinavia, down through Germany, across the Alps of Switzerland into the Balkans. It had been eleven years since my brother Jason's death. We started recording an album about him the year before with the Hydrogen Jukebox. Now there was a real urgency to finish it.

Back home in Philadelphia, things were buzzing. Matterz, Betty, and I decided to move out of the Tiberino Museum. We only had two rooms on the third floor, so we were pretty cramped for space. The Duke and Penguin went into renting a whole house with us on 5029 Pine Street. It was a three-story row home with an attic, a basement and a concrete backyard only two blocks away from a rehearsal space that the Hydrogen Jukebox was renting in an underground parking garage fallout shelter, perfect for finishing our recordings.

After eleven years, I had a feeling that the band's days were numbered, especially with the success of the traveling sideshow. There was a time when the two were one; however, the sideshow and the band were diverging. It was because of this I felt that we should record everything, just in case the end of the Hydrogen Jukebox was truly near. We were in the midst of recording two albums, one being all the songs we had written, inspired by Jason, since 1999, called *Dark Imagination Party*. The other was a newer collection of progressive songs called *Astro Brains*, a concept album about an alien invasion.

We turned our rehearsal space into a recording studio and laid down the basic tracks of drums, guitar, and bass. Jeff Newman was back in the band. We cut the wind section to Jim who played flute and Royce the clarinetist. At that point, the band was two sets of brothers: Jeff Newman and Bunny Savage on guitars, Matterz on bass, and I was the singer no longer playing an instrument. Styx Latte was on drums. We were still dedicated to playing Carnivolution at the Tiberino Museum once a month. Other than that, recording was our only focus.

It was May 2010, the beginning of the Carnivolution season. We had a lot of room in our new house for all the props created over the years. One room on the third floor was completely dedicated to puppets and circus banners. The Duke of Flies lived in the attic and Matterz had the third floor. I lived on the second floor at the front of the house with a nice roof deck. Betty had her own room at the back of the second floor. Penguin's room was in the middle with the number 666 screwed into the door. My orange cat Wigwam had the full run of the house.

In the beginning of June, weekend work started at Ripley's Believe It or Not in Times Square. On Saturday nights, we had the Squidling Brothers shows again at Cha Cha's. J.T. was completely obsessed with the idea of bringing Bob Dylan to Coney Island. Dick Zigun had rehired Insectavora and started a show starring her and Serpentina on Saturday nights to compete with us, called the Girlie Freakshow. He thanked me for doing the 'market research' for him regarding Saturday nights in Coney Island. This hurt the attendance at our show quite a bit. It was all in the spirit of the carnival and fair play in an unfair way.

Soon I received the bad news that J.T. was fired from Cha Cha's. He was replaced by a most unfriendly gangster. This caused us to have a major budget cut. We had to shrink the cast. Morale for the show was low. I still spoke to J.T. on the phone often. We became better friends and went out together to listen to live jazz.

At the end of Carnivolution that Friday night, most of the performers left without helping to clean up. Matterz, Styx Latte, Tommy Toons, Lunchbox, Joy Nightingale, and I stayed to break down. It was a lot of work to put all the band equipment and sideshow props in Styx's bus to unload the music equipment at the studio. Drinking whiskey didn't help with our tempers. Lunchbox had to drive me to Ripley's in Times Square early the next morning as well as get himself back to Long Island, and then onto Coney Island on Saturday night for Cha Cha's show. Styx had been upset for a while that the sideshow had taken a lot of the spotlight from the band, and that so many props and puppets had to be moved along with all the music gear. Matterz and Styx argued back and forth quite viciously while I stewed in the back of the bus. Years of frustration built up and made their way to the surface. Years of trying to accomplish the impossible success of the Hydrogen Jukebox. On our way to the studio, all the passionate debates with Styx on the right way to run the band ran through my head.

Styx joined the band seven years before, in 2003. He was a dedicated musician and engineer; we just always butted heads. I forget exactly what was said, but the way the words came out hit a nerve deep in my psyche. While unloading the amplifiers, PA, and drums, I just snapped and went berserk, leapt out the back of the bus, and open-hand punched Styx in the side of the head.

That was it; the band was over. It was the last straw for Styx. He annoyed me as much as I annoyed him.

Instead of hitting me back, he just looked at me and said, "I dedicated my life to this band for seven years, and this is how you repay me?" There was nothing else to say. We all silently unloaded the van, knowing the end had come for the Hydrogen Jukebox.

The recordings were unfinished. After some reflection and cooling down, Styx agreed to help finish engineering *Dark Imagination Party* out of respect for my brother Jason. However, *Astro Brains* would remain unfinished. I wished I was cooler, but my spirit was in flames. Once again, the elemental fire licked its lips.

I could feel the Misfit Mother of Death crying inside me as the baby Squidling became not so much a baby anymore. I was and am very grateful that Styx went through with finishing *Dark Imagination Party* that year. It was not an easy journey. There would be no Hydrogen Jukebox anymore at Carnivolution; we had to find different bands to play the rest of the summer while we focused on the sideshow.

Chapter 15
Faster, Faster We Ride

It all went down at the R Bar in the Lower East Side of Manhattan. Just after the band broke up, Albert Cadabra invited me to be a part of a show for a friend's 60th birthday. Frank Henenlotter wrote and directed bizarre movies like *Basket Case* and *Frankenhooker*. Frank asked Albert to make him the strangest, craziest show possible for his birthday.

For burlesque we had Apathy Angel, Ms. Tickles, and a new boylesque performer named Go-Go Harder. He had the body of an exotic dancer with the spitfire attitude of a glitter queen. A clash of punk rock and disco. Then there was the weirdo sideshow freak part of the party including Albert, Rose Wood, and me. Rose Wood had the build of a carpenter and a passion for baking with elements of clown, drag, and body modification. She was the mother of all motherfuckers.

The place was packed when Rose took the stage. Albert had gotten the entire crowded room to sit on the floor. Frank Henenlotter was thrilled, sitting with his friends all around.

The opening chords to Muddy Waters's mannish-boy song "I'm a Man" came on and Rose came out with pinched lipstick lips. She wore a tangled wig of blonde locks, a half-cut Hooters shirt, and a short skirt surrounded by raccoon tails. Her tongue darted around the top of an open bottle of whiskey. The bottle was placed on the stage. Rose presented her body with a defiant deliciousness. Hulkish muscles flexed unintentionally when she tore her Hooters shirt off to reveal her breast implants with muscles rippling around them. Muddy Waters sang "I'm a man" as Rose lifted her raccoon tail skirt and smacked her penis from one leg to the other.

The audience screamed wildly, except for one man who seemed to be high on cocaine right near the front. He stood up as if the performance wasn't happening and talked loudly to a friend sitting next to him. Albert tapped me on the shoulder and whispered, "Hey Jelly, can you get that guy to sit down? The best part is about to come up."

I walked over in a crouched position, trying not to block the view, and said softly in the man's ear, "Can you please sit down? There is a show on." He did not acknowledge me or Rose. He went on talking loudly, continuing as if the whole thing wasn't happening. He seemed so disturbed by the idea of Rose Wood that he was trying to create a drug-induced distraction. I put my hand on his shoulder and with a little force tried to push him to a seated position. He resisted, so I pushed a little harder. He punched me in the face.

Rose Wood pulled a condom out of her ass with a stretch and a pop. When I was punched, I fell back a bit into some other members of the audience. Everyone started getting up, pushing and pulling. It was mayhem. Rose just kept on dancing in the midst of an ignited bar brawl. I was so angry after being punched, I picked up a bar stool and raised it above my head. As I was swinging it at the man who had punched me, I felt many hands grasping me and the bar stool.

The same thing was happening to the man that I tried to hit with it, but the hands on him were not leading him to safety like the hands on me were. They forcibly pulled him out of the room and ejected him from the bar in a violent way. Frank Henenlotter had a brother who was both a police officer and a biker, the type of guy who dealt with the Hells Angels and the Pagans. I was later told that he took care of things outside after the man was ejected.

As we were pulled apart, Rose Wood sat on the bottle and lifted it with her ass muscles. She swung it between her legs with her hands on her hips. Rose removed the bottle from her ass and took a long swig. She then added to the pandemonium by spitting the whisky out into the audience like a fire breather with a billowing mist. People scattered, trying to avoid the spray.

After the show, Rose thanked me for what I had done. "Normally, I would have karate-chopped that guy, but my chest is still healing from surgery," said Rose. "People come at me all the time in my act, it hits certain individuals that way. I like what you are doing with your sword swallowing as clowning. I work at a place down the street from here called The Box; you should come see what we are doing there as my guest, and I can help you set up an audition."

J.T. showed up at the end of the party's loud and lovable lunacy with powder on his nose. He showed all the people at the bar his lumpy "penis finger." His white hair was greased back, and his smile was grinding its teeth. I told him how much he was missed at Cha Cha's.

He held up a glass of whisky and said, "Fuck that fat bastard; we are going to get Bob Dylan to come perform at Coney Island! What are we doing this for!?" He yelled and threw the whisky back into his face. His big, crazy blue eyes got wider with the burn of the alcohol at Frank Henenlotter's 60th birthday party.

I was overwhelmed with a proposal to organize a sideshow for a nationwide Coney Island rockabilly tour, along with maintaining weekends at Ripley's Believe It or Not and Saturday nights at Cha Cha's, as well as house painting during the week. Working seven days a week all summer long I was exhausted, but at least I made enough money to buy the Squidling Brothers a fifteen-passenger van for touring.

We named the van 'Beatrice Pretenhour' after my great-great grandmother, the mother of my great-grandfather William Tucker, who married Anna Lally from Galway, Ireland. The story that Anna had passed down about her mother-in-law, Beatrice Pretenhour, is that she had "ruined a priest." She felt so guilty about it that she carried her mattress up and down the stairs during sleepless nights. The story was passed to my grandmother Dorothy Kolb, who told it to her children. Then my mother told it with great humor to my brothers and me. Since Holland was the first country outside of America that we were invited to perform in, and Beatrice was Dutch, I thought this would be a lucky name to carry us on our adventures.

The Squidling Brothers were about to cover many miles, zigzagging all over the United States with the rockabilly tour from the end of July to the beginning of September. A lot of job juggling raced through my head. Luckily, I had many friends who could keep everything going while I popped in and out of the tour.

Jim Kydonious, the flute player from the Hydrogen Jukebox, kept the painting crew together. Betty Bloomerz took my spots with Albert Cadabra at Ripley's on my tour weekends. She also helped host the show at Cha Cha's. The Squidlings who went on the tour were Matterz, the Duke of Flies, the Illustrated Penguin, and a Detroit burlesque dancer clown who also played ukulele, Hayley Jane.

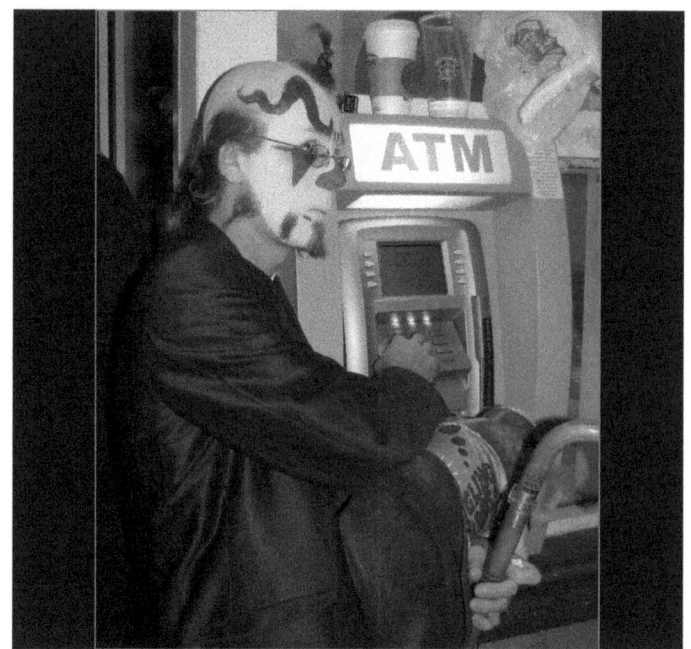

Cockabilly tour, 2010 (Strange Eye)

Paul Holland of Viva Le Vox on accordion, 2010 (Strange Eye)

Polly Punkneck and Penguin, 2010 (Strange Eye)

Penguin, Matterz, and Jellyboy, 2010 (Strange Eye)

Penguin, 2010 (Strange Eye)

Scarecrow Jenkins of Viva Le Vox on stand-up bass, 2010 (Strange Eye)

Hick'ry Hawkins, 2010 (Strange Eye)

Jellyboy and Penguin, 2010 (Strange Eye)

There were five bands on the road with mutated music, ranging in style from country, punk, fifties rock 'n' roll, and some dark bizarro psychobilly leaning towards the psychedelic. We had Hick'ry Hawkins and the Panty Sniffers, Viva Le Vox, Guitar Bomb, the Holy Roller Sideshow, along with Jason and the Punknecks. The official title of the 2010 tour was the Coney Island Cockabilly Roadshow. The tour was a little too ambitious with five bands and a sideshow, needing a lot of fuel and a lot of food. There were thirty-seven shows in about a month and a half. It looked good on paper, but there were too many groups and the money the shows generated was basically enough to get from town to town, with little to no profit. I had to miss the first week of the tour that went through upstate New York, Ohio, Kentucky, Indiana, and into Alabama so I could work at Ripley's and square away all my responsibilities.

The Squidling Brothers had to do short sets in between all the music while the bands changed equipment behind us. We were the face of the festival, the part that made it Coney Island, with sideshow stunts, burlesque, and a carnival-style emcee introducing everything. Because of this, Ben offered a higher percentage of what we earned as a whole. Otherwise, I wouldn't have agreed to go along.

I joined the tour in Baton Rouge, Louisiana, picked up from the airport by the Squidlings in Beatrice and shuttled directly to the venue. I had always wanted to go to Baton Rouge because I thought the name was so beautiful. It translates to "red stick" because of the red cypress trees that grow around there that mark tribal hunting grounds in the Bayou; more beautiful in French than English. "Red stick" was deep in the deep end of the Bible belt. The religious right wing made laws in Louisiana, except in the oasis of debauchery called New Orleans. Baton Rouge law would not allow burlesque on stage in a venue that served alcohol. In fact, they would not even allow dancing with clothes on that was sexually suggestive, so Hayley Jane played a few songs on the ukulele that night instead of doing burlesque.

We were poised to play the Dragon's Den in New Orleans. August in New Orleans is hot and humid, making humans into sweaty swamp slime. Hot and irritable, we had a group meeting, all the bands standing in a circle on a patch of grass in the French Quarter. Clown makeup from the night before was melting off my face. The meeting was held because the first week of shows were far less successful than anyone had anticipated. We were like a raiding party with no treasure. No fortune, no glory, just six groups on the road over many miles.

The Squidling Brothers had been offered forty percent of all the money made on the tour. We also sold t-shirts and had two dings to get tips from the audience. The staple gun act helped with blood money; a hat passed to staple the strangest, most sensitive part of the body. We had also borrowed a Coney Island style blade box from a magician whom I worked with at Ripley's from time to time.

Our business plan was to let these "dings" like the staple gun and blade box cover our travel expenses, so the individual members of the group could be paid even cuts from the door when we carved up the money at the end of the night. Because of our high percentage of the earnings, plus our other ways of making money, the Squidlings were the only group able to survive. The bands were only making ten percent of the door each plus record sales. When they all found out through the grapevine how much we were making compared to them, they were very unhappy.

It was hot, like being slowly cooked, with mosquitos on the prowl. The show creator, Ben Wilson, was in the band the Holy Roller Sideshow. Lots of pressure was on him for the tour to work out. I felt like we could have had a private discussion about it, but it was sprung on us as an emergency meeting where our sideshow was "thrown under the bus," and blamed for the bands not making enough money. The meeting ended in a lot of yelling and bickering. The Duke of Flies was about to get violent. Penguin and Matterz had to step between him and the bass player of the Holy Rollers. In the end, I offered to give up fifteen percent to be distributed among the bands, and Ben's band dropped off the tour. It eased tensions, but I refused to share the staple gun and blade box. We needed those because they were more reliable than the door, which was unpredictable and split too many ways.

Ben stayed on as the tour manager and played a little with the band Guitar Bomb. New Orleans was a town that could give and take away in a major way, depending what side of the mojo you were on. Penguin and the Duke were both abducted by girls they met at the show that night, and Matterz and Hayley Jane found a new place to sleep.

I ended up being taken to a place named Voodoo Alley, off a street called Elysian Fields, by my friends Stumps the Clown and Amzie Adams. Stumps was a performer with the End of the World and the Know Nothing Family Zirkus Zideshow during the Nomadic Festival; Angel had been a part of it in the 1990s. Stumps could play the bayou blues on steel guitar and was a professional clown of avant chaos art with Xs tattooed over his eyelids, always dressed like an old-time gentleman. Amzie had long, white hair with a beard to match. He was a famous local painter who also played psychedelic blues on electric art guitars. He wore a marching band jacket and a top hat with an eyeball on it. I figured we all ended up in the right place that night.

There was a voodoo temple full of shrines and candles in the garage painted brightly, full of years and magic. It was a compound where quite a few local characters lived. I was taken to a little shack to sleep. The nights were hotter than I could really handle; it was 110 degrees that day. There were no screens in the shack. The windows were open, and mosquitos were everywhere. I fell into a deep sleep inside the mosquito net that hung from the ceiling over the bed.

I woke up in the middle of the night drenched in a puddle of my own sweat with a dry mouth. Night creatures chirped and sang layered sounds of the Mississippi River delta as I staggered out of bed. Moonlight illuminated the room through an open window. When I walked into the kitchen, I reached into the sink to get a glass to rinse out; at least fifty palmetto bugs came scuttling out of the drain. The fearsome beetles looked like giant cockroaches with long antennae and wings. They formed a sentient mob that covered the walls, ceiling and floor. I became completely still. The insects gained confidence as they inched toward me. I made one sudden move and said "Boo!" They scattered in fear and ran back into the drain. I quickly rinsed the cup, filled it with water and went back to bed, safely under the mosquito net that was there to protect from more than just mosquitos. In the morning before breakfast, I took a cold wash in the hose spigot. Most of the makeup was washed away, minus some black around the eyes to protect me from the supernatural.

While I was away, the cast I hired for the Cha Cha's show ran into some trouble with getting paid, so we canceled all shows for the rest of the summer until the Rockabilly Festival would converge on Coney Island for Labor Day weekend. The roadshow rolled up through the south, through Georgia and the Carolinas.

Somewhere in that time, I had to leave the tour by plane again to get back to New York to work at Ripley's and do an unexpected benefit show at Coney Island for my friend Spliff, who had just been in a horrible car accident while on tour with Disgraceland in Texas.

One of the tires had blown while they were driving full speed. The car flipped around a few times on the highway. Everyone got severely injured. Ji Ji was pregnant at the time, but the baby was safe. Spliff was hurt the worst. He was helicopter-lifted to the hospital with a broken back and brain trauma that put him into a coma. Betty Bloomerz and I joined with some of Spliff's best friends like Orbi Orbism, the Mighty Lunchbox, and Spliff's brother, Joe Snake, to make a ritualistic benefit show. We attempted to bring Spliff out of his coma through the magic generated by our daring stunts. Joe Snake pierced Betty Bloomerz with long pincushion needles. Orbi Orbism put hooks in my back for a flesh suspension.

Spliff had spoken to me about his dream to have a sideshow on hooks, so Orbi and I decided on an aerial sideshow that was so intense that I damaged the Coney Island blade box and electric chair with my flailing feet. I swallowed a sword while hanging from the ceiling with big fishhooks tugging up on my shoulder blades. Orbi swung me over the audience and made gravity disappear. I hung a suitcase of rubber chickens from mental floss fish tubes which spun so fast that the suitcase raised up level to my face.

When the show was over, we received word that Spliff the Amazing Amazonian Affliction had actually opened his eyes and came out of the coma. He still had a long way to go to get out of death's clutches: he needed surgery on his back, and he had to have part of his skull opened to relieve the swelling in his brain.

While I was away in New York, the festival went through Georgia and the Carolinas. After an emotionally intense week, I met back up with them. The final stages of the tour went through Virginia, Maryland, and D.C., up the coast through Philadelphia, New Jersey, Connecticut, New Hampshire, Massachusetts, and Rhode Island before settling in on Coney Island. The performance at Sideshows by the Seashore was sold out, just standing room only on the outskirts of the theater. Even J.T. showed up to take part and watch after being estranged from Coney all summer.

At the end of the show, J.T. stapled money to my head and we had a long embrace. I had no idea it would be the last time we would ever see each other. A few days later, he was found dead in his house, surrounded by his record collection with his model train set upside-down on the ceiling above him. The photo of J.T. stapling my head was placed on the coffin at his funeral by Norman Blake, the official Coney Island photographer.

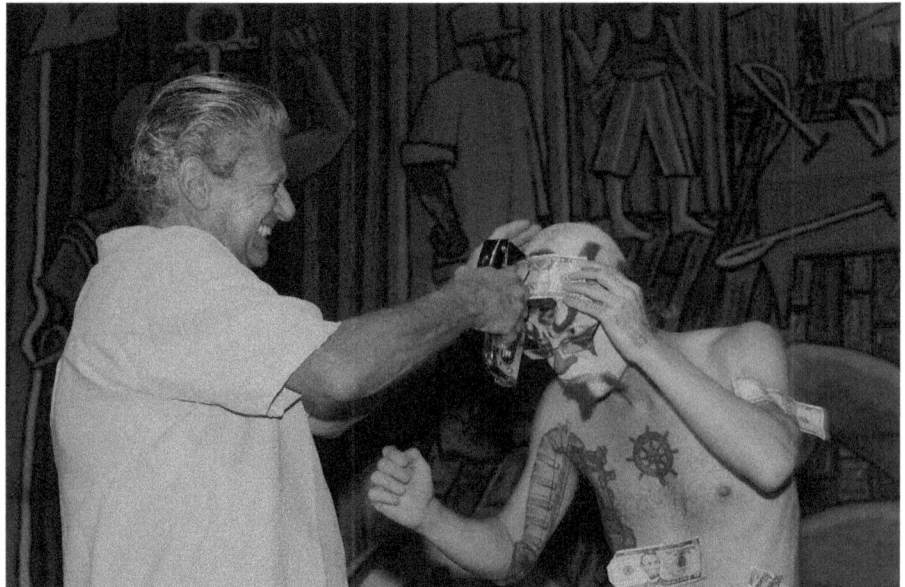

J.T., the manager of Cha Cha's stapling money to Jellyboy's head, banner by Marie Roberts, Sideshows by the Seashore, Coney Island, 2010 (Norman Blake)

September house painting shot by, and before I knew it, we were on the road again with Beatrice. This time it was Betty Bloomerz, the Duke of Flies, Penguin, Matterz, and me on a long tour that would make us a lot of money. We started in Florida, then aimed northwest for Detroit and Theatre Bizarre. On the way up from Florida, we got a phone call that the police and the fire department had shut down the Theatre Bizarre grounds. The show was moved to a single stage at the Fillmore Theater, where we would meet with Enigma. Theatre Bizarre was a totally different experience when all the acts were crammed together on one stage. Previously, they had been intentionally placed in many different zones. The amount of work that went into moving the magic from the grounds to the theater overnight was backbreaking.

After Theatre Bizarre, our tour took us down south, back to Huntsville and New Orleans for Halloween. We performed in Austin, Phoenix, Las Vegas; up the Pacific coast from Los Angeles to Portland; then to Oakland before heading east on Route I-80 towards Philadelphia.

We didn't check the weather before deciding to take the quickest way back, straight across the middle of the country. It started snowing heavily as we were leaving California into the mountains of Nevada. The flakes were giant, piling deep along the highway and in the towering evergreens, weighted down with white as far as we could see. We had to stop and put chains on the tires to roll over the mountains into Utah, where we were able to get out of the storm for a little while.

The blizzard caught up to us again in the long, flat plains of Wyoming in a town called Little America. Visibility was so bad, people pulled to the side of the road. I was in and out of sleep with my glasses on in the back bench seat when we crashed. There was a long skid with no traction as Matterz tried to avoid the end of a five-car pileup. Our van hit a pickup truck full of Christmas presents that flew back and scattered all over the road. My face smashed into the seat, causing a black eye and making me bleed from the edge of my eyebrow. Everyone else was buckled up, with some whiplash from the abrupt stop.

Our van was totaled beyond repair, with the hood all bent and the engine smashed. We waited for a tow truck in the cold with the other people involved in the accident. I thought about Spliff's accident in Texas. The tow truck driver was a friendly Jamaican man named Mr. Brown whose demeanor put us at ease. He put one of the presents in our bent-up hood and said, "Merry Christmas." We piled into his truck. He drove us and towed our broken van to the nearest motel.

We had to scrap Beatrice and somehow find another way to get home quickly because the storm was not letting up. If we didn't leave by the next morning, we would be snowed into Little America, Wyoming, and wouldn't make it back home in time for Thanksgiving. We made phone calls, got some food, and found a scrapper to come take the van and pay us one hundred dollars for it. We also decided that renting a U-Haul moving truck would be the cheapest, quickest way home because all of our sideshow props and treasures from the road weren't exactly legal. That night, in the motel, we opened the present Mr. Brown had put in our hood and were shocked to find it was a rubber chicken in a cheerleading costume with a wonderful scream. We named her Cleopatra.

Bright and early the next morning, we rented the U-Haul, packed all of our equipment inside along with three of the bench seats salvaged from Beatrice. There were five of us, and only three people could fit in the front cab. Betty and I decided to ride in the back with the equipment, cuddled to keep warm, wrapped in a thick quilt we bought at Walmart on the way out of town. Matterz was so shaken up but focused; he drove us straight back to Philadelphia, only stopping for fuel, bathrooms, food, and energy drinks. We made it back in time for Thanksgiving in one piece, once again, only minus our beautiful, rusty van.

Chapter 16
The Elemental

Albert Cadabra and I were booked to do shows on New Year's Day at Ripley's Believe It or Not in Times Square. We didn't go anywhere as a group to perform that New Year's Eve. I stayed alone at Albert's house with his best friend Ruby the Wonder Dog and watched Frank Henenlotter's *Basket Case* series as 2010 became 2011, while Albert performed and partied in New York City. *Basket Case* is a three-part saga about a boy born with a parasitic twin with whom he has a telepathic connection. When he was just a child, his brother was forcibly removed from his body by surgeons. When he was older, he and his brother got revenge: together they tracked down the surgeons and murdered those responsible. My night was spent sitting around and sipping whiskey while petting the Wonder Dog. I rang in the New Year on the roof alone except for Ruby and watched the fireworks from Albert's rooftop in Queens.

On New Year's Day, Albert and I were shut down early by the police because our Ripley's shows were drawing such large crowds that no one could pass by. I remember going across the street to get coffee cakes and seeing a drunk man passed out on the sidewalk, his pants pulled down with a bottle in his hand. People walked by on the crowded sidewalk in a daze of overstimulation. Albert and I couldn't stop laughing.

Instead of going to Europe that winter, we decided to take a tour of the United States from February through March. It was important to Roc that we experience Europe fully in the spring. I took the month of January to study yoga with a daily practice, because being on the road so much was taking its toll on my body. We'd made enough money from the October/November tour to buy another vehicle, an Atlantic City Jitney shuttle bus. We modified it by removing seats and adding a bed that doubled as a counter, with everything welded in place to feel like a mobile living room. There was overhead storage and a lot of room in the back for our sideshow props.

The friend who helped us weld the bus from our sketches was also a weapons expert for movies. He had an old rifle that he modified for me to swallow. It was a Remington target rifle from the 1950s. He shortened the stock, sawed off the sight, removed the firing pin, and welded the barrel smooth. I was not able to swallow it right away, but I took it on the tour so I could practice on the road. It was like learning to swallow swords all over again. The barrel of the rifle would lock up in my throat. I wanted to do it in memory of my brother Jason, to cheat death with a rifle for him. That would take a lot of preparation of both emotional and anatomical understanding to do. Not only that, but it is also always dangerous to challenge death, even when it comes to honoring someone's memory. You never know what you might be inviting into your life!

Along with the Jitney bus and the rifle, we made a new website. I worked with my friend Lance to fabricate an improved blade box that could collapse into a rolling case full of lightweight aluminum blades. The box was made for the road to be set up quickly, with eleven slots and slits. Instead of wood sides, we made a red curtain that was attached with the power of Velcro. It had six PVC pipe legs. The design was from "ancient China," but the parts were clearly from Home Depot. It was laser cut into existence at a theatrical fabrication shop.

We figured since we had a bigger vehicle, why not take a bigger crew? Consequently, on top of Matterz, Betty Bloomerz, Penguin, and the Duke, we added Maray Fuego on the squeezebox and Bunny Savage to play comedic songs. After another ambitious and successful coast to coast tour, of sleeping in strange and sometimes dirty places, the reality that all seven of us were covered in scabies could not be denied. It hit home hard on our three-day drive back across the country. We researched and discovered that the cure for scabies was a topical cream called Permethrin. It is a poison that kills scabies and their eggs. We had to quarantine all our clothes and bedding in the bus for over a week to make sure they had no food source. We held up in our house on Pine Street, covered in Permethrin, feeling the microscopic spider mites crawl out of our skin to die. It was a nightmare that the seven of us Squidlings shared together.

I wasted no time hitting the rooftops of Philadelphia to paint in early April until the first two weeks of May. We planned the story for the new Carnivolution season, along with a six-week tour through Europe and Scandinavia from the day after the first Carnivolution show until the end of June.

Betty Bloomerz was asked to be a part of a real circus tent show in Finland with a contract from May until August. It was called Cirque Dracula and she'd perform as a vampire bride. It was too good to pass up. She and I had a long talk about it; I didn't want to hold her back, but I also had a bad feeling that I couldn't shake. I asked her not to go because I thought if she went, it would somehow change everything. The show was in a tent full of mirrors and dining booths. The pay would be great and so would the publicity. It was a real step up for her from the kind of tours we had been making. I was thinking about Hellzapoppin and how that tour had led to Betty's sword swallowing injury, scared of us being separated for another summer. In the end, she took the job.

Directly after Carnivolution, Matterz, the Duke, Penguin, and I packed our bags to fly to Oslo, Norway, for our spring tour over the ocean with Pain Solution. The plan was to meet with Roc there and take a boat across the Baltic Sea to Finland where Betty would be, to deliver her 27-inch serpentine sword. It was too big for her luggage and a very important part of her act.

We performed at Blitz with Pain Solution once again. Before the show, I stood in the dressing room above the stage, looking out of a window at the growing audience. A girl approached me, and what she said took me completely off guard.

"Were you in a mask at the PervoSirkus last year?" she asked. "You seem familiar. I had sex with a man in a mask and never found out his identity, and I was hoping it was you."

I had been focused on my ritual pre-show daydream, so I looked carefully at her, really noticing her for the first time. She had a delightful gleam in her devilish stare. Blue ice with fire peeking around the sides looked into me, searching for the answer to her question. Still half in a daydream, I imagined the scenario she was describing, in a place I never was, wearing the mask I never wore.

I said, "No, that wasn't me. I was never at the PervoSirkus, but I kinda wish I was!"

"Dammit!" she exclaimed, "I was sure it was you. I guess I'll never know who it was." She put her hand up over her face, a little embarrassed. There was a thick black line tattooed up her arm, like a corkscrew.

"I will, however, be at PervoSirkus this year," I said. "I won't be wearing a mask; I'll be as you see me now, Jellyboy the Clown. Maybe I'll be wearing a trench coat with nothing underneath, so I can be a Pervo at the Sirkus. What's your name?"

"Rajn: not like *rain*, more like *rind*," she laughed, making me blush under my clown makeup. "I'm Håvve's poster slave; I put up posters for your show all over town while wondering if you were the masked man from last year's Sirkus. And now I know! Have a great show tonight, I can't wait to see it. Nice meeting you, Jellyboy."

I didn't see Rajn after the show that night, but I did go out drinking with Pain Solution and a punk rock girl who ran sound for the show. I had met her before at the Køpi in Berlin, and I remembered having a crush on her and not knowing what to do about it. The more we drank, the more she and I talked.

"Are there islands north of Oslo?" I asked.

"There are a few," she said. "The coolest one is called Svalbard in the Arctic Sea."

"Are there polar bears on Svalbard?" I asked.

"Lots of polar bears there," she said. "In fact, you can't leave the main town of Longyearbyen without a rifle because of it. Why do you ask?" She took a drink of her beer and waited for my response.

"Well, it's kinda crazy," I said. "When I was a teenager, I had a past life regression hypnosis session. I imagined I was in a medieval village in northern Norway. We were on a fjord with a dock that had lots of longships, the kind a group of people would row. I was this guy with crazy, long red hair and a wild beard, in a village of all-blond people with straight hair. I was wearing a coat made of animal skins with a sword by my side. I remember saying goodbye to my wife and dog because I was going off on a voyage with my boat and a crew of men. We got caught in a storm, and it knocked us off course. We wrecked out on some island, north of where I had started. My entire crew died and turned blue in the frost. There was nothing to do but walk off into the snow in search of food. I ran into a polar bear and drew my sword. We fought, and it knocked my head off my shoulders with its paw. I saw this blue, electrical spirit rise out of my body, screaming, not wanting to accept death."

"You should definitely go to Svalbard," she said, laughing and drinking more beer. "That was an intense hypnotism."

We talked until the bar was closing, when I said, "I'm going to be in town tomorrow. Maybe we can get together, and you can show me around Oslo."

"Who says you'll lose me tonight?" she said and put her arm around me. "You're coming to my place to drink rum and hot cocoa."

When I left the bar, it was still basically light outside; it was that perpetual light or some form of twilight. During that time of year in Norway, the sun never really set. It would almost fall behind the mountain, but just shoot back up again before the darkness could come back.

Roc, Matterz, the Duke, Penguin, and I boarded a ferry to Finland across the Baltic Sea. We stayed out on the deck with a bottle of rum and the cold sea wind on our faces.

We stared out, looking into the waves as far as could be seen, through white clouds lit somewhere between sunset and sunrise.

Waiting at the docks was Jussi Paradise: he was a friend of Pain Solution and the Enigma, so he was a friend of ours. He ran a piercing shop in Helsinki that performed surgical body modifications, and he was also a creative sideshow performer. He was covered in a colorful patchwork of tattoos that leaked up onto his cleanly shaven head. Jussi had just married a sword swallower named Lucky Hell. She was a tattooed lady from Australia who said she hated the sun, so she moved to Finland. Jussi had booked us a show and a hotel room in the center of the city. He also arranged it so that after our performance, he would drive us to Turku, Finland, to meet up with Betty Bloomerz at Cirque Dracula.

Betty was giddy with joy when we rolled into town with her serpentine sword. Her show wasn't up and running yet, so we all sat in on a rehearsal to watch her as one of Dracula's brides. The tent had razzle-dazzle, with wooden floors, dining booths, and mirrors everywhere under a big top. We then sat in on Betty's rehearsal, the sideshow performers off to the side, watching sword swallowing take the main stage. There wasn't much time for all of us to hang out, much less for Betty and me to be alone together before we had to go catch our boat to Sweden.

It was a party cruise liner full of wealthy families. Our little crew did not fit in at all, which made drinking while getting lost together on the ship lots of fun. We found our way through casinos to a dance party led by a live cover band.

Our cabin was compact, with bunk beds that folded out of the walls for a drunken night's sleep. The boat landed in Stockholm. We rented a minivan to drive across Sweden to Gothenburg to meet friends of Penguin, who had set up a show for us at a motorcycle club. We performed for an audience of bikers known as the Knights of the Innocent MC, along with some Hells Angels, followed by an all-night party in the twilight gleam of the midnight sun with a massive bonfire. I made the mistake of trying to keep up with these Viking motorcycle gangs as they brought out drink after drink, and a special bottle of Motörhead wine. By the end of the night, I was in the "help club" and asked the leader of the Innocent MCs, who was afraid of clowns, for headache medicine. One young biker got so drunk by the fire he nearly fell in after losing consciousness. The Duke caught him by the back of the shirt, pulling him out just in time before he got crispy.

I closed my eyes for what felt like a few minutes in our guest's sleeping place. Before I knew it, people were up serving breakfast and coffee. The plane to Slovenia was calling.

We entered a land of medieval architecture, a previous Soviet territory in what was once Yugoslavia, in a region known as the Balkans. Our show was at another former military compound occupied by punks and graffiti called Metelkova. It had been a squat, turned into a counterculture art space surrounded by a sculpture garden, with painted graffiti murals on the buildings. People there made the most delicious blueberry schnapps.

We drank thirstily and stacked our cups high on our table at a little speakeasy in a hidden pocket of Metelkova. Ljubljana was the city where we found this treasure trove of wondrous color, in the center of Slovenia, bordering Italy, Austria, Hungary, Croatia, and the Adriatic Sea. Larz Vagas drove us onward through unknown countryside, between thruways, and the narrow farmland roads of northern Italy.

The Northern Alps appeared like a tidal wave of rocks covered in ice that crashed into the flatlands. I felt tiny in the mountains where the Carthaginian General Hannibal tried to take an army of elephants across. We listened to Roc Roc-It DJ while we ate cheese, bread, and pesto. From Switzerland, we drove along the part of Germany that borders France towards the Netherlands.

Great things were waiting for us in Amsterdam. Pim had organized another show at the Pacific Parc. He invited a magician named Ramana from Senegal to watch our show with a group of Indian street magicians and fakirs. The troupe had traveled under the leadership of a man named Raj Kumar, the guru of the Delhi School of Magic, to earn money for their village. I was so nervous to perform in front of real fakirs that I vomited when I swallowed the rifle barrel, but they absolutely loved it, saying it was their favorite part of the show because it was so real. They laughed like children in delight the entire time. If we were ever in India, they would host us; we exchanged contact information, intending to meet again.

Smelly the Clown of the Carnival of Hellucinations introduced us to a performer named Princess Tweedle Needle, a young punk covered in triangle tattoos who liked pain. She was a road manager who drove bands around Europe. What she really liked to do was pin feathers to herself with long, hollow needles, remove them, and bleed. She joined us for a show at a pirate squat where she lived and made sure we ate Dutch potato fries with mayonnaise. We talked about touring together in the near future. Larz and Roc drove the van to Berlin while the Duke, Penguin, Matterz, and I flew back to Oslo where we had started the tour, for the PervoSirkus with Pain Solution.

It was a wild installation of pain fetishes. In one room, there was BDSM and people playing with fire on each other's bodies. In another room, a man in a kilt named Odvar

Iron Balls had his testicles twisted, stepped on, and kicked by girls in big shoes. Ballerinas were tied up, suspended from the ceiling. There were private play booths behind black curtains, where people could go to be alone together. And then there was us, the self-made freaks, the natural born freaks, and the clowns, brought there to entertain the kinksters as the Sirkus part of the PervoSirkus. I was in clown makeup, a black trench coat, and a pair of spandex pants with black polka dots popping out of fluorescent green fabric.

Rajn came right up to me; in her grip she held a leash with a girl attached to it. She handed the leash off to a friend and said, "Hold my slave for a little while." She got close to me, wrapped her arms around me, inside my trench coat, and kissed me in front of Håvve the Headmaster. He looked shocked, and he was not one easily made to feel this way, as the organizer of such an event.

Rajn took me by the hand to a private booth. I could hear people having sex in the booths right next to us, behind thin, black fabric walls. Rajn and I kissed as if we were possessed by the spring fires lit by witches. She took off her erotic underwear, which was all she had on, and then she climbed into my trench coat with me.

I wanted to have sex with her until I noticed a man dressed like a vampire, masturbating while he peeked through the curtains at us. From the neighboring wall, Rajn's slave also peered in, with a mad-eyed, long-bearded man covered in tattoos, inside her from behind. The slave girl came over and grabbed me between the legs. I was feeling slow motion panic interlaced with desire; I didn't know what to do, because I was only interested in Rajn.

Rajn said, "What's the matter? Is this too weird for you, clown?"

"A little," I said, frozen inside the trench coat with Rajn and her slave, surrounded by two masturbating men. "I want to, Rajn, but not like this. I just want to watch you get dressed."

She seemed a bit shocked but kept eye contact with me as she slowly put her clothes back on. I asked if I could go home with her, but she was too intoxicated by the PervoSirkus, and I lost her that night in the chaos of the party. Later that evening, I stared at the twilight reflected off the water, as the nearby stream ran away in magical illumination, standing alone, just outside the doors of the PervoSirkus.

Meanwhile, in Philadelphia, the Carnivolution went on under the care of Tommy Toons, with everyone but the Squidling Brothers.

It was written into the storyline that we were quarantined due to space-scabies, temporarily lost in another dimension. Upon our return, there was no time to unwind before jumping back into things full-time with Albert Cadabra at Ripley's Believe It or Not. I hadn't rented a place yet because I was hoping Albert would let me stay with him. He had just started dating a girl named Danger Doll, so he really wanted his privacy. I decided to couch surf with different friends each night while I looked for a room I could afford to rent. My days off were spent in Philadelphia. I liked hanging out in an old cemetery which had become overgrown on the edge of West Philadelphia that was full of broken masonic tombstones from the 1700s and 1800s.

Tommy Toons as Alpha Mouse McDonald, Carnivolution, The Ellen Powell Tiberino Museum, Philadelphia, 2011 (Lunchbox)

J.T. was on my mind. I could hear him say, "What are we doing this for?" in the Coney Island bar where it was always Halloween. I took out an ad in the *Village Voice* for a tribute show that said, *"Jellyboy and John Thomas present from beyond the grave: the Squidling Brothers in Coney Island."* The photo was me in a Batman mask with Insectavora drinking wine through a tube in my face. J.T.'s tribute show, in loving memory, was set for July 3 at Sideshows by the Seashore.

Insectavora and Jellyboy, 2009 (Lunchbox)

After a long, hot day of work at Ripley's in Times Square, I went out drinking with my oldest childhood friend, Brian Levinson. We lived across the street from each other from the time we were five years old until we went to college. He attended Yale on a scholarship and went on to win the trivia show *Jeopardy* while speaking in a Sean Connery voice to Alex Trebek. I was going to stay the night at the apartment of another friend but ended up having too much fun drinking for free with Brian at bars, where he was well known as the host of trivia nights. We talked and laughed, drank beer after beer, and smoked a pipe out on the back patio of a bar near Brian's apartment. When the bartender shouted last call, we staggered back to his place in Sunnyside, Queens.

The last *Game of Thrones* episode of the first season was on HBO. We watched Daenerys Stormborn burn herself and a witch alive next to her cursed husband, Khal Drogo, and three dragon eggs. Since she was a fireproof Targaryen, she emerged unharmed from the flames with her clothes burned off as the mother of dragons. The fire-breathing reptile babies with wings nursed on her as all the Dothraki Army bowed in reverence.

I slept in Brian's library that night, completely unaware of the terror I was about to face while dreaming of fire, smoke, and dragons. I wouldn't have woken up if Brian hadn't screamed my name. Smoke was everywhere and I could hear the crackling of flames. I first thought it was a double dream until I stood up and walked to the door. The heat bit into my skin like hundreds of tiny, sharp teeth. Brian ran berserk in the middle of the living room. The walls were on fire all around him. I didn't have my glasses on, and thick smoke distorted my sense of distance. Brian shouted, "Follow me! Let's get out of here! It's too big to fight!"

Time slowed down. As he ran for the door, I watched fire drip from the ceiling and fall on the back of his neck, paralyzed from the shock of the heat. Never before had I felt something so hot! When Brian opened the door, a backdraft oxygen blast of flames shot into the room as the door was slammed shut behind him from the force. Immediately I focused on the fire headed for me: in slow motion I leapt out of the way in the direction of the bathroom, the only place in the apartment where the fire had not reached.

Dressed in extremely flammable black show pants, I was careful to hop over floorboard flames with naked feet that danced fast. I'd pulled a cotton tank top up over my face with one hand to attempt to filter some of the smoke. Completely focused on the moment in slow motion while thoughts sprinted inside my head, a whole life of memories flashed along with faces and thoughts of people I loved. Would anyone understand what happened? I saw my vest melted to an exercise bike. At that moment I thought, *"This is it. I'm going to die, and I've never been to Asia."*

I thought about my mother and father, about Betty Bloomerz in Finland, and my brother in Philadelphia. No one would understand what really happened and no one would know my story. *I'm going to die, and I've never had any children.* To avoid burning my feet and pants, I jumped into an old claw foot bathtub and crouched low. The bottom of my shirt was still over my face. The fire followed me into the bathroom like an elemental serpent. It began to drip down, straight for my face in slow motion, which gave me the reaction time to throw an arm up. My head, arms, and shoulders were on fire. I quickly sloughed it off, and burned my hands in the process, but I didn't feel any pain.

Reached through waves of thought. Past, present, future, all equally in clear focus. Saw lights shine through the smoke. Figured time was up on earth. Being suffocated and devoured by a constrictor snake that was pure elemental fire. In its grip, jaws dripping down hot digestive juices on my skin. The Misfit Mother of Death slapped me in the face to keep me awake as I burned. Beams of light came closer through the smoke. Not the light at the end of the tunnel, but two firefighters with a life preserving respirator mask.

I was carried like a battering ram, headfirst, face down. The floor passed under as they ran out the door, descending the stairs. I felt weightless in their cross-arm carry. The firefighters gently placed me on the sidewalk. Covered in soot and burns, Brian sat on the front steps of his building. I'd always loved fire, but this was too much!

On the ride to the hospital, the paramedics cut off my clothes. They asked questions to assess my level of shock. "What year is it?" "Who is the president of the United States?" "What year were you born?" I could hear them talking on the radio about my condition. It didn't sound good, but I felt fine. It was around four in the morning on July 3.

I spoke up, to the surprise of the paramedics. "I'm fine," I said. "They got me out of there. I can't go to the hospital! I have a show tonight in Coney Island. I've got to work at Ripley's Believe It or Not this afternoon."

They looked surprised. I had answered all the questions well, but they realized I was not in touch with the reality of the situation. I tried to sit up and one of the paramedics pushed me back down. "You are not fine. This is very serious," he said.

I began to panic as the other paramedic came at me with a needle. I tried to fight but was held down. The needle went into my arm, and I was gone.

I wandered lost through snow and ice. An armored man with long white hair and one eye emerged from the frost. Odin immediately backhanded me with his metal gauntlet, airborne through fields of green. A paradise of rolling hills in a land of eternal spring. The face of my grandmother looked down from the blue, her facial features made of clouds. My mother's brother, Kenny, who had recently died, farmed the land. He walked up and said, "Pop a squat." I sat with him in the grass. John, my aunt Margie's son who died near the end of high school, drove up on his four-wheel, all-terrain vehicle. I felt a tap on my shoulder, turned around, face to face with my brother Jason. "It's not time for you to go," said Jason. "Our family needs you more than ever. Don't try to follow us." As amazing as it was to see my brother again, I had no intention of following him, but fell deeper into the dream of a chemical coma.

I felt a wind wash over on the beach at Coney Island, tied to a bed on display at an art bazaar. A friend was singing sweet songs, strumming her acoustic guitar. Another girl stitched colorful, broken pieces of glass into my arm. Lost and confused, I pushed a button and drove my bed into the ocean. Albert Cadabra came to visit me there. We smoked cigars under the water and exhaled smoke bubbles, talked about show business like two old vaudevillians. He pushed my bed out of the ocean and back onto the beach.

"I can't find my way home," I said. "Can I stay with you tonight, Albert"?

"Sorry J.B.," said Albert. "You have to stay here tonight on the beach. I'll come visit you again tomorrow."

After Albert left, I was alone for a while. The sun set and I started to get cold. Matterz and Penguin walked up and pulled a blanket over me for warmth.

"I'm so glad you guys found me. I can't find my way home. Can I stay with you tonight?"

"No, you can't," said Penguin. "Sorry, Jelly, you have to stay here on the beach."

They walked away. I was alone as the sun disappeared into the ocean's horizon.

In the nighttime, pirates came to try to rob my blood. I drove the bed back into the ocean, managed to get untied, and swam to an underwater bunker, chased by evil mermaids. Harpies beat me up badly, pulled the feeding tube out of my nose, and disconnected the medicine bags. Gasping for air, I realized I was being kept alive by a machine. There was a tube that went into a slit in my neck where I got oxygen pumped in. Matterz and Penguin chased the attackers away for a rescue, almost too late.

"If you ever want to make it out of here, you *have* to cooperate," said Penguin. "You kicked a nurse. They are going to keep tying you to the bed and there won't be a thing Matterz and I can do about it."

I was convinced there was a chainsaw conveyer belt in my throat which held the secret to sword swallowing. I guarded the information with my life, for Betty Bloomerz. X-ray techs with long necks and fish faces tried to take pictures of it against my will, and used vacuums on my throat and lungs, kept alive on machines so they could learn what I knew. Shrunken plastic toy airplanes stuck to the skin of my fingers in long, melted, translucent strings. I was abused by nurses with fish gills and night janitors with eyes that glowed.

In between the invasions, visitations from friends would take the darkness away. My brother handed over a paper and a pen. I wrote a blackmail note to the X-ray technician.

The words floated all over and off the page. Tried to catch them and stick them back onto the paper, everything slightly out of order.

Couldn't tell the difference between being asleep and being awake, between a dream or a double dream. Woke up on the set of an action movie with video cameras all around, turning into a computer. A giant robot tore off the roof of a little house where I hid just off the Coney Island boardwalk. A chase ensued. Drove my bed as fast as it would go, dodged laser beams from giant 1950s robots. Screamed out, "I want to talk to the producer! I need a more suitable role for my talents!" A few of the camera men heard and stopped shooting the scene.

They took me to see the producer who sat behind a large wooden desk in a cluttered office. The producer wore a white coat and a blue hair net. He introduced himself as Kevin and pushed a button on his desk.

Some beams of light through smoke became a hologram of Brian Levinson. Brian had tears in his eyes. "I can't stay long," he said. "You have to get better. I hope you can hear me; get better." He was crying uncontrollably until he disappeared. My eyes got so heavy they couldn't stay open.

I woke up chained to the floor of a boat next to a metal cutout of a clown eating an ice cream cone. A Jamaican woman moped around me and said I better learn to behave myself. Even though she wanted to unlock the chains, she didn't have a key. We were in the ocean, bobbing up and down in the waves. I could see the Coney Island amusement park on the shoreline. Nurse Kevin, the tall, dapper movie producer in a blue hospital gown came out of a door below deck with a clipboard. He took a key out of his pocket to unchain me.

"You're Jellyboy the Clown," he said. He read from his clipboard. "We are going to make you feel human again, starting by taking this catheter tube out of your penis. Then a shave and a shower, of course. Now that we know who you are, we have a much better role for you. Much more suited to your character." A team of nurses came in who were not monsters. They removed the catheter which made me instantly feel better. I was wheeled into the shower room. After being hosed down with warm water, Kevin shaved my face.

A doctor with a bowtie took the ventilator tube out of my neck. He had a scalpel in his hand. When the tube was removed, I spit up blood. The hole in my neck was filled temporarily with a little voice box that made me sound like a robot. The doctor with the bowtie asked my name. With a vomit of blood spit, I said, "Jellyboy the Clown," then proceeded to sing a Billie Holiday song like an android. Little by little they weaned me off the drugs. I came to realize I had been in a chemically induced coma for about a month on a cocktail of painkillers, narcotics, antipsychotics, and amnesia medications to help with the trauma and pain.

Everything changed quickly once I could talk. While lost in hallucinations, many people had come to visit. In the beginning, my parents, my aunt Margie, and Brian Levinson's mother and uncle tried to drive to the hospital to visit us from Lancaster when they were in a car accident! My mother broke a few ribs and punctured a lung, and the others were all right. We had to wonder how much bad luck one family could have.

Lots of friends had been coming to visit, getting to know the hospital staff. Benefit shows were put together all over the country, as well as a few in Europe while I was in the coma. Albert Cadabra and Anya Sapozhnikova put on a huge show at the House of Yes, and even Donny Vomit and Heather Holliday did an act. Hearing all the news was emotionally overwhelming: the tears could not be held back. I was so grateful for the love and support while I navigated hallucinations in the drug-induced coma.

As a result of the carbon monoxide poisoning from smoke inhalation, I had blood transfusions and was filled with saline for the first couple of weeks to defuse the poison in my blood. The burns were out of their bandages, covered in scabs, still hot to the touch like an intense sunburn that wouldn't go away. My head, face, and hands were burned crispy, but I didn't need any skin grafts. None of the burns were third degree—more like a second and a half degree, so the nerves were damaged but growing back. My body temperature went up and down, from shivering to sweating.

I had thought that possibly after watching *Game of Thrones* in my drunken haze, I had poured gas all over the house and lit it on fire in some sort of bizarre, psychotic episode. I wouldn't know the real cause of the fire until I was recuperating; Brian had fallen asleep with a cigarette on a synthetic blanket where one spark caught fire, he tossed it aside after he thought he extinguished it and passed back out. He woke to try to fight off the fire that now engulfed the rooms, shouting to wake me as he realized it was beyond his control. The last time I saw him, he had been hit on the back of the neck by flames that dripped from the ceiling, just before the door slammed shut. I just wanted to see Brian, hug him, and let him know it was all ok; we survived and would always be friends. I thought he felt bad enough about it without feeling any negativity from me. I was happy to be alive and able to see him again. Brian's ears were badly burned, and he had to get skin grafts on the back of his neck, but he was otherwise all right. He didn't take in as much smoke as I did. Inside, my lungs and throat had been burned from the hot ash. The hospital vacuumed black tar from my lungs while I was out, believing the beach was my home in the land of delirium and hallucination daydreams. I wanted to get off the pain medicine to feel what was really happening.

Over the course of the first week of being able to speak again, we dwindled the lines down in my arms and got rid of the mainline medicine. Psychologists and physical therapists came to visit regularly. I began to walk with a walker and passed the chew test, which meant I could eat solid food. The doctors removed the feeding tube. Fruit never tasted so good when I got my first bite of pineapple. Matterz brought a falafel and a can of orange soda for my first meal of non-hospital food. Orange soda had been part of my hallucinations, so it only seemed right to give the unconscious mind what it wanted. A friend had made a mix of music that constantly played on a radio from an iPod on shuffle. This was a big source of inspiration. It was also the reason why I was singing Billie Holiday in a robot voice after the ventilator tube was removed.

Albert Cadabra came often while I was in the coma. I told him about us smoking cigars under the water. He told me about the benefit show at the House of Yes. It was so exciting that he and Anya made out afterwards. After the night of the fire, he had been waiting for me all day at Ripley's to show up for work, and was thinking I had been arrested until he got a call from Matterz, who had just got a call from my father when he pulled up for the show we were supposed to do on July 3, in memory of J.T. in Coney Island.

News of the fire reached people on a delay because neither Brian nor I had identification on us at the time. Brian's family called my parents, who called Matterz. The show at Coney Island never happened: Matterz rushed off to the hospital, where he learned there was a good chance I wouldn't make it.

The day after I was burned, Albert Cadabra didn't recognize me when he first walked in until he saw the ship's wheel tattoo Enigma had done on my chest. The tubes, the bandages, and the saline made me look bloated. Mixed with the hospital shaving off my hair, Albert had to do a double take. He thought for sure I wasn't going to live. However, there we were, five weeks later in the hospital, laughing and crying about it.

I convinced the psychiatrist and the nurses that I should be released early. The hospital was driving me out of my mind. I felt like a prisoner there. Even though they saved my life, I couldn't shake the trauma of being tied to the bed on all those drugs. The antipsychotic meds had side effects that caused me to come out of the coma like a deranged sleepwalker. I was the one who tore the cables out, tried to fight the hospital staff who tied me to the bed for my own protection. The psychiatrist wept when I told her the story of the fire, the hallucinations, and my family's car accident on their way to visit. I told her about Jason's suicide in 1999.

Betty Bloomerz would return from Finland soon and I didn't want to be in the hospital when she got back. At the end of my sixth week in the burn center, Kevin the nurse recommended that I be released early. Nights were the hardest to get through. The side effects from a synthetic morphine called Dilaudid caused more hallucinations and temperature fluctuations. Since it wasn't being administered by IV anymore, I was able to pretend to take the pills, hiding them on the side of my teeth and spitting them out when the nurse left the room. The physical therapist also gave her approval to release me.

Matterz was on his way over the Manhattan Bridge in our Atlantic City Jitney to fetch me when a cable under the bus snapped. Luckily, he was able to get safely to the other side of the bridge. It poured rain outside all day. The bus was towed to a mechanic. Matterz went to rent a car for my rescue mission. My cousin Peter, whom I hadn't seen since childhood, came to visit out of the blue while Penguin and I waited for Matterz. All the paperwork was finalized for my release and the fire alarm went off. We laughed about escaping the hospital with a fake nose, mustache, and glasses as a disguise. This would be preferable to a fire evacuation, but we would take whatever we could get. Our escape was sanctioned, following all protocol.

When Matterz finally arrived in the rental car, we all went down to the lobby and handed in my discharge papers. They gave me a pair of scissors to cut the hospital bracelet off my foot with shaky hands. It had been raining all day, but when we stepped out of the hospital, the last drop hit the pavement and the sky cleared. Matterz was so excited he ran over an orange cone. I told the traffic guard I had just been released from the burn unit, it was a wonderful day to be alive, and we were sorry about the cone.

We drove straight to Coney Island to drop Penguin off with Insectavora and the sideshow building manager, Patrick. The New York air smelled like hot summer garbage, but I didn't mind. The feeling of freedom overwhelmed my every cell. Withdrawal from the medication settled in with tremors. In the past week, I had fooled everyone by deciding to go off the meds cold turkey. Upon escaping the hospital, I could not stop shaking, even though I had a huge smile on my face.

After leaving Coney Island, I laid down in the back of the car for the long ride to my parents' house in Lancaster, PA. I crawled into bed with them that night and cried like a little kid. The effects of withdrawal from the meds caused amplified emotions. It felt like growing up all over again, squished into one day. My Aunt Margie, who was a nurse, came to visit every day and helped me with physical therapy. My muscles were atrophied from six weeks in bed. Walking was slow, like an old man riddled with arthritis. I loved sitting in my parents' back sunroom in their rocking chair, observing the birds and the bugs interacting with their garden.

One day, Brian and I had a long talk about the fire while listening to *The Only Living Boy in New York* by Simon & Garfunkel on repeat, like we used to do in high school when we were having deep conversations.

Matterz picked up Betty Bloomerz from the airport. I was nervous to see her after so much had happened that summer. I warned her about my scars over the phone, but they didn't bother her at all. Betty stayed over the night she came back, then went to have some time with her mother in Harrisburg for a few days.

In September, we had a big party at the Squid house on Pine Street. Many old friends came over to celebrate with us, but I ended up going to bed way before the party was over. Friends laughed on the roof deck attached to my room; I always enjoyed the sounds of a party, and I drifted off to sleep.

I figured the best way to heal was to push through the fatigue and stay true to the mission of being a professional artist. The first show back was at the September Carnivolution. I missed the June, July, and August episodes of my own creation. Betty Bloomerz and I were meant to return to Carnivolution at the same time; however, there was major flooding where her mother lived in Harrisburg, so she was stranded there.

It felt strange returning to Carnivolution without Betty after the fire and then a flood. The adrenaline of it all pushed me through fatigue and heavy movements. I helped unload the bus into Tiberino's yard, hung the banner line, tested the PA system, and put clown makeup on with a shaky-handed brush. The makeup was set with powder along with a new second face called Neck Man, whose mouth was the scar from the ventilator, just above my collarbones in the center of the neck. My Adam's apple was his nose, and his eyes went up the bottom of my jaw line.

During Carnivolution, the long-nosed Masked Perfesser was in charge of the jail break out of hell to the land of the living. Over his shoulder in a black sack, fireworks went off as he danced. Inside a sack with a backwards devil mask on, I began to panic, inhaling the pyrotechnic smoke. I squirmed and yelled, kicked free from the sack off his shoulders, emerged from the bag to chain smoke cigarettes and spin a fire baton. Five cigarettes were smoked at once. They were put out, human ashtray style, on different parts of my body, the last one extinguished on the ventilator scar after a few theatrical puffs on Neck Man's lips.

Shortly after Carnivolution, we did a show at the House of Yes. I swallowed a sword for the first time since the fire, worried that the neck scar would somehow interfere with the path of the blade. It went right down smoothly with no trouble at all.

The road was calling! In October, Betty Bloomerz finally reunited with the Carnivolution. She had fallen under the spell of a vampire puppet named Dicksidious Dribliticus. I burned him to death with sunlight released from a box of Quaker Oats. Betty and I were once again together in the Carnivolution universe, but ready to hit the road, in the here and now on actual earth, in the Squidling Brothers Atlantic City Jitney.

There was nothing more I would rather do while climbing back to life than hit stages around the country. We headed out through Pittsburgh and Indianapolis to Theatre Bizarre in Detroit. It had a new permanent home in the world's largest Masonic Temple. The building took up an entire city block. It was a marvel of architecture inside and out, with mazes of secret intricacies in every square inch. The many theaters, hallways, secret passageways, and staircases were overrun by red devils, black shadows, pumpkins, goats, and clowns. The ritual masquerade led by a marching band into a carnival takeover was laid out before us on a silver plate.

In the splendor of these dark-carnival, royal halls of days gone by, we received the sad news of Spliff's passing. He had ventilator-related pneumonia. After a year and a half fighting for his life, his struggle was over. In respect to his memory, we poured out our drinks in the parking lot of Detroit's Masonic Temple. I'd gone to visit him with Lunchbox shortly after getting out of the hospital. He was asleep on pain medicine, kept alive on a ventilator machine as I had been over the summer. His mother was there watching over him. We talked to him even though he seemed to be in and out of consciousness; I knew from experience that it makes a difference. He died the second week of October 2011. The Misfit Mother held him close as a nexus point to continue his work in death. He was my friend and an inspiration to many.

Everywhere we toured felt like a celebration that I had survived. The roads took us south through Raleigh, Greensboro, and Fayetteville in the Carolinas. Two full nights in Huntsville at the Flying Monkey Theater. It was as if I had come back from the dead with a chance to witness my own funeral. Death's door wouldn't let me in; instead, it had me linger at the portal touched by both worlds. We returned to New Orleans, Austin, Tucson, and Phoenix, where I wore a long, blue Civil War trench coat to protect the burned skin on my arms. Sweating in the desert heat was preferable to the sting of the sun's rays where there was no longer pigment for protection.

The west coast welcomed us from Los Angeles, to San Francisco, Eureka in the redwood forest, to Portland, Oregon. There was a show at a firehouse in the small town of Eugene on the way back to Oakland in the San Francisco Bay. We turned east for a long journey in the Jitney back to Philadelphia. Healing on the road was the way to go. Adrenaline from adventure with live audiences gave me strength for further travels.

Thanksgiving, Christmas, and New Years were calm, cozy celebrations of life moving into 2012. We spent New Year's Eve with a small group of friends on Pine Street, engaging in light to heavy hearted contemplation, preparing us mentally for the travels ahead. Life was unpredictably short, so we had to live it fast.

Chapter 17

Squidlings Around the World

We stood on a precipice, our future unfurling in front of us. To start off 2012, Matterz and I were going to turn our annual tour in Europe into a trip spanning the circumference of the Northern Hemisphere, going completely around the world! Logistics would be our biggest challenge as we faced this daunting task. We would fly to Germany, where we would meet with Roc Roc-It, Larz Vegas, and Princess Tweedle Needle, who we'd kept in touch with after meeting in Amsterdam. As a driver for a company that planned tours for rock bands, she could get us a good deal through "Just Like Your Mom" van rentals. The next five weeks would take us through eight countries: Germany, Austria, Slovenia, Croatia, Serbia, Switzerland, Belgium, and Holland. Although Betty was feeling weary from so much travel, she wanted to tour with us through Europe, head back home, and then meet us again on the west coast of the United States.

We wanted to contact the fakir magicians and take them up on their offer to host if we ever passed through India. Roc-It wouldn't be able to get a visa there, but we could get him a ticket to join us later. Matterz and I could get all our immunity shots and paperwork for visas with the guru of the Delhi School of Magic as our sponsor. The guru knew all about my fire through emails, and he knew of my desire to travel to Asia because of a vision I had in the flames. He promised to show us around Delhi and take us to meet the magicians at their village. He also said that he would see to it that Matterz and I would make it to the Himalayan Mountains, where friends of his would look after us.

After India, our plan was to meet Roc-It in Japan, where we would book a two week stay in a hotel in Tokyo's red-light district. With no ability to speak or write in Japanese, we were looking for places to make shows, but having absolutely no luck. We thought that physically being there would make the difference with getting booked, to see what we were made of, in a country and culture that we had never experienced before.

A friend of ours from California would use the Atlantic City Jitney to drive a busload of furniture and belongings from Philadelphia to Oakland, so our ride would be there when we flew back to California. Betty and Penguin would meet us for a tour up the west coast, through the redwood forest, to Portland, Oregon. After that, the four of us would drive across the country, back to Philadelphia.

There was so much of the world to explore. We never knew how much time we had, though I felt protected by spirits daring me to take it further in Jason's memory. He became a part of me, and we always traveled together, carrying each other through different worlds. I wanted to go as far north as Iceland, Greenland, and Svalbard; go as far south as Tasmania on the bottom of Australia; to Madagascar; to the end of the world in Argentina; all the way to Antarctica, where the Penguin Boy would be the emperor on the key edges of the South Pole; to walk the sand dunes in the deserts of Abu Dhabi; to swim in the Dead Sea and float like a turtle.

Of course, our story would need to be told, and we were DIY filmmakers ready to document our travels. Matterz was already working on a documentary called *A Clown's Recovery*, inspiring us to capture our travels and edit them into adventure stories. We were going to record our upcoming global tour with a new documentary called *Squidlings Around the World*. The monster-birth's tentacles were compelling us to carry the Squidling Brothers Circus Sideshow to all seven continents. I was feeling like myself again, only with something new that I learned when I was in a coma, a new perspective on life. I couldn't help but think about how my childhood mirrored my adult life.

When I was in second grade, I went to Catholic school for the year and became known as the class clown.

One day, I put a ski mask backwards on my face and played Run, Catch, and Kiss with some of the girls, chasing them blind and kissing them with no mouth, nose, or eyes. Sister Mercedes saw me and grabbed me by the arm, parading me into every single one of the classrooms as punishment. To the other children, she said, "This is what a fool looks like!" Fortunately for me, her plan to humiliate me backfired, because the other kids thought it was hilarious. After that, I got so much respect from them, and it was the first time I realized that humor could be my armor, my superpower to help me cope with difficulties. Becoming a clown felt so effortless, because I didn't have to do anything other than be myself while other people told me it was wrong, or probably not that smart.

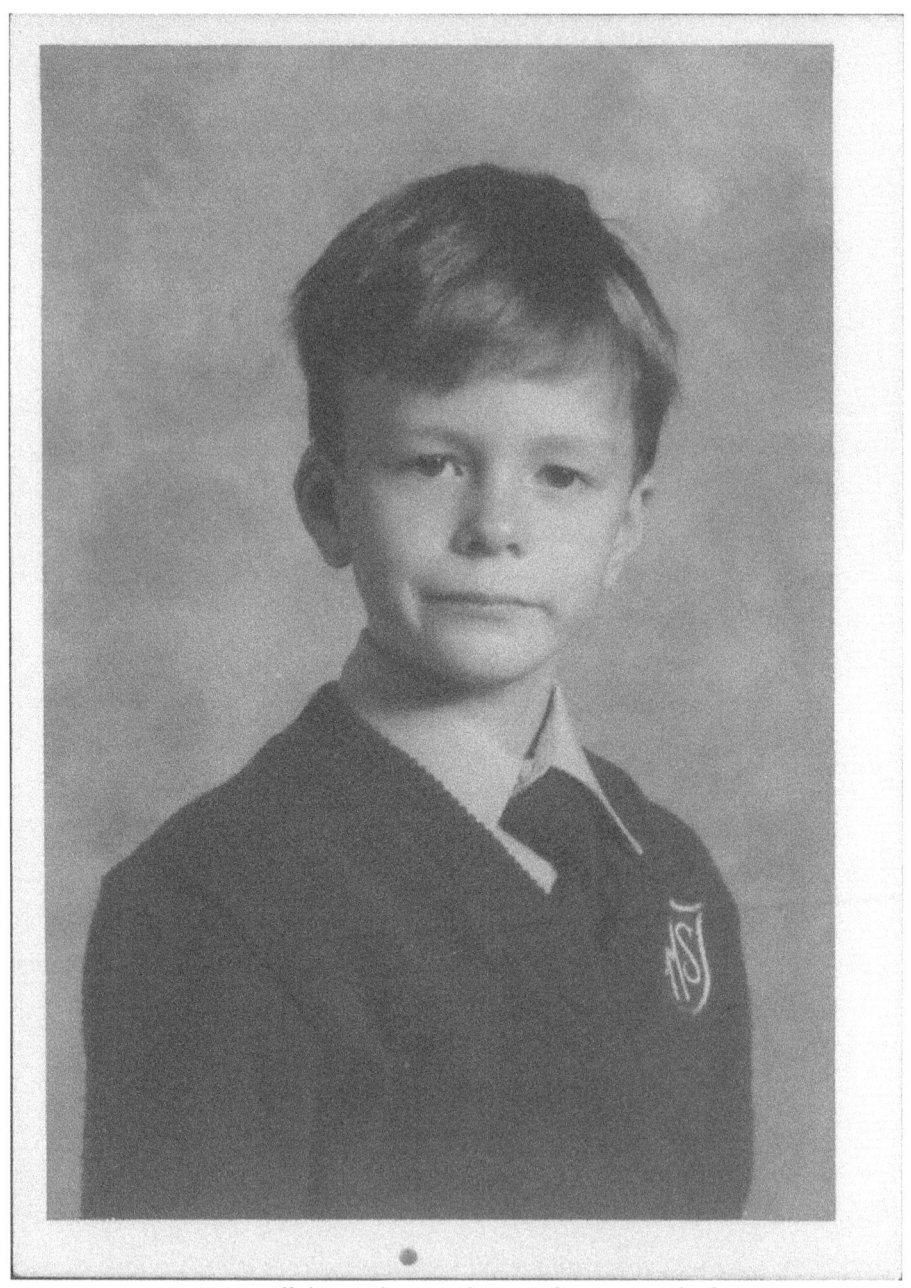

Young Jellyboy at the Sacred Heart elementary school

Young Jellyboy aka Eric Broomfield (Vicky Broomfield)

Danger Mania treehouse (Vicky Broomfield)

When we were preteens, Matterz and I played a game called "Danger Mania" with our neighbor Brian Levinson.

We stole things from nearby backyards, desperate for the thrill of it, for the wrongness of it. Our father had built us a treehouse when we were small, and as we got older, we co-opted that space into an angsty fortress against boredom and the looming terror of adulthood. We stole a package from our neighbor, sure it was drugs, money, or both, only to find it contained mere lawn mower engines. Our only solution was to change our disappointment into a weapon, turning the engines into whips that we cracked around our heads. Into adulthood, I continued to chase that feeling of transforming the taboo, of pushing myself up against the limits of possibility and creativity.

Around that same time, Brian and I were playing around on the river near our home. The river had flooded, so I made a raft to surf on it from an inflatable sled. I was ready to push out onto a limitless ocean of what could be, off to a place I had never been. Brian made the possibly smart decision to abort when he realized that the current was too strong, and the water was moving way faster than we expected. Meanwhile, I was only using a baseball bat for a paddle and got washed all the way out to Mahwah, New Jersey, finally ditching the bat and paddling with my hands and feet, towing my useless raft behind me. Brian thought I had possibly drowned, but before his shorts were dry, I made it all the way back to the shore and walked home. He was relieved and happy to see me.

We echoed this situation years later, when he got out of the fire much faster than I did. That feeling of being swept out to sea by the chaotic, torrential power of the future unknown loomed over me. As I stood there getting ready to board that plane to go around the globe, I felt an inevitable undertow magnetizing me towards the future, pushing me towards comedy, and pulling me through chaos.

From my teenage dream of rock 'n' roll to the spark of the circus, searching for the strange after my brother's suicide, my quest had thrown me into the fire of adventure at the edge of life. Death closed the door in my face where the Misfit Mother awaited those who broke the mold from the heat of liquid metal. Wrestling with hospital hallucination memories, I wondered, *"Did I die in the fire? Is this just the afterlife, or am I still in the hospital, trapped in an illusion of the way I wished things to be?"* I came to the conclusion that it was all too real to be a simulation of medically induced consciousness, or a bizarre echo of desire after death. When I stood in the airport with Matterz and Betty to start this epic, world-tour adventure, I put all my doubts aside to embrace what was coming.

I was looking back, before moving forward into the unknown mist of the future. I could see the ember of the circus, glowing with an intelligence that compelled me to jump into a whirlwind, searching for the reason *why*. I'd picked up a piece of my brother Jason's skull in 1999 by the blood-soaked unicycle under his bed, near the splattered wall where his surrealistic paintings hung. I made contact with the Misfit Mother of Death, blindly following her lead into music and art, all while trying to make peace with the whisper of the alien assassin, who caused my brother to feel that we would be better off without him.

I carried Jason with me through the fog that led the Hydrogen Jukebox to Ithaca, where I met Angel, who passed me the circus spark that grew into Carnivolution. Tentacled mutations led to Red Stuart the sword swallower on the jazz floor of Tower Records, who invited me to the Philadelphia tattoo convention, where I met Enigma after seeing his picture in a book. Simultaneously, I crossed paths with Spliff and Roc-It from Disgraceland, who had joined forces with the Coney Island Circus Sideshow. In a trailer behind a roller coaster, I met Albert Cadabra, who brought me to Ripley's Believe It or Not. Somehow, with the circus spark flying around in the whirlwind of New York City, I met the elemental fire face to face, only to be snatched out of its jaws by the guardians of fate.

I was a raw nerve antenna, now broadcasting to a wider and wider circle. My frequency stepped out of the lemonade, drinking shade, and sneezed at the dying sky as the sun and the moon were out at the same time. Looking up into the light of the sky always gave my nose a tickle, as if I was meant to live in a cave, but life was leading me out of the underground shadows into more adventures. With healing burns and forming scar tissue, a little on the crispy side, I was ready to take the ride.

I looked at Matterz before boarding the plane that would take us around the world and said, "We're really doing this, brother."

There was a time when Jason, Matterz, and I sat around a campfire, drinking to the future.

On the top of a mountain in our old town of Suffern, Jason said, "One day people will be coming to our shows, watching our movies, and reading our stories."

That dream kept us going through the hardest of times, and we never, ever stopped. Together, we three brothers got on the plane, and then we went around the world!

Jason holding Eric and Matt Broomfield (Vicky Broomfield)

Afterword: The Creative Process

I had the idea to make a handwritten book while on the road in 2004. Things felt so profound when it all started for me in the world of sideshow; I felt like my life had turned into a tale that needed to be recorded. At first, I was writing things down as they happened, but quickly experiences overwhelmed me and there was no way to keep up. I made outlines in sketch books of main events, adventures, and characters. Whenever there was a long flight or train ride or just some down time, I would meditate to achieve a state of self-hypnosis where I could visualize the time, place, and people, reliving it all while writing.

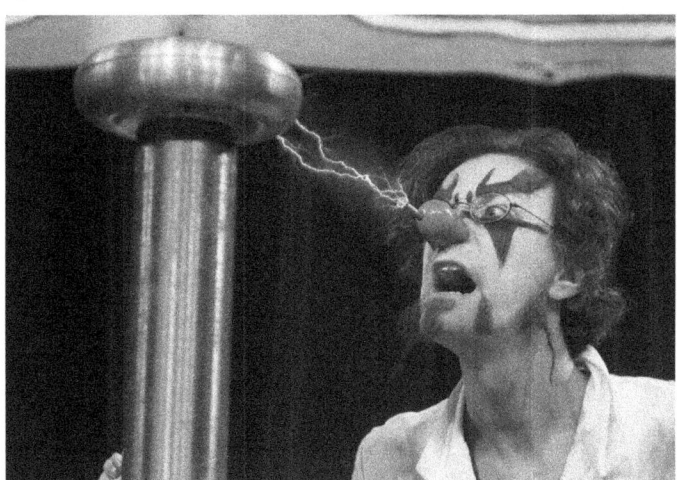

Jellyboy performing the electric blockhead clown nose with his Tesla coil, Sideshows by the Seashore, Coney Island, 2017 (Norman Blake)

I'm a slow typer and a bad speller, so my Aunt Marie volunteered to type the notebooks over the years as I finished them. After I was rescued from the fire in 2011, the book took on a new urgency, because near death, I had a deep regret that no one would know my story.

Taking off on a flight to travel around the world while still healing seemed to be a natural ending for the book, although many interesting and unexpected things have happened since 2012. Matterz and I decided to make travel documentaries to chronicle what came after the end of this book. The *Squidlings Around the World* documentary emerged from this.

In 2014, my friend Katya Kadavera, who had her entire body tattooed as a leopard by Katzen the Tiger Lady, made me a Tesla coil in exchange for teaching them to sword swallow. She now swallows swords regularly at the Uranus Sideshow Museum in, you guessed it, Uranus, Missouri. The tesla coil fits in a suitcase and can be checked as baggage on a plane. I've taken it to Japan a few times; I've taken it to Europe and Dubai in the UAE, where security thought it was a falcon detector! I've been called down to airport basements by police in several countries for having a Tesla coil as well as a rifle in my suitcase.

One bizarre time in 2016, I was flying from a Tel Aviv tattoo convention to New Orleans to run a grind show for Mardi Gras. There was a transfer in Kiev, Ukraine. When I landed, there was a note in my suitcase from the Ukrainian police. Luckily, I was with a friend from Belarus who translated it for me: the police had taken my rifle. The Tesla coil was taken apart and a fire penis that I had in a pair of American flag underwear was missing. Håvve from Pain Solution linked me with his friend in Ukraine named Pavlo Klets, who combined hook suspension with bungee jumping. Pavlo helped get me a lawyer named Anna who recommended we bribe the police to get the rifle back, and she was successful!

The only problem was, I had to go to Kiev to get the rifle because it couldn't be sent in the mail. I found a cheap flight after getting documents made saying that the rifle had been demilitarized for use as a theater prop. I met Anna by a McDonalds in downtown Kiev, where she gave me the rifle wrapped in cloth. Later that night, after I had a chance to see the city, she came with me to the airport to bribe some more police and get me on the flight with my rifle. I got a lot of writing done for this memoir during long trips like that.

After years of hanging around Coney Island doing night shows and recommending other performers for the grind show, I was brought in as a cast member from 2017-2021. Dick Zigun made me his right-hand man, casting the show and making the schedule. Marie Roberts, the famous painter of the Coney Island banner artwork, even painted me a human banner line suit, full of classic freak art. It's the one I'm wearing on the cover of this book! Along with the suit, she also painted me a Squidling Brothers Coney Iceland banner. I'd become fascinated with Iceland while working at Coney, and I booked some shows there for some reason I couldn't put my finger on. In 2018, I finally went to Reykjavik for the first time, and I met the woman who would become my wife.

Earlier that year, I fell off a roof while sweeping the gutters breaking both feet, and fracturing my spine. I was in a wheelchair for six months, with lots of painful healing. During that time, I finished the handwritten part and got it all typed. In 2021, during the pandemic lockdowns, I sent the book to a professional editor who helped with grammar and spelling, as well as plot and character development. It took me about a year to work through all the notes.

At that time, I was unsuccessfully searching for a publisher and agent. The book wasn't ready to be published, as it was too long at 400 pages, and a bit confusing at times. Outside Talker Press agreed to pick up the book if I cut it down to approximately 250 pages. I had to make big decisions to cut out performers, places, lovers, family, and friends. I decided to cut out tangents to the storyline that was now emerging through the editing process. I cut out some fights, some relationships, and my opinions about politics. If you are one of the people who were part of my life and not included in this story, you know who you are, and I apologize.

James Taylor of *Shocked and Amazed!* edited the 400-page version by mistake, but I am glad he did, because I put back in some of what was cut, using that manuscript as a reference. Basically, Jim Moore, the publisher of Outside Talker Press, sent a printed book to James, who marked it with a red pen and sent it back to Jim. It was then faxed page by page to me in Iceland, where I got married and have been living since the end of 2020, so I could plug those edits into the computer.

None of the editing process would have been possible without the technical support from my wife Heida, who has been helping me navigate the digital world and letting me use her laptop to write. After faxing and plugging in the notes, my one-and-a-half-year-old son got ahold of the book and scribbled all over it with some crayons, so I decided to ritualistically burn it, because the pages were not numbered, and it was a mess! But all was not lost, because Jim gave me the original manuscript with James's red pen on it in Coney Island around Halloween. I read the book all the way through, editing along the way, adding details while naming the chapters in November through January, 2023-2024. James took the 250-page version back for a final editing pass.

My long-time sideshow friend Jenn O. Cide read a review copy of the book and offered to be an extra set of eyes for some proofreading. She helped with a continuity restructure amidst several brainstorming sessions, right before I turned it in for layout and printing. In the eleventh hour, she jumped in to give the book exactly the polish it needed, plus a bit more after that. Jenn had the idea for the seventeenth chapter to tie everything together, to clarify where we were going, and where we had been. Another miraculous connection from the Misfit Mother of Death came to pass, as we worked for days corresponding between Reykjavik and New Orleans. Marc Hartzman, author of the *American Sideshow* Encyclopedia, also kindly donated his time to give us some final proofing notes..

In this book, I represent the people as I experienced them, but I made some name changes for personal reasons. Despite these changes, the essence of the characters and their experiences remain authentic and true to life.

The book is now finished, 20 years after it began! It was a convoluted, highly polished process of travel and writing while isolated, and at times broken, that has brought us to bring *Memoirs of a Coney Island Clown* to life. You can find glorious color versions of these photos on our Squidling Brothers website. It would mean the world to me if you would let me know how you feel about this book. If you enjoyed it, please pass it down the line to friends, write a review, or talk about it on Amazon, and be sure to check out the other Outside Talker and Squidling-related books and movies!

Jellyboy with fireworks sword swallow, banner by Marie Roberts, Sideshows by the Seashore, Coney Island, 2009 (Norman Blake)

squidlingbrothers.com

outsidetalkerpress.com

About the Author

Jellyboy the Clown tours the world with the Squidling Brothers Circus Sideshow. He's worked for Ripley's Believe It or Not and the Coney Island amusement park as a sword swallower and fire breather.

After witnessing his older brother's struggle with schizophrenia and losing him to suicide, Jellyboy and his younger brother Matterz turned to art as therapy. They produced *A Clown's Recovery*, *Squidlings Around the World*, and a horror movie, *Freakshow Apocalypse: The Unholy Sideshow*, as well as several albums with their band the Hydrogen Jukebox.

In 2011, Jellyboy spent five weeks in a coma after being rescued from a burning building in New York. Ironically, the accident had nothing to do with fire breathing.

Jellyboy has a degree in the study of world religions with a minor in modern dance. Adventuring in Icelandic nature over rocks and rivers, he discovered a love for lava, the aurora borealis, and writing novels. Being a burn survivor who enjoys the shade, Jellyboy found the love of his life in Reykjavik, where he now lives with his wife, three stepchildren, and son. To find out more about Jellyboy, visit squidlingbrothers.com.

www.ingramcontent.com/pod-product-compliance
Lightning Source LLC
Chambersburg PA
CBHW061734070526
44585CB00024B/2671